D0553820

CYBERMAPPING
and the Writing of Myth

PETER LANG
New York • Washington, D.C./Baltimore • Bern
Frankfurt am Main • Berlin • Brussels • Vienna • Oxford

Paul Jahshan

CYBERMAPPING
and the Writing of Myth

PETER LANG
New York • Washington, D.C./Baltimore • Bern
Frankfurt am Main • Berlin • Brussels • Vienna • Oxford

Library of Congress Cataloging-in-Publication Data

Jahshan, Paul.
Cybermapping and the writing of myth / Paul Jahshan.
p. cm.
Includes bibliographical references.
1. Information society. 2. Cyberspace.
3. Virtual reality. 4. Myth. I. Title.
HM851.J34 303.48/34—dc22 2006034894
ISBN-13: 978-0-8204-8885-1
ISBN-10: 0-8204-8885-2

Bibliographic information published by **Die Deutsche Bibliothek.**
Die Deutsche Bibliothek lists this publication in the "Deutsche Nationalbibliografie"; detailed bibliographic data is available on the Internet at http://dnb.ddb.de/.

Cover design by Joni Holst

The paper in this book meets the guidelines for permanence and durability of the Committee on Production Guidelines for Book Longevity of the Council of Library Resources.

29 Broadway, 18th floor, New York, NY 10006
www.peterlang.com

Printed in Germany

Table of Contents

INTRODUCTION

Although cyberspace has become, in the last twenty years, a reality in the daily life of millions of human beings, there have been very few genuine attempts at mapping the new virtual world. What exist are ephemeral, day-to-day, even hour-to-hour map renderings of network traffics which, while very useful for the smooth conduct of everyday online business, are too transient to be adopted as long-term models.

This book is a response to what I perceive to be the inadequacy of the existing ways of mapping cyberspace and an attempt to formulate a long-lasting blueprint through which our *understanding*, our *theorizing*, and our *practice* of cyberspace can be anchored on solid grounds.

I will consider how modern and especially contemporary critical theory have paved the way to the emergence of virtuality; what is actually meant by seemingly interchangeable terms such as virtual reality, the new media, cyberspace, the matrix, and simulation; how attempts at mapping cyberspace have fallen short of the requirement for a stable long-term theoretical framework; how and when the mapping of cyberspace began and how the new space begged a new map to accommodate a new body; how cyberspace can be seen as the last contemporary bastion of myth; how this mythical space survives through writing and is, in itself, a writing, an *écriture*; and finally how, in the cyber-polis, cyber users can map new practices that thwart power centers.

The debate has been one-sided enough to prevent a quiet and clear-headed assessment—or, for some, re-assessment—of cyberspace. On the one hand, Neo-Luddites have repeatedly—and many times convincingly—pointed at the imminent dangers facing humanity after the "machine" has taken over. In apocalyptic scenarios of varying credibility, the human race gradually disappears or is driven "underground." On the other hand, techno-junkies have hailed—with equally convincing terms—the computer age as the harbinger of liberation, total equality, enlightenment, and absolute truth. I believe that as long as the "geomapping" of cyberspace is not seriously investigated, both camps, the technophobes and the technophiles, will remain at loggerheads for quite some time before a re-appraisal is effected.

This re-assessment, more than two decades after the creation of cyberspace, I propose to envision through the prisms of myth, writing, and the polis. Yet this must remain an obvious contribution to the on-going dialogue feverishly taking place around this essentially new and challenging mode of existence we have come to designate as cyberspace.[1]

It will be soon clear that I don't intend—nor would I be able to even if I wanted—to approach this topic from a technological angle. My aim is to invite further research in the area, and as such it is essential that this be followed by further concrete analyses which will fill the shortcomings associated with an undertaking of this scale. This book is primarily intended for the critical, cultural, and literary theorist and, above all, for the inquisitive reader who, no doubt, is wondering about the nature of the new world we, as humans, have been hastily ushered into.

NOTE

1 John Perry Barlow, in "The Best of all Possible Worlds," *Communications of the ACM* 40.2 (Feb. 1997), 68–74, begins his essay by cautioning that, thirty years after the creation of cyberspace, the wildest forecasts have been given a sound "thrashing" by reality and that his "one certain prediction" for the next fifty years is that "practically anything [he says] of it now will seem silly by then" (69).

CHAPTER ONE

After the Break

> That is perhaps the greatest problem of all. Life as we know it has ended, and yet no one is able to grasp what has taken its place.
>
> Paul Auster, *In the Country of Last Things*[1]

It is difficult to argue against the fact that our twenty-first century has witnessed the emergence of a different breed of human beings under the sign and aegis of the information age. It is also true that the survival of the fittest theory has now to be expanded to mean, almost exclusively, the survival of the electronically fittest. Pierre Lévy, already in 1990, was saying: "We live one of those rare moments when, through a new technical configuration, that is, through a new relationship with the cosmos, a new style of humanity is being invented."[2] The new technical "configuration," following in the wake of changes in critical interpretative techniques, has rendered classical notions of reading and writing, of space and time, and of reality itself, dangerously obsolete. Lévy announced that "[h]istorical transcendentalism is at the mercy of a boat trip. Let social groups scatter a new means of communication, and all the balance of representations and images is transformed."[3] In 1997, Lévy was again speaking of a shift from one humanity to another which, though still undetermined, was not fully accepted as a topic to be discussed, questioned, and aimed at.[4] What the new technologies are heralding is no less than the "brutal" acceleration of the "process of hominization" brought about by the new techniques of communication through the creation of virtual worlds. The process of emergence of the human species, far from being over, is just passing through its apex.[5] What is being glimpsed, to Lévy, is the new ability to think collectively this adventure, as a "space of Knowledge" has been added, thanks to the new technologies, to the three classical spaces of Earth, Territory, and Trade.[6] Talking about the relationship between the new technologies, collective thinking, and the new space, he said:

> The role of the computer and that of the digital techniques of communication is not to "replace mankind," neither to come close to a hypothetical "artificial intelligence," but to favor the construction of collective intelligences where the social and cognitive potentials of each and every person are permitted to develop and expand in a mutual relationship.[7]

Never before, he added a year later, have the changes in technology, economy, and customs been so fast and so destabilizing to the human race.[8]

J. Hillis Miller, talking about the new directions to be taken by the journal *Critical Inquiry*, insisted on the importance of change and on the study of "the effects of the new media on the sensibilities, the ethos, the interior life of our citizens," adding that it is "not just a description of the new media or an analysis of their products, along the lines of film studies for cinema, but a reflection on what sort of citizens the new media will produce or are producing."[9] Marshall McLuhan, who was equally impressed by the changes taking place in the twentieth century, stated, as far back as 1958: "We are moving very rapidly and at high speed naturally from an area in which business has for, say a century, been our culture, to a situation in which culture is going to be our business."[10] On a more extreme note, Mark Dery compared the new technological/informational changes to a complete lift-off toward altogether different realms: "Escape velocity is the speed at which a body—a spacecraft, for instance—overcomes the gravitational pull of another body, such as the Earth. More and more, computer culture, or cyberculture, seems as if it is on the verge of attaining escape velocity."[11] Even more dramatically, Michael Heim—probably the most mystically-minded writer on cyberspace—agreed with Dery when he prophetically said: "Plugged into electric power and computer chips, the human race in this last decade of the twentieth century is preparing to lift off from nature into another—electronic—space."[12]

Modernism and, more obviously, postmodernism and post-structuralism, have proved to be the uncanny pioneers of the new technologies which have culminated in cyberspace. Jacques Derrida mentioned, in his "Structure, Sign and Play in the Discourse of the Human Sciences," an "event" which had the form of a "*rupture* and a redoubling,"[13] an idea taken up by Fredric Jameson in 1984 when he posited postmodernism on the "hypothesis of some radical break or *coupure*" to be traced to the end of the 1950s or the beginning of the 1960s.[14] But Jameson, almost twenty years later, also believed that whereas the moderns "were obsessed with the secret of time," the postmoderns are obsessed with that of space[15] and added, in the context of the new spatial configuration and the information age we live in, that

> [i]nstant information transfers suddenly suppress the space that held the colony apart from the metropolis in the modern period. Meanwhile, the economic interdependence

of the world system today means that wherever one may find oneself on the globe, the position can henceforth always be coordinated with its other spaces. This kind of epistemological transparency no doubt goes hand in hand with standardization and has often been characterized as the Americanization of the world (if not its Disneyfication).[16]

Indeed, Lévy believes that we have "dreamed, and perhaps sometimes attained, especially since the middle of the 1980s, a desirable software space which is open to explorations, to connections to the outside, and to singularizations."[17] The new spaces raise issues not only with outside "connections" but also with the nature of the connections themselves. Miller, in 2000, perfectly saw the potential presented by the new technologies:

Moreover, these new telecommunications technologies, so many new devices for raising ghosts in a new way, also generate new ideological matrices. They break down, for example, the barrier between consciousness and the objects of consciousness presupposed in Hegel's *Phenomenology*.[18]

Yet even Derrida's *coupure* is not enough to describe the new technology and the new spaces—cyberspaces—that have emerged as a result. Bruce Sterling, in the now famous "Manifesto of January 3, 2000," said: "The central issue as the new millennium dawns is technocultural."[19] Similarly, Friedrich Kittler describes the new age in terms of a change in writing and points to the early seventies as "the last historical act of writing" to have happened with the design, by Intel engineers, of the first integrated microprocessor. So big is the change that Kittler has to admit that we do not know, at this stage, what our writing does.[20] Lévy questions as well the appropriateness of our present means of interpretation:

[t]he conditions which used to make of critical and objective truth the norm of knowledge are quickly undergoing transformation...Theories, with their norm of truth and with the critical activity which accompanies them, give way to *models*, with their norm of efficiency and the apropos judgment which presides over their evaluation. The model is not put on paper, an inert support, it now appears on a computer.[21]

The apparent volatility of the new technologies is what has probably made attempts at fixating or anchoring our bearings an arduous task to say the least. Yet it is without doubt the massive, *en force* influence of postmodernism and post-structuralism that has paved the way for the decentering of solid, tangibly identifiable, points in the space(s) of writing.

It is first of all an *actual* decentering of the subject that mostly identifies the spaces created by the new technologies. Marjorie Worthington describes the new virtual realities as having created a new kind of subject, almost identical to what has been called the "postmodern subject."[22] Jameson was more radical as to the new space we occupy and, as early as 1984, sounded these prophetic words:

> I am proposing the notion that we are here in the presence of something like a mutation in built space itself. My implication is that we ourselves, the human subjects who happen into this new space, have not kept pace with that evolution; there has been a mutation in the object unaccompanied as yet by any equivalent mutation in the subject.[23]

Continuing in the same vein, but advancing to the problem of mapping, Jameson pointed out that "postmodern hyperspace" was allowing us to go beyond "the capacities of the individual human body to locate itself, to organize its immediate surroundings perceptually, and cognitively to map its position in a mappable external world."[24] It is interesting to note that it is only with the advent of cyberspace that the postmodern self can practically be seen as forcibly deconstructed. Frances Dyson says that cyberspace is "established as an 'other' place to enact the deconstructed self: a self whose multiplicity and ambiguity is continually reinforced as the body seems to increasingly inhabit the dematerialized world that technology creates."[25] Dyson also attributes the obsession with space to "Western ocularcentrism," the conflation of being with objects;[26] and the postmodern interest with space is doubled by a cyberspace which is, uncannily, both a space and a non-space. And as the concept of the deconstructed self helped to problematize the very essence of the unity of the self, the advent of cyberspace has likewise problematized the nature of space and the nature of matter occupying that space, and consequently problematized the nature of the relationship between the two. Using the story of Odysseus and the sirens, Maurice Blanchot was able to throw light on why the "other," any "other," is seen as a threat:

> What was the nature of the Sirens' song? What was its defect? Why did this defect render it more powerful? Some have always answered: it is an inhuman song…But others say that the enchanting was stranger even: it was only reproducing the habitual song of man, and since Sirens, who were only beasts, beautiful because of the reflection of feminine beauty, could sing like men sing, they rendered the song so strange that the suspicion of the inhumanity of any human song would be present to the mind of those who were listening.[27]

Is cyberspace such a beautiful yet terrible beast, able, by its inherent vacuity, to make us question our assumptions of physical space as ultimate presence? The suspicion of nothingness looms large whenever cyberspace is used oppositionally to real physical space. Blanchot's famous answer to where literature was going can be interestingly applied to cyberspace: where is space going? Space "is going towards itself, towards its essence which is to disappear."[28]

Such dramatic actualization of what was hitherto safely relegated to the realm of theoretical speculation has inevitably led to the resurgence of a kind of cyber-Luddism and technophobia. In 1960, Marshall McLuhan ended his essay, "Effects of the Improvements of Communication Media," with the following insightful words:

> Many people are terrified at the speed of information movement in our electronic time which brainwashes whole populations on the one hand, and eliminates long established roles based on highly specialized knowledge. The interpenetration of Gutenberg and the electronic galaxies is naturally very destructive at many levels.[29]

McLuhan, way before the explosion of the information age, had judiciously brought together writing—Gutenberg—and galaxy-mapping. I will show here how pertinent this vision is today.

In 1999, Jodi Dean gave voice to the fear of decentering when she said that we had become repeatedly and fearfully reminded that new technologies are threatening to destroy reality. Not only a symptom of Luddite technophobia,[30] these fears come, according to Dean, from people as diverse as Slavoj Žižek, Mark Slouka, and R. U. Sirius (Ken Goffman), who share the fear that the new technologies, from cable television to software programs, disrupt the distinction between the natural and the virtual.[31] AI expert Ray Kurzweil shocked the world in July 2000 at the ACM (Association for Computing Machinery) Siggraph conference in New Orleans when he excitedly announced that although "[t]he natural world has had some interesting qualities to it...we can create a more interesting world which will become more and more compelling and realistic as we go through the 21st century." The punch line was probably his decade-by-decade predictions as to the state of things beginning with 2000: ending in 2050, he calmly assured his listeners that by that time, "[t]he bulk of thinking...will be non-biological."[32] Yet, as Tyler Stevens pointed out in 1996, the changes should not come as a total surprise:

> [W]e are already used to dealing with digital, intelligent life in the form of digital representations of other humans. A good number of us set our biological clocks by when we are able to login and when we can read our e-mail. We are used to narrativizing our lives, ourselves, for our on-line friends, many of whom we've never met; it's a small step to asking how we know that our correspondents are cognizant, conscious, aware, "real." How do we know, by what heuristics do we discover, that our correspondents are sentient? By what standard of measurement could we gauge, in this age of the "intelligent" machine, that our interlocutors are, in a word, "human"?[33]

It is very probable that the lack of bearings inherent in the space(s) of the new technologies is the main culprit behind the mounting fears. Reality, at least, boasts of recognizable and theoretically mappable territory. In virtual reality, information has suddenly taken the place of actual physicality.

Yet other voices have sought to redress the balance and to show that picturing any technology in general and the new technologies in particular as evil can be vastly detrimental to human progress. On the most mundane level, cyberspace has helped people communicate with each other in what would otherwise be a world gradually closing in on itself. Janet Moursund uttered these simple words about her experience in a virtual world called Sanctuary:

> I have been asked for advice, and I have been given information. I have listened to stories of trivial daily events and of major life crises, incidents of loss and grief and of elation and triumph. I have talked with different "individuals" from the same multiple personality household, and learned to recognize them by the way they express themselves. I've petted a kitten, rubbed the ears of a baby dragon, received bunches of flowers, and been hugged and comforted when I spoke of having had a bad day. For me, as for the others who come there, SANCTUARY is real.[34]

To Lévy, the advantages of cyberspace exist on more than one level: the recreation of social networks through exchange of knowledge, the listening to and the valuation of singularities, the establishment of a more direct and more participatory—hence more genuine—democracy leading to the enrichment of individuals, to the invention of new forms of cooperation and, ultimately, to the heralding of collective intelligence.[35] The new technologies also prove to be a fertile ground for the construction and the resurgence of myth. Lévy again: "The products of modern technology, far from being used instrumentally and computationally only, are in fact major sources of the imaginary, entities fully participating in the institution of perceived worlds."[36]

Luddite critique conveniently forgets that there has never been a *natural* or *non-technological* society in the first place. François Dagognet suggests that the debate about whether nature is becoming technologized is based on a false dichotomy: namely that there is a category called "nature" and a category called "technology." Dagognet argues, in a deconstructionist-like method, that on the contrary, the category "nature" has not existed for thousands of years, "not since the first humans deliberately planted gardens or discovered slash-and-burn farming."[37] Lévy is aware of this fact and adds: "Those who condemn the information age would never think of criticizing the printing press or even less writing. It is because the printing press and writing (which are technologies!) *constitute* them too much."[38]

Lévy also laments the situation where the problematization of issues of politics and power is sacrificed, by some, on the altar of Luddism:

> Technology embodies with them the contemporary form of evil. Unfortunately, the image of technology as evil power, ineluctable and separate, shows itself not only to be false, but catastrophic as well…*A priori* morally condemning a phenomenon artificially separated from the collective future and from the world of significations (of "culture"), this conception forbids to think, at the same time, technology and techno-democracy.[39]

It is clear that the new technologies are more than just a handy tool and more than a lethal weapon threatening to take over the world of the humans. As Dery judiciously says, the "technophile-versus-technophobe debate" is rendered futile upon close inspection: the computer is a "Janus machine," both an "engine of liberation" and "an instrument of repression."[40]

Lévy, however, for all his laudable acumen and insight into the relationship between human culture and technology, and for his contribution to the ongoing debate with his concept of cognitive ecology, stops short of presenting a model allowing twenty-first-century human beings to come to terms with the new spaces they have been invited—or, some would say, forced—to tread. It is my contention that only when the bearings of the cyber-traveler have been, if not fully defined, at least put within a *theorizing framework*, that the prevailing confusion can be cleared. As I will show, cyberspace fills the mythical void by re-creating an already-there virtual reality through the magical/mythical medium of writing with the city as model.

But first things first. Familiar and not-so-familiar terms such as *virtuality*, the *new technologies*, and *cyberspace* mentioned above need to be re-defined in the context of this book. New terms like *matrix* and *simulation* will also be introduced.

It is appropriate to begin with Miller who, far from shying away from the advances of the new technologies, boldly put virtual reality on a pedestal which was hitherto occupied by literature:

> Radio, television, cinema, popular music, and now the Internet—these are more decisive in shaping citizen's ethos and values, as well as in filling their minds and feelings with imaginary worlds. It is these virtual realities rather than strictly literary ones that have most performative efficacy these days to generate people's feelings, behavior, and value judgments.[41]

What are, then, these "virtual realities" Miller speaks of? *Webster's Encyclopedic Unabridged Dictionary of the English Language* defines "virtual" as the following:

> 1. being such in power, force, or effect, though not actually or expressly such.

and

> 2. *Archaic*. having the inherent power to produce certain effects.[42]

Even at this very basic stage, it is important to note that two elements are immediately discernible: absence and fiat. It is this combination of power and unlocatability which gives cyberspace and cybermapping qualities we associate with, on the one hand, classical myths and, on the other hand, with contemporary critical theory notions of *écriture*.[43]

One of the earliest and most lucid attempts at defining virtuality is Richard Norton's 1972 essay "What is Virtuality?" in which he stated that the term "implies an immediate, if tacit, admission that something is not the case in fact. But something else *is* the case and this something else is quite practicable. Is there power in a virtual reality? Yes, indeed there is."[44] Another interesting point he made, and this years before the explosion of the new technologies, was that "[a]ll virtual events are then actual events *in terms of* themselves but virtual events *in terms of* the actual realities for which they are the alternatives."[45] In other words, cyberspace is an entity which exists *in itself*, as reality exists *in itself*. The problem arises when the rules and laws we apply—or the rules and laws we see being applied—in one world conflict with those of another. The term "virtual reality" (VR) was first coined by Jaron Lanier, one of the "gurus" of cyberspace, and has recently been defined as "a real or simulated environment in which the perceiver experiences telepresence."[46] In the same context, Arthur Kroker and Michael A. Weinstein define virtual reality as "the dream of pure telematic experience" which, begun "in the cybernetic shadowland of head-mounted scanners, wired gloves, and data suits," has now become "the electronic horizon of the twenty-first century."[47]

Simplistic attempts, like those of Julio Bermudez and Debra Gondeck-Becker, see "classical reality" as the natural world we live in, whereas "digital space," which they equate with a "virtual place," is a world with functions not necessarily following or referring to classical reality. It is an "immaterial world" offering alternative experiences to those of classical reality.[48] More to the point, architect Peter Eisenman sees the virtual as "a condition in real space that contains the oscillation between past and present time, between figure and ground, between smooth and striated space."[49] This inter-penetration or complementarity is also quite lucidly problematized by Philippe Queau in his "Virtual Multiplicities":

> The word "virtual" comes from the latin [sic] virtus, virtue, which itself comes from the latin [sic] vir, man. As for the word "real" it comes from the latin [sic] res, thing...The virtual is neither the opposite of the real (the unreal) nor the opposite of the actual (the potential). The virtual is like the leavening in dough. It unites and combines the poles, the forms and the forces, but only in order to transform them...It

> constitutes, in the true meaning of the word, an "intermediary" reality—a metaxu—as Plato said.[50]

Lévy points out that *virtus* also means strength and power: in scholastic philosophy, what exists potentially and not actually is known as virtual; virtuality and actuality are, in fact, only two different ways of being.[51] Language is, first of all, a virtualization process which keeps what is alive prisoner of the here and now and opens up the past and the future; we humans constantly inhabit a virtual space the moment we use language. Second, all of our technology, from the beginnings of humanity, is the materialization of a virtual possibility and without that virtualization no technology is possible. More, rituals, religions, morality, laws and rules are social mechanisms set up to virtualize relations built on power, pulsions, instincts, and desires. Finally, to Lévy, art, the summum and pride of humanity, is the ultimate result of virtualization, since it "sits at the crossroads of the three great virtualizing and hominizing currents, namely language, techniques, and ethics." Art "fascinates because it puts into play the most virtualizing of all activities."[52]

The virtual, if properly defined, bears almost no relation to the false, the illusory, or the imaginary. The virtual, in fact, is not the opposite of the real; far from it, it is a mode of being "fecund and powerful," which allows the blossoming of creation and opens up mines of meaning under the "platitude of the immediate physical presence."[53] It is this new "mode" which forms Lévy's key concept as it is developed more clearly in his subsequent works: the virtual is not a particular mode of being, it is the "process of transformation" from one mode of being to another, a "heterogenesis," a "welcoming of otherness" on the same lines as the process of hominization mentioned above, and not, as one may think, the alienation so feared by some.[54]

Virtualization is not derealization; on the contrary, it is an "identity mutation" where the ontological self sees its center of gravity moved from its traditional anchoring point.[55] The process of self-discovery through virtualization allows humans to "step outside," to be "out there"; they "deterritorialize themselves."[56] Brian Massumi sums up Lévy's contribution to the dialogue on the virtual by acknowledging his emphasis on the "participation" in the virtual of earlier technologies like writing and his distinction between various terms like the actual, the possible, and the potential as "an integral part of any thinking of the virtual."[57]

Lanier takes the definition one step further and rhapsodizes about the different meanings of virtual reality: "A delinquent disassociation from the truth…A protean, all-encompassing triumph of creativity…An ecstasy or epiphany brought about by technology…A transcendent perspective brought about by technology."[58] But it is here that problems begin to appear. What was, with Lévy, a mode of being or a progression, threatened with others the concept of physical, tangible reality altogether. Mark Poster refers to discussions about a virtual reality which "so destabilizes the real that the real itself is understood as 'virtual,' as provisional, constructed," and reality can then be seen as "always already virtual."[59]

The new technologies which I have been mentioning until now in a rather general context can be equated, maybe for the first time in the history of human culture, almost exclusively with media. Why this is important to my thesis is the fact that the new technologies, media, information and the space in which these three blend—and in which the distinction between them remains blurred—form what is also called cyberspace. Geert Lovink is aware of the link and says, in his "From Speculative Media Theory to Net Criticism," that the Net is the "medium to end all media," the "Metamedium," yet bemoans at the same time the lack of current cyberspace theory. To Lovink, the media theory of the 1980s was a discourse of "The End" presented within the context of cyberculture by writers such as William Gibson, Steward Brand, Timothy Leary, Howard Rheingold, and theorists such as Norbert Bolz and Friedrich Kittler who took up the pioneering works of Marshall McLuhan. Yet, "net criticism" and "cyber discourse," born of the works of those thinkers, is still, to him, a fledgling discipline.[60] David Silver, in his introduction to cyber studies, traces three stages or generations in the new discipline in the last fifteen years of the twentieth century: popular cyberculture, when the Internet was seen as the new frontier; cyberculture studies, when virtual communities attracted academic scholars; and critical cyberculture studies, which dealt with issues of identity and digital discourse.[61]

McLuhan, of course, became famous for his 1964 essay "The Medium is the Message" in which he explained the title by saying that

> it is the medium that shapes and controls the scale and form of human association and action. The content or uses of such media are as diverse as they are ineffectual in shaping the form of human association. Indeed, it is only too typical that the "content" of any medium blinds us to the character of the medium.[62]

Comparing the electric light to a communication medium, he added that the message of the electric light "is like the message of electric power in industry, totally radical, pervasive, and decentralized."[63] If one were to forget the span of years, this would read like a description of the Internet. McLuhan also foresaw, more than forty years ago, the uncanny *physicality* of what will later be called cyberspace as long as it is the *medium* itself which is under scrutiny: "If the formative power in the media are the media themselves, that raises a host of large matters...Namely, that technological media are staples or natural resources, exactly as are coal and cotton and oil."[64]

Such was the influence of McLuhan's theories that even today the fascinating link between the two modes, "real life" and "virtual reality," is still discussed in the context of media theory. John Armitage, in his "Resisting the Neoliberal Discourse of Technology: The Politics of Cyberculture in the Age of the Virtual Class," wonders how, if the medium is indeed the message, it is able to exert such power over human beings who are willing to exchange their corporeality for virtuality.[65] Indeed, one has only to listen to Sterling rhapsodizing, in the ISEA (Inter-Society for the Electronic Arts) 1995 conference, about the new media:

> Media is an extension of the senses.
>
> Media is a mode of consciousness.
>
> Media is extra-somatic memory. It's a crystallization of human thought that survives the death of the individual.
>
> Media generates simulacra. The mechanical reproduction of images is media.[66]

The allusion to Jean Baudrillard—and to Walter Benjamin—is clear and not gratuitous. Cyberspace is the simulacrum *par excellence* and the new media, here synonymous with the new technologies, are equated with an array of simulacra behind which *nothing*—for this is the definition of simulacra—is hidden. Baudrillard, in his seminal *Simulacra and Simulation*, eloquently said:

> The medium itself is no longer identifiable as such, and the confusion of the medium and the message (McLuhan) is the first great formula of this new era. There is no longer a medium in the literal sense: it is now intangible, diffused, and diffracted in the real...One must think instead of the media as if they were, in outer orbit, a kind of genetic code that directs the mutation of the real into the hyperreal.[67]

While I agree with Baudrillard that what *was* the medium is now "intangible" and "diffused," this does not mean that we should not attempt to map or, at least, to come up, with a *theory* upon which such mapping can be undertaken. But what exactly *is* cyberspace? After the first Conference on Cyberspace was held in 1990 at the University of Texas at Austin and the text of the papers gathered in *Cyberspace: First Steps*, the marriage of cyberspace to virtual reality was, as Marie-Laure Ryan puts it, "ratified,"[68] and the path made clear for definitions, enunciations, and theories of cyberspace. Martin Dodge and Rob Kitchin, in *Mapping Cyberspace*, define cyberspace as "navigable space," from the Greek *kyber*, and refer to Gibson's *Neuromancer* as the original source. To them, cyberspace is better seen as a collection of continuously expanding spaces.[69]

Indeed, for the most commonly and most-widely used definition of cyberspace, one has to go back to Gibson's pioneering 1984 cyberpunk novel *Neuromancer*, still now the inspiring bible of cyber fans.[70] Gibson, in probably one of the most quoted passages in all his novels, writes:

> 'Cyberspace. A consensual hallucination experienced daily by billions of legitimate operators, in every nation, by children being taught mathematical concepts . . . A graphic representation of data abstracted from the banks of every computer in the human system. Unthinkable complexity. Lines of light ranged in the nonspace of the mind, clusters and constellations of data. Like city lights, receding . . .'[71]

In the sequel to *Neuromancer*, *Mona Lisa Overdrive*, the third volume of what is known as the Sprawl Trilogy, further explanation is given:

> *There's no there, there.* They taught that to children, explaining cyberspace. She remembered a smiling tutor's lecture in the arcology's executive creche, images shifting on a screen: pilots in enormous helmets and clumsy-looking gloves, the neuroelectronically primitive 'virtual world' technology linking them more effectively with their planes...As the technology evolved, the helmets shrank, the video terminals atrophied.[72]

Cyberspace is accessed, in the Gibsonian world, by connecting through the "static-wall," and "into cluttered vastness, the notional void of cyberspace, the bright grid of the matrix...like an infinite cage."[73]

Many names have been given to what Philip Elmer-DeWitt calls "that shadowy space where our computer data reside." DeWitt mentions the Net, the Web, the Cloud, the Matrix, the Metaverse, the Datasphere, the Electronic Frontier, the Information Superhighway. But DeWitt adds that Gibson's contribution, or coinage, has proved to be "the most enduring" among "the millions of computers jacked into the Internet."[74] Mike Featherstone and Roger Burrows see cyberspace as "a generic term which refers to a cluster of different technologies" and identify three main variants: Barlovian cyberspace, Virtual reality, and Gibsonian cyberspace which can be further described as "a city of data, a Borgesian library of vast databases containing all a culture's deposited wealth, where every document is available, every recording playable and every picture viewable."[75] To Lévy, cyberspace is the "moving space of interactions between knowledge and knowers of deterritorialized intelligent collectives."[76] More prosaically, cyberspace is, according to John Perry Barlow, "that place you are in when you are talking on the telephone."[77]

The connectivity feature looms large in Michael Benedikt's essay "Cyberspace: First Steps":

> Cyberspace: Accessed through any computer linked into the system; a place, one place, limitless; entered equally from a basement in Vancouver, a boat in Port-au-Prince, a cab in New York, a garage in Texas City, an apartment in Rome, an

office in Hong Kong, a bar in Kyoto, a café in Kinshasa, a laboratory on the Moon.[78]

Benedikt gives cyberspace a labyrinthine quality: "Its horizons recede in every direction; it breathes larger, it complexifies, it embraces and involves. Billowing, glittering, humming, coursing, a Borgesian library, a city; intimate, immense, firm, liquid, recognizable and unrecognizable at once."[79] Ryan takes up the corridor-like feature of cyberspace (which she also calls "Cyberia" or "Cyberelia") and says that instead of being traversed point by point like Cartesian space, it is traveled by jumps and "seemingly instantaneous transportation"; that it is not finite but "infinitely expandable"; that since it is non-physical, it is equally distant from all points. As such, its size and/or area expand and change continually and cannot, therefore, be mapped. Cyberspace becomes then "the closest approximation of the mystical circle whose center is everywhere and circumference nowhere: every user regards his home site as the heart of the system, and there is no limit on how far the system can reach."[80] Cyberspace is the twentieth-century's monument to a totalizing vision, just as the cathedral was in the Middle Ages and the encyclopedia was in the Age of Enlightenment. The ideal of the total work is transformed into the idea of universal intertextuality: every individual text is linked to countless others. In the electronic age, as Ryan says, "the text literally becomes a matrix of many texts and a self-renewing entity."[81] If the cathedral and the encyclopedia were monuments constructed according to a specific vision of reality, cyberspace is, to some, a gigantic laboratory set up to examining that reality itself. Heim is often quoted saying that cyberspace is not a mere breakthrough in technology; with its virtuality, "cyberspace is a metaphysical laboratory, a tool for examining our very sense of reality."[82]

Behind the obligatory literariness and cyber-fantasy, one can see why such vistas have mesmerized cyber fans and theoreticians of cyber-culture alike. The fascination of *willingly* and *consciously* entering into a world of "nonspace," into a world similar to that of the mind, is irresistible. For the first time in human history, humanity can attain, without the use of mind-altering techniques or drugs, to a realm where the limit is only the extent of the imagination. Myth, as I will show in more detail later, is an essential element in any mapping of cyberspace.

Robert Nirre is more mundane in equating cyberspace with the Web: "You type: you connect. Your computer nuzzles into another and sucks off a loving, coded flow. You follow a link, you traverse, you search, you back out again." Yet even Nirre, a programmer, launches, quite like Gibson himself in *Neuromancer*, into the following mesmerized description:

But what is this, exactly? Clearly it isn't amenable to our spatial understanding. There

> is neither a physical nor even a conceptual space. There are places but nothing between them, no interspatiality; one navigates a sprawling agglomeration of webbed-together billboards, of insides without exteriors, of islands of hyperdense information adrift on etherealized seas.[83]

Roy Ascott, during the ISEA 2000 conference, preferred to lump the physical and the informational together in what he calls the new Big Bang, the combination of "Bits Atoms Neurons and Genes" together as the new media universe, a universe of "moist" media, the coming together of the silicon domain of computers and the wet biological world of living systems. Ascott devises an interesting new name for this convergence, calling it "natrificial" space, the union of nature and the artificial.[84] A year later, Ascott formally dubs the basis of the new art of the coming century "Moistmedia," a "transformative art concerned with the construction of a fluid reality."[85]

Clearly some framework has to be put in place in order to hamper—or, better, to situate in a theoretical framework—the enthusiasm of sometimes unbridled fantasies. In some extreme cases, writers have put forth scenarios that are nearer science-fiction than reality: Hans Moravec, first in conjunction with KurzweilAI.net, gave a picture of the future where beings will totally lose their geographical boundaries, establishing connections only as informational entities in cyberspace, finally becoming a bubble of Mind expanding at almost the speed of light.[86]

This is not say that theoreticians have not seriously poured over the problem. Lévy, for instance, has fruitfully compared cyberspace with architecture and urbanism. Instead of structuring physical space, the programmer "organizes the *space of cognitive functions*" such as information, memory, evaluation, decision, conception, etc.[87] Yet he also says that technology is a dimension, "cut out by the mind, of a heterogeneous and complex collective future in the city of the world."[88] What Lévy is doing here, and one wonders if he is successful at it, is desperately trying to get away from the whole problem of mapping, and attempting to replace it with a space of functions which will try to mirror the cognitive abilities of the human race, lumping together the mind, physical dimensions, and urban mapping. Yet one has to be fair: the conundrum is not to be easily solved: a "space of cognitive functions" is still a space where human beings go to, or connect to, everyday more and more frequently. But where do they actually *go*? What and where is this new "dimension" and how can it be mapped in urban-like fashion without it being possessed of physical existence?

Can the problem be with the subjects themselves? What if, according to Gilles Deleuze and Félix Guattari, we were not one but many? The two authors begin their famous *Mille Plateaux* with the following announcement:

"The two of us wrote Anti-Oedipus together. Since each one of us was several, there was already quite a crowd...We are no longer ourselves...We have been aided, aspired, multiplied."[89] Would the dissolution of the individual self be more conducive to a better understanding of the non-physicality of cyberspace? In this context, Dyson writes that the cyber experience occurs as flows of data and the "as if you are there" is becoming a "you are there." One is "in cyberspace, not watching it, one is a navigator, a netizen, not a viewer." The gap between signifier and signified, Dyson says, between viewer and viewed, and between real and representation is quickly narrowing.[90]

But this is hardly new. Postmodernism and post-structuralism had already done away with classical concepts of the author and Roland Barthes, Jacques Derrida, and Stanley Fish, just to mention a few, had already shattered the notion of the innocent and passive reader. The individuated author and the individuated reader belong to historical fallacies. But the dissolution of the individual, or the convergence of many individualities into one, poses the same problems mentioned above, those of a "global brain/mind" which would pulsate with all the sucked-in individualities willing to donate themselves.

While no one can question the plausibility of such scenarios, critical and/or cyber theorists try to encompass the many attempts and strive to come up, if possible, with unifying theories about the nascent cyberspace. It is not enough—and ultimately counter-productive—to just resort to the old answer that cyberspace's confusion is inherent in its essence and that any attempts to map out cyberspace are doomed to failure. As my thesis unfolds, it will be clear that such endeavor is not only possible but also highly rewarding in terms of our positioning in cyberspace.

The "matrix" is yet another term offered in the attempt to pin down the nature of cyberspace. Derived from the Latin *mater*, it boasts the following definitions:

> 1. that which gives origin or form to a thing, or which serves to enclose it.
>
> 2. *print.* a mold for casting type faces.
>
> 3. a mold made by electroforming from a disk recording, from which other disks may be pressed.
>
> 4. *Archaic.* the womb.[91]

What is indeed interesting in these definitions is the concept that the matrix is *that which comes first*, that which gives birth to, the *origin* of things; an idea which, if applied to cyberspace, is immediately and irrevocably outrageous to our whole protological views of the universe. How can cyberspace possibly be the master mold from which our physical reality was subsequently produced?

Here, of course, we rejoin cyber-fiction movie hits like, among others, "The Matrix," "Existenz," and "The Thirteenth Floor," where the relationship between physical reality and virtual reality is turned upside down.[92] It is true that western philosophy, since Plato's metaphor of the cave, has been entertaining such notions and has been toying with the attractive idea that our world is but a reflection of a higher order of things. Yet, even to philosophical minds, cyberspace as matrix, *for all to try and experience*, is an awesome and quite impressive notion to accept. But is the term "matrix" as an alternative to "cyberspace" easier to picture? In the matrix as Gibson sees it, the physical and the abstract mix, the objective and the subjective are interchanged: "In the nonspace of the matrix, the interior of a given data construct possessed unlimited subjective dimension; a child's toy calculator...would have presented limitless gulfs of nothingness hung with a few basic commands."[93] Nothingness and nonspace again present the reader with almost insurmountable problems. Short of being a mystic, it is highly dubious that a passage such as the following from *Neuromancer*'s ending would make much sense:

> 'I'm not Wintermute now.'
>
> 'So what are you.' He drank from the flask, feeling nothing.
>
> 'I'm the matrix, Case.'
>
> Case laughed. 'Where's that get you?'
>
> 'Nowhere. Everywhere. I'm the sum total of the works, the whole show.'[94]

The ultimate nature of the matrix is the undifferentiated dissolution of the self in the grand scheme of things. In the matrix, no more dualities, no more oppositions. As Baudrillard says in his "Clone Story":

> The Father and the Mother have disappeared, not in the service of an aleatory liberty of the subject, but in the service of a *matrix called code*. No more mother, no more father: a matrix. And it is the matrix, that of the genetic code, that now infinitely "gives birth" based on a functional mode purged of all aleatory sexuality.[95]

The matrix as replacement for "Father" and "Mother" is seen in Gibson's second part of his trilogy, *Count Zero*, where the protagonist is pictured in his infancy as a boy who had been acquainted with holodecks and who had experienced "mankind's unthinkably complex consensual hallucination, the matrix cyberspace," a plane "where the great corporate hotcores burned like neon novas, data so dense you suffered sensory overload if you tried to apprehend more than the merest outline.[96] Cyberspace as *beyond* echoes the matrix as *before*, the origin of all things, where even the sexes are undifferentiated. The fantasy and utter magic of these two notions can only be expressed in a discourse which re-invents and re-inscribes myth in the new dimensions of the new technologies. Baudrillard is aware of this when he writes:

> It is the fantasy of seizing reality live that continues—ever since Narcissus bent over his spring. Surprising the real in order to immobilize it, suspending the real in the expiration of its double. You bend over the hologram like God over his creature: only God has this power of passing through walls, through people, and finding Himself immaterially in the beyond.[97]

And it is here that the twin concepts of simulation and simulacra appear in connection with the tantalizing problem of reality vs. virtuality or "realspace" vs. cyberspace. Kurzweil, in another futuristic scenario, envisions full immersion into virtual reality by sending millions of nanobots to nerve fibers with the job of suppressing signals coming from real senses and placing them on hold. The nanobots, complete with instructions, will then take over and present a fully immersing simulation to our senses.[98] The illusion would be perfect, the graphics pristinely "real," and the switching from one world to another totally seamless. Instead of entering into a simulated world, we would be, body and all, the simulation itself. Instead of entering into cyberspace, we would become part of cyberspace itself as we are now part or reality. Instead of leaving our bodies *behind* us, we would take them with us. Our bodies, instead of remaining physical bodies only, would become cyberbodies; we would have actually *grown* cyberbodies. The knowledge of new world(s) created by simulation would be as filling as that experienced in real life, if not more. In fact, Lévy believes that "knowledge by simulation" is "undoubtedly one of the new means of knowledge brought about by informatized cognitive ecology,"[99] and assures his readers that computerized simulation lets us explore more complex and more numerous models than those afforded by our limited memory and mental imagery. Simulation, to him, "does not refer to some un-realization of knowledge or of our relationship to the world, but rather to augmented powers of imagination and intuition."[100]

All of the above does not fit very well with the dictionary definition of simulation which gives the Latin *simulatio*, "a pretense," as the origin of the word. Furthermore, "simulation" is:

> 1. the act or process of pretending; feigning.
>
> 2. an assumption or imitation of a particular appearance or form; counterfeit; sham.
>
> 3. *Psychiatry*. a conscious attempt to feign some mental or physical disorder to escape

> punishment or to gain a desired objective.[101]

It is clear why "simulation" was—and still is, despite the fervent efforts of its adherents—seen as the representation of a sham reality, incomplete and *supplementary*, a *margin* which is, ultimately, dispensable. Baudrillard accepts the dictionary definitions given above but gives them a specific twist: to simulate is "to feign to have what one doesn't have" and implies an absence. Yet he warns that things are not that simple and quotes the Littré: "'Whoever fakes an illness can simply stay in bed and make everyone believe he is ill. Whoever simulates an illness produces in himself some of the symptoms'," and simulation therefore "threatens the difference between the 'true' and the 'false,' the 'real' and the 'imaginary'."[102] Dissimulating is hiding what is, simulating is showing what is not. The first, as Baudrillard says, "reflects a theology of truth and secrecy," the second "inaugurates the era of simulacra and of simulation, in which there is no longer a God to recognize his own, no longer a Last Judgment to separate the false from the true, the real from its artificial resurrection."[103] Simulation is not mere counterfeit, mere sham, mere faking; it is not a playful one-time happy-go-lucky journey into a cheap imitation of reality, an ersatz realm on the computer screen or apprehended through VR goggles. Simulation, in Baudrillard's term, is a "strategy of the real, of the neoreal and the hyperreal."[104] What is even more dangerous, in the Baudrillardian socio-political worldview, is that simulation, by showing a thing which is not, by consciously showing it as imaginary, is in fact hiding the truth that *it really is* and what is referred to as real *is not*. The famous Baudrillardian Disneyland analogy makes this clear:

> Disneyland exists in order to hide that it is the "real" country, all of "real" America that *is* Disneyland...Disneyland is presented as imaginary in order to make us believe that the rest is real, whereas all of Los Angeles and the America that surrounds it are no longer real, but belong to the hyperreal order and to the order of simulation.[105]

Can the above be transposed to cyberspace? Can we safely show that cyberspace exists in order to hide that it *is* the real space? Can we say that cyberspace is presented as imaginary in order to make us believe that the rest is real, whereas all of real space that surrounds us is no longer real but belongs to the hyperreal order and to the order of simulation? Is the imaginary of cyberspace a deterrence machine set up in order to rejuvenate the fiction of the real in the opposite camp, in this case in real life? Hence the representation of cyberspace as debility, as infantile degeneration; hence the relegation of cyberspace to long-haired teenagers, to pranksters, to immature but dangerous crackers, hence the overwhelming dominance of the gaming industry in cyberspace.

True, this scenario is daring, but not devoid of interesting ramifications.[106] What if cybermapping turns out to be, in the final analysis, the mapping of reality itself or, better to say, the mapping of our hyperreality? Is it true that, in Baudrillard's words, "[t]he universe, and all of us, have entered live into simulation"?[107] Can the following scene from *Count Zero* become a reality in the near future: "He spent most of those three months in a ROM-generated simstim construct of an idealized New England boyhood of the previous century...You could smell the lilacs, late at night"[108]? Would simulation become so real that we could, in an instant, be transported to a world so real that even the senses would be fooled? The following scenario, also from *Count Zero* sets the picture:

> As her fingers closed around the cool brass knob, it seemed to squirm, sliding along a touch-spectrum of texture and temperature in the first second of contact...A confusion of small details, her own memory of a drunken art school picnic warring with the perfection of Virek's illusion. Below her lay the unmistakable panorama of Barcelona, smoke hazing the strange spires of the Church of the Sagrada Familia.[109]

If we have indeed entered live into simulation, it is all the more urgent to map our bearings or, more importantly since we are dealing with shifting essences, shifting allegiances and self-substituting modes of representation, to devise a new mapping strategy that goes beyond the vagaries of the moment in a constantly changing dimension. Far from being awed at the prospect and daunted by what appears to be insurmountable difficulties, we could, even with Baudrillard, agree that "[t]his is where seduction begins."[110] Barthes' injunction that "[i]t is not the 'person' of the other which is necessary to me, it is space: the possibility of a dialectic of desire, of an *unpredictability* of jouissance"[111] is appropriate in a study which takes cyberspace as a textual construct. Indeed, it is not necessarily the "person" of cyberspace which I have in mind, rather it is, paradoxically, its space, i.e., the myriad possibilities offered by a theory of cybermapping among many potential others. Graham Allen, in his book on intertextuality, writes the following words: "What to many might seem counterintuitive in Barthes's treatment of literary books becomes obvious, inevitable and even 'natural' when dealing with hypertext systems."[112]

One clear conclusion to be drawn from the above is that cyberspace as a new field of study is rife with theoretical possibilities and is fully open to the gaze of cultural and critical theorists. Ryan's edited volume on cyberspace textuality contains these revealing words by Espen Aarseth about the race not only to conquer cyberspace *per se* but also the theoretical field of cybertheory itself:

> [T]he race is on to conquer and colonize these new territories for our existing paradigms and theories, often in the form of "the theoretical perspective of <fill in your favorite theory/theoretician here> is clearly really a prediction/description of <fill in your favorite digital medium here>." This method is being used with permutational efficiency throughout the fields of digital technology and critical theory, two unlikely tango partners indeed. But the combinatorial process shows no signs of exhaustion yet.[113]

Featherstone and Burrows echo the importance the new technologies have on contemporary theory and on the representation of the reality we live in: "The writings which have emerged on cyberspace, cyberbodies and cyberpunk over the last decade are replete with utopian, dystopian and heterotopian possibilities. For some, this entails the assumption that we are about to enter a new era."[114]

Three noteworthy attempts are currently being made to map cyberspace, all of them spearheaded by Dodge, director of the Cyber-Geography Research initiative. A researcher at the Centre for Advanced Spatial Analysis (CASA) at University College, London, Dodge and his team produced, until 2001, a web page called "Mappa.Mundi Magazine"[115] which presented, every month, a different map of the Internet and of related cyberspace geographies. Among the maps are "Mostly Cloudy, Clearing Later: Network Weather Maps" which showed, graphically, network lines superimposed on actual geographical maps of different countries, with "weather" forecasts using the specialized jargon of weather reports; "Mapping the Geography of Domain Names," which showed areas of concentration of the more than 20 million domain names[116] registered on the Internet also superimposed on real maps, with the aim of identifying decision-making areas; "The UK Academic Map," online since 1994 which gave a visual directory of universities and colleges in the UK, also based on geographic maps.

Dodge also maintains a page entitled "Cyber-Geography Research" at http://www.cybergeography.org. He introduces CyberGeography as

> the study of the spatial nature of computer communications networks, particularly the Internet, the World-Wide Web and other electronic "places" that exist beyond our computer screens, popularly referred to as *cyberspace*. Cybergeography encompasses a wide range of geographical phenomena from the study of the physical infrastructure, traffic flows, the demographics of the new cyberspace communities, to the perception and visualisation of these new digital spaces.[117]

As mentioned above, the indefatigable Dodge has also written, with Kitchin, two books on the subject, *Mapping Cyberspace* (2000) and *Atlas of Cyberspace* (2001).[118] The latter contains more than 300 images of dazzling beauty which, according to the authors, can be printed out and framed for aesthetic effect. The overall aim is both technical and artistic, as the table of contents moves from questioning the ways we can view the images to mapping infrastructure and traffic, mapping the web, mapping conversation and community, to finally imagining cyberspace. Kitchin describes, on his homepage, the aims of the book:

> The maps in the Atlas of Cyberspace are important as they are powerful in framing our conception of the new virtual worlds beyond our computer screens. More and more of our time and leisure and business activities are spent in virtual space and yet it is a space that is difficult to comprehend and mentally visualise...Other maps in this collection are simply beautiful to look at, possessing powerful aesthetic qualities in their own right.[119]

To Dodge and Kitchin, their atlas can help users, services providers, and others interested in network operations, to understand the "various spaces of online interaction and information" and get a "unique sense of a space that is difficult to understand from navigation alone."[120] Dodge and Kitchin use cartography to classify and represent information that would otherwise be too large and too complex to comprehend, especially in the case of cyberspace. More interestingly, the authors are aware that any mapping in general and the mapping of a brand new space like cyberspace in particular involve decisions of inclusion and exclusion which will in fact construct a cyberspace tailored to the cultural, historical, and judgmental values of the cartographers themselves. They say:

> It has long been recognized that mapping is a process of creating, rather than revealing, knowledge...In other words, a map is imbued with the values and judgements of the people who construct it. Moreover, they are undeniably a reflection of the culture and broader historical and political contexts in which their creators live. As such, maps are not objective, neutral artefacts but are constructed in order to provide particular impressions to their readers.[121]

Steve Branigan, expert in computer and network security and vice president of engineering at Lumeta Corporation has co-authored a paper entitled "What Can you do with Traceroute?"[122] in which the Unix network utility Traceroute is used for mapping purposes. Lumeta Corp. has devised a visualization algorithm in order to help them understand their daily databases. While the generated visualizations take no account of geography, they do however produce stunning color-coded images highlighting domain names, autonomous systems, routeable/non-routeable network addresses, leaks in corporate perimeters, mergers-and-acquisitions activities, small home networks, and anomalies associated with them. Art galleries have expressed interest in these generated visualizations, some of which were installed at the entrance of the Glasgow Science Centre in July 2001.[123]

Lévy initially proposed to construct hypertextual maps through diagrams and graphics but ended up getting bogged down by details and fell prey to the false analogy of comparing cyberspace to real space. Quite simplistically, he wrote:

> One can also construct global two-dimensional maps which show only available paths from one single node: whether it is the starting document, the root of the hypertext, or the active current document. Let us imagine a road map of France where would be represented only the roads leading from Bordeaux to other cities while in Bordeaux, from Toulouse to other cities while in Toulouse, etc. At any time, visual complexity would thus be reduced to the minimum.[124]

Yet Lévy then affirms, paradoxically, that "to the regular movement of the page succeeds the perpetual movement of folding and unfolding of a kaleidoscopic text."[125] How can a kaleidoscopic text be made analogical to a map of Bordeaux and Toulouse?

Lévy—at least in his early writings,—Dodge, Kitchin, and Branigan, among others, have undoubtedly pioneered the field of cybermapping yet, upon looking at the maps produced, one can wonder about three intimately related problems:

One, most of the maps are time-bound, i.e., they are either historical, depicting some network state dating a few years back or, on the contrary, so "current" that they are only valid the moment they are produced. What is more serious is that when they are printed they are already outdated. It is true that the "Mappa Mundi" project gave updated, online maps, but the problem remains the same. The issue of forecasting is also problematic: how can one accurately predict network movements? Can the tools, terminology, and methodology of weather forecasting be used in cybermapping with similar results? The very changeability of networked technologies renders the above mapping attempts at best a precarious endeavor.

Two, most of the maps presented tend more to be on the quantifiable side and thus leave little place for theory. A theory, according to *Webster's Dictionary*, is "a coherent group of general propositions used as principles of explanation for a class of phenomena" and "a particular conception or view of something to be done or of the method of doing it; a system of rules or principles."[126] What are the principles which can help us explain the phenomenon of cyberspace? What is the particular conception or view of cybermapping and the method of coming up with a mapping theory? More importantly, how do *we, the human species in the twenty-first century,* use these maps to get our bearings in cyberspace? The above maps are as useful to the cyberspace navigator as a night photograph of car traffic on a busy lane. Dazzling, yes, but how useful to the newcomer?

Three, the visually aesthetic appeal produced by such maps probably will, in the long run, be detrimental to a serious attempt at mapping cyberspace. Flashy and stunning postcards produced with sophisticated photographic equipment do not do justice to what is presented to the naked eye (which, by the way, is also a sophisticated photographic equipment complete with filters and zooming lenses). To pursue the analogy above, a postcard, however flashy, is only useful insofar as the newcomers are aware of the framework lying behind the taking of the photograph, insofar as they know that behind the tracer-like car lights there are actual cars, that the lights in the night sky, produced by increased exposure time are, to the naked eye, a compilation of stationary moments, insofar, finally, as they know that behind or below bewildering sights lies a city the inhabitants of which have learned to navigate almost effortlessly. If postcards and photographs are esthetically pleasing, it is because *we know what lies behind them*. In a world yet unknown to us like cyberspace, we cannot yet afford this luxury.

Have we not yet fully realized the impact of cyberspace on our lives? Are we amusing ourselves with pretty graphics instead of trying to look for inner frameworks and mechanisms? Michel E. Doherty, Jr., in his "Marshall McLuhan Meets William Gibson in 'Cyberspace'," raises a very pertinent issue:

> [S]ince the totality of (post)modern culture has not yet interiorized virtual technology, we cannot define, much less critique the "realm" of cyberspace. In fact, if cyberspace does not exist—at least not in ways we can yet talk about sensibly—then, hell! What's the point of talking about it at all? Well, cyberspace *is* being created—or perhaps it is being discovered—and it is in the process of being interiorized.[127]

As we are the first generation of cybernauts, it is our duty to seriously map the yet-uncharted territories of cyberspace. If this new space does not, as Doherty says, exist in ways we can yet talk about sensibly, can we not at least *read* it as a text is read and extract from it a *grammar* or, better, a *grammatology* of cyberspace? McLuhan wrote that "Alexis de Tocqueville was the first to master the grammar of print and typography. He was thus able to read off the message of coming change in France and America as if he were reading aloud from a text that had been handed to him."[128]

Cyberspace *is* the print and typography revolution of the twenty-first century. Are we able to master its grammar and from there read the message of coming change? Dyson accurately says that as the Renaissance maps reduced the known three-dimensional world to its two-dimensional representation, the technology of virtual reality is again reducing our two-dimensional ways of mapping into a "numerical series composed of just two binaries." This series of reductions, from the Renaissance to the present age, has allowed, paradoxically, the handling of the infinite horizons of cyberspace.[129] It is in the same vein that Massumi suggests a new concept of mapping better adapted to the new virtual spaces, based on a topographical vision of cyberspace. Defining topology as "the science of self-varying deformation," he concedes that since a topological unity is multiple (because in constant deformation), it is theoretically impossible to actually diagram and follow every step in a topological transformation.[130] Massumi's approach, then, is diametrically opposed to that of Dodge and Kitchin in that it openly acknowledges the dynamic nature of cyberspace and the problematics inherent in every mapping, and tacitly expects that the issues surrounding the mapping of cyberspace will reshape our concepts of mapping in general.

Where are we in now in the stage of cyberspace mapping? Even Dodge and Kitchin acknowledge the fact that we are in the infancy of cybermapping, saying that at present, it is fair to state that "cartographers of cyberspace are at the same stage as the cartographers at the start of the Renaissance period," in addition to the fact that, unlike the Renaissance cartographers, we are not even in possession of blueprints.[131] Lévy, in a more recent reappraisal, says that the form and content of cyberspace are "still partially undetermined," and that the mobile maps of these fluctuating spaces belong to *terra incognita*, adding, with Massumi, that even if cybernauts were able to achieve the immobility required to get more precise bearings, the virtual landscape itself would continue to flow, to swirl, and to transform the gazer.[132] Lévy's cartography, then, short of being a topographical attempt, is content to map a "space of knowledge," a sort of "anthropological cartography."[133] To achieve this, Lévy has come up, with his colleague Michel Authier, with the concept of the "Ciné-carte," a sort of hypercard which would trace the cybernauts' progress in the moving world of signification as they become part of the collective intelligence of cyberspace; the hypercard would be the record of that interaction between this collective intelligence and its navigation in the informational universe.[134] In 1997, Paul F. Starrs, in "The Sacred, the Regional, and the Digital," stressed that "cyberspace is one realm where geographers ought to bestir themselves to consider how information has become tantamount to space and is in the process of becoming an actual place."[135]

Yet, unbridled theories can be as nefarious as no theories at all. Countering the hype generated by cyberspace, Cameron Bailey, at the ISEA 1995 conference, was sounding the warning siren: "Faced with the delirious prospect of leaving our bodies behind for the cool swoon of digital communication, the leading theorists of cyberspace have addressed the philosophical implications of a new technology by retreating to old ground."[136] Bailey is here referring to the happy-go-lucky expeditions to a new world where major concerns such as race, gender, and class are put behind. Similarly, theorists have been gazing not at the moon but at the finger pointing to it, allowing themselves to be misled by bright colors and fireworks. David Gelernter, in his "The Second Coming—A manifesto," articulates this danger:

> "The network is the computer"—yes; but we're less interested in computers all the time. The real topic in astronomy is the cosmos, not telescopes. The real topic in computing is the Cybersphere and the cyberstructures in it, not the computers we use as telescopes and tuners.[137]

At this moment, there is no theory of cyberspace which can offer a solid framework from which we can map our bearings and thence map our progress. *Cybermapping and the Writing of Myth* constitutes an attempt at reading the ways we can map cyberspace along the same lines offered by David Bell and Barbara M. Kennedy in their *Cybercultures Reader*, which is to "understand the ways in which cyberspace…is currently being experienced and imagined."[138] Trying at the same time to keep away from the hype surrounding cyberspace, it is helpful to keep in mind Behar's wise warning that "with tempered reflection, reasoned argument, and empirical study we can be saved from the excesses of hype that so severely mystify and distort the actual implications and consequences of cyberspace developments."[139]

As a critical theorist, my approach will be governed by questions of writing and as such I will treat cyberspace as an ultimate text which is being constantly and infinitely re-written by its users. One of the recurrent ideas will be that postmodernist and post-structuralist theories have suddenly seen themselves actually translated into cyberspace. Cyberspace is thus the very fertile testing ground of the seminal theories/writings of Walter Benjamin, Jacques Derrida, Roland Barthes, Michel Foucault, Italo Calvino, Jorge Luis Borges, Fredric Jameson, Jean Baudrillard, Paul Virilio, Jean-François Lyotard, Gilles Deleuze, Félix Guattari, Hakim Bey, and many others. Writing—*Écriture* in a Barthean sense—will form, along with the twin concepts of myth and the city, the backbone of this investigation. Cyberspace, as I will try to show throughout, fills the contemporary mythical void by re-creating an already-there virtual reality through the magical/mythical medium of writing with the city as model.

The following chapter, "Beginnings," covers the development of cyberspace up to the present time and also presents the history of cyberculture studies;

Chapter three, "New Maps for a New Body," looks at maps in general and at mythical maps in particular in order to find out how they can lead to a better understanding of cybermapping;

Chapter four, "Cyberspace as Myth," shows that myth, far from being absent from our contemporary lives, has resurrected in cyberspace. Myth also provides a working framework for a theory of cybermapping;

Chapter five, "Cyberspace as *Écriture*: the Metaverse," forms, with chapter four, the centerpiece and hub around which this whole investigation rotates. Cyberspace, when approached through writing, proves to be yet another textual space with its unique features. Cyberspace as a new form of writing *is* mappable space;

Chapter six, "Cyberspace as City," uses the city as model and locus of a writing of myth and of a mythical writing; and

Chapter seven, "Mapping Socio-Cultural Cyberspace," investigates ways in which issues of gender, race, class, authority and power, protest, anarchy and resistance to information oppression can construct maps and *islands* in cyberspace.

NOTES

1 Paul Auster, *In the Country of Last Things* (New York: Penguin, 1988), 20.

2 Pierre Lévy, *Les Technologies de l'intelligence: L'avenir de la pensée à l'ère informatique* (Paris: La Découverte, 1990), 18. All quotations from French sources appearing below have been freely translated by me.

3 Ibid., 17.

4 Pierre Lévy, *L'Intelligence collective: Pour une anthropologie du cyberspace* (Paris: La Découverte, 1997), 11.

5 Ibid., 11–12.

6 Ibid., 21–23.

7 Ibid., 25.

8 Pierre Lévy, *Qu'est-ce que le virtuel?* (Paris: La Découverte, 1998), 10.

9 J. Hillis Miller, "Moving Critical Inquiry On," *Critical Inquiry* 30.2 (Winter 2004), 414–20, 415–16.

10 Marshall McLuhan, "Speed of Cultural Change," *College Composition and Communication* 9.1 (Feb. 1958), 16–20, 20.

11 Mark Dery, *Escape Velocity: Cyberculture at the End of the Century* (New York: Grove Press, 1996), 3.

12 Michael Heim, *The Metaphysics of Virtual Reality* (Oxford: Oxford UP, 1994), xi.

13 Jacques Derrida, *Writing and Difference* (London: Routledge, 1997), 278.

14 Fredric Jameson, *Postmodernism or, The Cultural Logic of Late Capitalism* (London: Verso, 1992), 1.

15 Fredric Jameson, "The End of Temporality," *Critical Inquiry* 29 (Summer 2003), 695–718, 697.

16 Ibid., 701.

17 Lévy, *Technologies*, 64. See also Arturo Escobar's essay, "Welcome to Cyberia: Notes on the Anthropology of Cyberculture," *Current Anthropology* 35.3 (Jun. 1994), 211–31, which provides clear links between cyberculture and modernity/postmodernism and problematizes, among other things, ways in which a post-structuralist understanding of the body is to be constructed in cyberspace. Escobar's paper also reviews various types of cultural analysis conducted toward the articulation of what he calls an "anthropology of cyberculture."

18 J. Hillis Miller, "'World Literature' in the Age of Telecommunications," *World Literature Today* 74.3 (Summer 2000), 559–61, 559.

19 Bruce Sterling, "The Manifesto of January 3, 2000," *Whole Earth* (Summer 1999), 4–9, 5.

20 Friedrich Kittler, "There is no Software," *Ctheory* (Oct. 18, 1995), online at http://www.ctheory.net/ articles.aspx?id=74, as article a032 [Last accessed Oct. 12, 2006].

21 Lévy, *Technologies*, 135–36.

22 Marjorie Worthington, "Bodies that Natter: Virtual Translations and Transmissions of the Physical," *Critique: Studies in Contemporary Fiction* 43.2 (Winter 2002), 192–208.

23 Jameson, *Postmodernism*, 38.

24 Ibid., 44.

25 Frances Dyson, "'Space,' 'Being,' and Other Fictions in the Domain of the Virtual," in *The Virtual Dimension: Architecture, Representation, and Crash Culture,* John Beckmann, ed. (New York: Princeton Architectural Press, 1998), 27–45, 31.

26 Ibid., 33.

27 Maurice Blanchot, *Le Livre à venir* (Paris: Gallimard, 2001), 9–10.

28 Ibid., 265.

29 Marshall McLuhan, "Effects of the Improvements of Communication Media," *The Journal of Economic History* 20.4 (Dec. 1960), 566–75, 575.

30 Thomas Pynchon's "Is it O.K. to Be a Luddite?" in *The New York Times Book Review* (Oct. 28, 1984), 1, 40–41, gives an interesting overview of "Luddism" and how the meaning has changed throughout the years. To Pynchon, even the most die-hard Luddites will be hard-pressed to forsake their computers as knowledge is seen by all as power.

31 Jodi Dean, "Virtual Fears," *Signs: Journal of Women in Culture and Society* 24.4 (Summer 1999), 1069–78.

32 Ray Kurzweil, "The Human-Machine Merger: Why we will Spend Most of Our Time in Virtual Reality in the 21st Century," originally presented at the *ACM Siggraph Conference*, Jul. 2000. Later published as "Merging Human and Machine," *Computer Graphics World* (Aug. 2000), 23–24.

33 Tyler Stevens, "'Sinister Fruitiness': Neuromancer, Internet Sexuality and the Turing Test," *Studies in the Novel* 28.3 (Fall 1996), 414–33, 414.

34 Janet Moursund, "SANCTUARY: Social Support on the Internet," in *Mapping Cyberspace: Social Research on the Electronic Frontier*, Joseph E. Behar, ed. (Dowling College Press, 1997), 53–78, 61.

35 Lévy, *Virtuel*, 115.

36 Lévy, *Technologies*, 16.

37 Qtd in Allucquere Rosanne Stone, "Will the Real Body Please Stand up? Boundary Stories about Virtual Cultures," in *The Cybercultures Reader*, David Bell and Barbara M. Kennedy, eds. (London: Routledge, 2002, 504–28), 517.

38 Lévy, *Technologies*, 16.

39 Ibid., 12–13.

40 Dery, *Escape*, 14.

41 J. Hillis Miller, "Literary Study among the Ruins," *Diacritics* 31.3 (Fall 2001), 57–66, 57.

42 *Webster's Encyclopedic Unabridged Dictionary of the English Language* (New York: Gramercy Books, 1994), 1596. In this and other instances from the same source I have not necessarily kept the original numbering of definitions, giving them sequentially instead.

43 Paul Levinson, in his *Realspace: The Fate of Physical Presence in the Digital Age, on and off Planet* (London: Routledge, 2003), prefers to follow the pair "talking" and "walking" as he traces the development of cyberspace as opposed to "real space." Levinson's book is a clear diatribe against cyberspace and its excesses, as he writes in his preface: "Cyberspace…exceeds its humanity when it challenges the core of realspace, or the place where physical presence, not just exchange of information, is essential" (xii).

44 Richard Norton, "What is Virtuality?" *The Journal of Aesthetics and Art Criticism* 30.4 (Summer 1972), 499–505, 499.

45 Ibid., 500.

46 Mike Featherstone and Roger Burrows, eds., *Cyberspace/Cyberbodies/Cyberpunk: Cultures of Technological Embodiment* (London: Sage, 2000), 5.

47 Arthur Kroker and Michael A. Weinstein, *Data Trash: The Theory of the Virtual Class* (Montreal: New World Perspectives, 2001), 1.

48 Julio Bermudez and Debra Gondeck-Becker, "Emerging Architectures in the Virtual Scape: Architecture of (Im)Possibilities," *Sixth International Symposium on Electronic Art (ISEA),* Montreal, Canada (Sep. 18–22, 1995).

49 Qtd. in Cheryl Kolak Dudek, "Fiber/Cyber/Text," *Surface Design Journal* 26.2 (Winter 2002), 26–31, 31. The Eisenman original can be found in the *CCA Competition for the Design of Cities*, Canadian Center for Architecture, Montreal, Quebec, Canada, exhibited on Nov. 15, 2000–Apr. 1, 2001.

50 Philippe Queau, "Virtual Multiplicities," *Diogenes* 46.183 (Fall 1998), 107–110, 107.

51 Lévy, *Virtuel*, 13.

52 Ibid., 69–76.

53 Ibid., 10.

54 Ibid., 10, 23.

55 Ibid., 15–16.

56 Ibid., 18.

57 Brian Massumi, "Line Parable for the Virtual (On the Superiority of the Analog)," in Beckmann, *Virtual Dimension*, 305–21, 309.

58 Jaron Lanier, "Virtual Reality: A Techno-Metaphor with a Life of its Own," *Whole Earth* (Fall 1999), 16–18, 17.

59 Mark Poster, "Theorizing Virtual Reality: Baudrillard and Derrida," in *Cyberspace Textuality: Computer Technology and Literary Theory*, Marie-Laure Ryan, ed. (Bloomington: Indiana UP, 1999), 42–60, 44.

60 Geert Lovink, "From Speculative Media Theory to Net Criticism," *European Media Art Festival*, Osnabrück, Germany (May 7–11, 1997). Online at http://www.emaf.de/1997/vortrag_e.html [Last accessed Oct. 12, 2006].

61 David Silver, "Looking Backward, Looking Forward: Cyberculture Studies 1990–2000," in *Web Studies: Rewriting Media Studies for the Digital Age*, David Gauntlett, ed. (Oxford UP, 2000), 19–30. Fredric Jameson says in this context: "Besides the nomadic horde, I believe that another concept in the toolkit of late Deleuze can be seen as a variation on the ideal schizophrenic, and that is the enormously influential—and also relatively incomprehensible—theme of virtuality, which has been saluted as the first original philosophical conceptualization of the computer and cyberspace" (Jameson, "Temporality," 711).

62 Marshall McLuhan, *Understanding Media: The Extensions of Man* (London: Routledge, 1994), 9.

63 Ibid., 9.

64 Ibid., 21.

65 John Armitage, "Resisting the Neoliberal Discourse of Technology: The Politics of Cyberculture in the Age of the Virtual Class," *Ctheory* (Mar. 1, 1999), online at http://www.ctheory.net/articles.aspx?id=111, as article a068 [Last accessed Oct. 12, 2006].

66 Bruce Sterling, "The Life and Death of Media," *Sixth International Symposium on Electronic Art (ISEA)*, Montreal, Canada (Sep. 18–22, 1995).

67 Jean Baudrillard, *Simulacra and Simulation* (Ann Arbor: The University of Michigan Press, 2000), 30.

68 Marie-Laure Ryan, "Cyberspace, Virtuality, and the Text," in Ryan, *Cyberspace Textuality*, 78–107, 81.

69 Martin Dodge and Rob Kitchin, *Mapping Cyberspace* (London: Routledge, 2001), 1.

70 Paul C. Adams, in "Cyberspace and Virtual Places," *Geographical Review* 87.2 (Apr. 1997), 155–71, writes: "Gibson's vision has been prodigious. Today his influence is found in children's cartoons, Japanese movies, contemporary novels, and even screen savers—programs that turn an idle computer screen into graphic art" (165).

71 William Gibson, *Neuromancer* (London: HarperCollins, 2001), 67.

72 William Gibson, *Mona Lisa Overdrive* (London: HarperCollins, 1995), 55–56.

73 Ibid., 56.

74 Philip Elmer-DeWitt, "Welcome to Cyberspace: What is it? Where is it? And how do we get there?" *Time* (Spring 1995), 4–11, 4.

75 Featherstone and Burrows, *Cyberspace*, 5–6.

76 Lévy, *Intelligence*, 30.

77 Qtd in Elmer-DeWitt, "Welcome," 8.

78 Michael Benedikt, "Cyberspace: First Steps," in Bell and Kennedy, *Cybercultures*, 29–44, 29.

79 Ibid., 30.

80 Ryan, *Cyberspace Textuality*, 86.

81 Ibid., 14.

82 Heim, *Metaphysics*, 83.

83 Robert Nirre, "Spatial Discursions: Flames of the Digital and Ashes of the Real," *Ctheory* (Feb. 13, 2001), online at http://www.ctheory.net/articles.aspx?id=134, as article a092 [Last accessed Oct. 12, 2006]. See also Howard Rheingold, *Virtual Reality* (New York: Simon and Schuster, 1991).

84 Roy Ascott, "Moistmedia, Technoetics and the Three VRs," *Tenth International Symposium on Electronic Art (ISEA)*, Paris, France (Dec. 7–10, 2000), proceedings online at http://www.isea2000.com/ [Last accessed Oct. 12, 2006].

85 Roy Ascott, "Arts Education @ the Edge of the Net: The Future Will be Moist!" *Arts Education Policy Review* 102.3 (Jan.-Feb. 2001), 9–10, 9.

86 Hans Moravec, "The Senses Have no Future," in Beckmann, *Virtual Dimension*, 85–95.

87 Lévy, *Technologies*, 62.

88 Ibid., 219.

89 Gilles Deleuze and Félix Guattari, *Capitalisme et Schizophrénie 2: Mille Plateaux* (Paris: Les Éditions de Minuit, 1980), 9.

90 Dyson, "Space," 31.

91 *Webster's*, 884–885.

92 Jason Haslam, in "Coded Discourse: Romancing the (Electronic) Shadow in *The Matrix*1," *College Literature* 32.3 (Summer 2005), 92–115, writes in this context that "critics and fans of both the film and the subgenre have portrayed *The Matrix* as the first successful filmic translation of the imagery of cyberpunk, which is usually seen as being founded by, and epitomized in, William Gibson's 1984 novel *Neuromancer*" (92).

93 Gibson, *Neuromancer*, 81.

94 Ibid, 315–16.

95 Baudrillard, *Simulacra*, 96–97.

96 William Gibson, *Count Zero* (London: HarperCollins, 1995), 62.

97 Baudrillard, *Simulacra*, 105.

98 Ray Kurzweil, "Merging Human and Machine," *Computer Graphics World* (Aug. 2003), 23–24.

99 Lévy, *Technologies*, 137.

100 Ibid., 142.

101 *Webster's*, 1329.

102 Baudrillard, *Simulacra*, 3.

103 Ibid., 6.

104 Ibid., 7.

105 Ibid., 12–13.

106 See also Robin Hanson's "How to Live in a Simulation," *Journal of Evolution and Technology* 7 (Sep. 2001). Hanson poses the problem of whether we can know for sure that we are not living in a simulation ourselves. Others, like Brian Massumi in his "Realer than Real: The Simulacrum According to Deleuze and Guattari," *Copyright* 1 (1987), seriously doubt Baudrillard's views, disposing of them as fun reading and hyper cynicism. From a different angle, Laura J. Huey, in her "Policing the Abstract: Some Observations on Policing Cyberspace," *Canadian Journal of Criminology* 44.3 (Jul. 2002), is keen on assuring the judicial body that cyberspace is not mere simulacra, and that while cyberspace is an imperfect copy of the world, its spaces do mirror and duplicate existing realities of oppression and resistance.

107 Baudrillard, *Simulacra*, 159.

108 Gibson, *Count Zero*, 9–10.

109 Ibid., 24–25.

110 Baudrillard, *Simulacra*, 164.

111 Roland Barthes, *Le Plaisir du Texte* (Paris: Seuil, 1973), 11.

112 Graham Allen, *Intertextuality* (London: Routledge, 2000), 200.

113 Espen Aarseth, "Aporia and Epiphany in *Doom* and *The Speaking Clock*: The Temporality of Ergodic Art," in Ryan, *Cyberspace Textuality*, 31–41, 31.

114 Featherstone and Burrows, *Cyberspace*, 1.

115 Still online at http://www.mappa.mundi.net and also at http://mundi.net/maps [Last accessed Oct. 12, 2006].

116 According to "Domain Name School: The Domain Name Educator" online at http:// www. domainnameschool.com/domainnames.htm [Last accessed Oct. 12, 2006].

117 Martin Dodge, "Welcome to Cyber-Geography Research," "About" section, online at http://www.cybergeography.org/about.html [Last accessed Oct. 12, 2006].

118 Martin Dodge and Rob Kitchin, *Atlas of Cyberspace* (London: Addison-Wesley, 2001).

119 Rob Kitchin, "About the Book," online at http://www.kitchin.org/atlas/about.html [Last accessed Oct. 12, 2006].

120 Dodge and Kitchin, *Atlas*, 2.

121 Ibid., 3.

122 Steve Branigan et al., "What Can you do with Traceroute?" *IEEE Internet Computing* 5.5 (Sep.–Oct. 2001), 96.

123 "Lumeta's Brilliant Internet Map Featured at Glasgow Science Centre; Queen Elizabeth in Attendance for Centre's Grand Opening," *Business Wire* (Jul. 17, 2001).

124 Lévy, *Technologies*, 43.

125 Ibid., 47.

126 *Webster's*, 1471.

127 Michael E. Doherty, Jr., "Marshall McLuhan Meets William Gibson in 'Cyberspace'," *CMC Magazine* (Sep. 1, 1995), 4.

128 McLuhan, *Understanding Media*, 13.

129 Dyson, "Space," 32–33.

130 Massumi, "Line Parable," 306.

131 Dodge and Kitchin, *Mapping*, 71.

132 Lévy, *Intelligence*, 9–13.

133 Ibid., 147.

134 Ibid., 153, 183–85.

135 Paul F. Starrs, "The Sacred, the Regional, and the Digital," *The Geographical Review* 87.2 (Apr. 1997), 193–218, 198.

136 Cameron Bailey, "Virtual Skin: Articulating Race in Cyberspace," *Sixth International Symposium on Electronic Art (ISEA)*, Montreal, Canada (Sep. 18–22, 1995), later published in *Immersed in Technology,* Mary Anne Moser and Douglas MacLeod, eds. (Cambridge: MIT Press, 1996), 29–50.

137 David Gelernter, "The Second Coming–A manifesto," *Edge* 70 (Jun. 15–19, 2000). Online at http://www.edge.org/documents/archive/edge70.html [Last accessed Oct. 12, 2006].

138 Bell and Kennedy, *Cybercultures*, 1.

139 Behar, *Mapping Cyberspace*, 5.

Chapter Two

Beginnings

> We are come not only past the century's closing, he thought, the millennium's turning, but to the end of something else. Era? Paradigm? Everywhere, the signs of closure. Modernity was ending.
>
> William Gibson, *Virtual Light*[1]

Cyberspace has basically been depicted, until now, in three forms: as text-only, as text and graphics, and as graphics-only. The differences have been historical, technological, and preferential. Historically, the processor power necessary to produce smooth real-time graphics was lacking and text-only was the quickest and most stable way to present other worlds. As a consequence of text-only output, users had to input their interactions with the program in text as well.[2] As processor power increased, text output was matched with still graphics which would change as environments changed. With the introduction of the mouse, "clickable" graphics became the fashion and gradually took the place of text input. Graphics-only games launched the whole simulation industry into a new age where real-time graphical exposure was paramount to a totally immersing experience. Yet, "pockets of resistance" are still to be found, mainly comprised of purists who vehemently advocate text-only as the acme of cyberspace and the real realm of the mind.[3] I will show later how text, despite the vagaries or representation, has been and still is the prime element in cyberspace.

Cyberspace as technology can be traced back to the 1950s in non-digital form with a company called Avalon Hill which kept players awake for hours, even days, painstakingly engaging, on detailed table-top maps, in strategic and tactical warfare recreating battles from Gettysburg to Stalingrad. Players would go through intricate rules, timetables, and a myriad other variables regulating movement, terrain, line of sight, weather conditions, wind speed, etc. In 1973, Gary Gygax and Dave Arneson invented a new game which was to galvanize table-top players all over the world and create a whole new gaming genre known as RPG (Role-Playing Game): "Dungeons and Dragons." As opposed to the earlier table-top games, Dungeons and Dragons does not use a board and the only map is held by the "Dungeon Master" who divulges to the players their bearings as they progressively move from one area to another. The Dungeon Master doubles as storyteller since the players have only her/him to rely on while they fill a narrative space with their choices and actions. A typical D&D game would begin with the Dungeon Master giving a brief overview of the history of the place, whether it is a castle, a forest, or an antique city, whetting the players' appetite with a description of the fabulous treasures hidden therein, and then the dialogues would typically begin in the following fashion:

> –DM: You come out of the forest and you just see the castle of Mangoli in front of you. It is a huge building with high smooth walls surrounded by a moat. The path through which you have arrived stops in front of a gate. Nobody seems to be there. What do you want to do now?
>
> –Player 1: (looking at the other players) We decide to come closer, OK?
>
> –Players 2 and 3: OK, we come closer.
>
> –DM: Fine. The moment you cross the gate an iron grating suddenly falls behind you and blocks your way back.
>
> –Player 3: Zounds! We should have taken a wood log from the forest and we could have put it below the gate to keep a way out!
>
> –DM: While you're talking, from the gate to your left has just sprung out a small battalion of orcs. There are eight of them.[4]

As seen from the typical encounter above, most of the game is played in the imagination of the players. One of the early D&D manuals has this to say about imagination:

> The Dungeon Master imagines the setting, the story, the map of the dungeon where the players will be. He materializes the dungeon in a drawing. The players imagine themselves to be the characters who will enter the dungeon and play there…Potential spectators follow in imagination the great adventures also taking place in imagination![5]

As to the dungeon map, carefully hidden by the DM and revealed only as the players uncover new ground, the manual says the following: "The dungeon is the play area, drawn as a detailed map, inside of which will take place the actions and the combats the characters will go through. On this map is marked the placement of traps, treasures, and monsters."[6] Detailed instructions are given to the DM for the design of the dungeon and for the display of only bits of the map to the players, never the whole plan; as the players advance in the dungeon(s), old bits are withdrawn and new ones given.[7] More recently, the *Dungeon Master's Guide*, published by the "official" Wizards of the Coast, gives the following advice to the DM: "When one of the players is drawing a map as the characters explore a new place, give her a break. Describe the layout of the place in as much detail as she wants, including dimensions of rooms," but also warns: "Of course, when the PCs [player characters] are lost in a dungeon or walking through fog, the whole point of the situation is that they don't know where they are (or where they're going). In cases such as these, don't take pains to help the mapper."[8]

Table-top games, as they developed into D&D and RPGs on their way to becoming computer games, helped place—or replace—in the forefront three interconnected elements which are still key features of any cybermapping concept: one, myth suddenly came to be essential, as magic and fantasy realms proved to be the main attraction to players; two, the storytelling element became the only way to move the story forward: not only did the DM have to *verbally* describe the setting and the action, but the players also had to *tell* each others and the DM what they wanted to do—with the advent of the computer, speaking will be replaced by typing or, in other words, by writing; three, the concept of mapping, probably taken from the fog-of-war uncertainty of actual war games, evolved into something which will stay, in one form or another, the main problem to be dealt with in cyberspace: the map, instead of remaining a stationary entity, became a dynamic positioning device following the players *in the moment*, thus forcing them, first, to rely on their memory in order to remember what paths had already been taken and second, to rely on their imagination in order to anticipate what might lie ahead. These three elements, namely, myth, writing, and the dynamic nature of the map are, again, indissociable features of cybermapping.

With the spiriting away of the static, conventional map, the players' experience took on a slightly ethereal quality and forced participants to *interiorize* their bearings to the extent that they felt themselves actually *inside* the dungeon, actually fighting monsters and looting treasures.[9] Such translation might explain the attraction the game has held over players up until now with clubs and federations all over the world. But a hard blow was in store for the pen-and-paper purists: the coming of the computer on the scene would further change the way mapping was conceived.

In 1972, computer map plotter Will Crowther, husband of Pat Crowther who had found a secret passage in one of the most famous caves in the Bedquilt Cave area in Mammoth Cave, Kentucky, produced the first of what would be a long and venerable line of "Interactive Fiction" (IF) games, the famous “Advent.” In the words of Graham Nelson—the creator of *Inform*, one of the most famous development systems for the writing of text adventures,—Will Crowther “invented a new category of computer program and of literature,” a gaming genre rich in levels, details, and treasures.[10]

In 1976, Don Woods, working at the Stanford Artificial Intelligence Laboratory, discovered Crowther’s game on what was then the ARPANET network and offered to rework the cave system and stock it with more “magical” items and puzzles. Nelson judiciously remarked, in *The Inform Designer’s Manual*, that “there is a Crowther and a Woods in every designer, the one intent on recreating an experienced world, the other with a really neat puzzle which ought to fit *somewhere*.”[11] This marked the starting point, in cyberspace, of the actualization of the age-old dichotomy between reality and virtuality, between the actual and the potential, and between static and dynamic concepts of mapping.

By 1977, “Advent” was circulating everywhere and quickly became something of an addiction. The latest incarnation of the game can now be found online at the Interactive Fiction Archive, the pilgrimage place for IF aficionados created by Volker Blasius and maintained by David Kinder and Stephen Granade.[12] One of the latest versions, called “Adventure: The Interactive Original,” is dutifully credited to Will Crowther and Don Woods but also credits Donalk Ekman, David M. Baggett, and Graham Nelson for reconstructing it. The game begins in typical, time-honored IF fashion:

> At End of Road
>
> You are standing at the end of a road before a small brick building. Around you is a forest. A small stream flows out of the building and down a gully.
>
> >

The > sign prompts the players to input, through the keyboard, whatever they want to do and the map, again, is withheld from the player, only to be given on the spot after such commands as “look” or “examine place.” Yet the computer, taking the place of the DM, was different in two ways: first, it lacked the human element and blindly enforced the rules ascribed to it by the programmer and, second, the team-spirit which reigned in D&D simply disappeared. The player had become a single, solitary wanderer in the mazes of caves churned out on-screen by “Advent.” Instead of discussing their actions, players had to make do with the program’s limited vocabulary, called the “parser,” and soon learned they could also input abbreviated commands such as “n” for north, “s” for south, “w” for west, “e” for east, “d” for down, and “u” for up in order to move around the caves. Players were free to draw their own maps as the game advanced since it invariably involved a lot of back-tracking. In fact, such was the need for mapping that additional software was later specifically designed to help in the drawing of rooms, hallways, and other map features. The "Frobot Magic Adventure Mapper," the "Interactive Fiction Mapper," "Mapper," and "MapMaker," to name just some of the most widely used, added a new dimension to mapping by spiriting away the last remnant of "physicality" from the game, in this case the pencil and paper. Mapping was done either by entering information onto the mapping software, or was performed automatically on screen, the player having only to step into a room or a hallway in order for the mapping software to update the digital map. Whichever the method, mapping had entered cyberspace. As Mark J. P. Wolf pointed out in this context, the player "has a stake in the navigation of space, as knowledge of the video game's space is often crucial to a good performance." [13] Furthermore, what were noisy, sometimes boisterous gatherings around a big table laden with paper, pencils, charts, and the obligatory drinks and sandwiches, plus the continuously rattling sound of unusually-shaped dice, became a totally silent head-to-head exchange of written words. It had, in fact, become a *contest of writing*.

Yet what drew players away from the social gatherings of D&D was a certain kind of magic which was lacking from the human-to-human encounters: what was probably the illusion—illusion because behind the "machine" existed a very human game designer—of trying to "beat the machine," trying to overcome not a human mind with all its frailties and idiosyncrasies, but the cool, inert, unthinking force of matter, binary electrical signals hiding beneath human-like written words. Mankind's greatest dream, that of mind controlling matter was, for the first time in the history of humanity, at the fingertips of almost any individual. Players became not only adventurers in the game they were playing, but also humans re-enacting the age-old ritual of mind over brute force. Back in the 1970s, cyberspace indeed began to fill the mythical void by re-creating virtual reality through the magical medium of writing.

But cyberspace, with "Advent," was little more than a makeshift space with boundaries pre-set by the programmer and with characters the responses of which were limited to the extent of their parser. When all was said and done, when puzzles were solved and treasures scavenged, there was little to do in IF apart from signing off for good and beginning a new game. Surely, this could not be all of cyberspace. Roy Trubshaw and Richard Bartle, at the University of Essex, took over where "Advent" had left and devised, in 1979, "Essex MUD," short for "Essex Multi-User Dungeon." The Essex MUD was only the first of many MUDs (later on the "Dungeon" was transformed, elegantly, into "Dimension" as it had to acquire, for many, more respectability) to spring later, lasting until the late 1980s. To the usual mapping descriptions of "Advent" was added a crucial change: players were no longer solitarily fighting computer-generated orcs and goblins; they connected through phone lines and/or networks and met, through their characters, together. The realms were now filled with human beings and it is from that time on that cyberspace became a social reality. Later, the gaming elements were found to attract less participants than expected, and little by little users would meet to chat and discuss other issues as well. MUDs took a new turn in 1990 with the creation, by Pavel Curtis, of LambdaMOO, the first social MUD accommodating users who would construct a real world in cyberspace. MUDs that were devoted to gaming quickly saw the potentials of social gathering in cyberspace and followed suit, producing a bevy of MUDs devoted to education, programming, science, anthropology, literature, and other fields. But the map was still there, and it was indispensable. What had been a hitherto mythical space inhabited by unreal denizens and fantastically convoluted mazes filled with deadly traps was transformed, overnight, into a similar meeting place where, instead, serious academic discussions were being held.

In fact, more than twenty-five years after the creation of "Essex MUD," immersive online communities are alive and kicking. The first electronic urban environment, "Habitat," was designed in 1986 and could accommodate 20,000 users simultaneously. "Regions," as they were called, were inhabited by "toons," representations of users as blocky images with a torso, legs, arms, and head. They could also be represented as taking different positions such as standing and walking. The landscape where these toons—also called "avatars," but more on this later—existed was made up of simplistic renditions of houses on green grass under a blue sky. As Michael Ostwald remarked, "Habitat became more than a poorly rendered computer game, it was an interactive environment, a place with its own currency, newspaper and traditions."[14]

The most famous of these new cyber-environments is undoubtedly "Active Worlds,"[15] started in 1995, and now accessed through the Internet at http://www.activeworlds.com. In their own words, Active Worlds,

> the web's most powerful Virtual Reality experience, lets you visit and chat in incredible 3D worlds that are built by other users. Think you have what it takes to build your own world or Virtual Reality game? Active Worlds is the place for you, where in minutes you can create fascinating 3D worlds that others can visit and chat in. The Active Worlds Universe is a community of hundreds of thousands of users that chat and build 3D virtual reality environments in millions of square kilometers of virtual territory.[16]

Virtually anything can be done on Active Worlds. For business-oriented users,

Active Worlds can help them "[c]reate massive amounts of buzz, sell products, support customers...perform interactive product demos, and conduct on-line corporate training and other e-learning initiatives." For shoppers, a lot is offered:

> If you love to shop you will find plenty to do in Active Worlds. @mart, the first "real" 3D virtual mall in cyberspace is designed to resemble a modern shopping mall...With over 100 stores selling a wide range of products, @mart is a unique e-commerce experience.

Since Active Worlds is a full cyberspace world, customers can buy either "traditional" products for their "real life" needs or "virtual" products they can use in Active Worlds. For the gaming enthusiast, the choices are only limited by the imagination, ranging from trivia games to bowling, soccer, chess, and bingo.

The educational side is not forgotten, though, witness the creation of whole worlds called "Active Worlds Educational Universe" (AWEDU) which host, in full graphical rendering, simulations of architecture departments from famous universities to science labs and ThinkQuest projects. Participants include the Art Center College of Design (California), Bologna University, the Boston Architectural Center, Canterbury Christ Church University College, Cornell University, George Washington University, Harvard University, Indiana University, Loyola University, the National Defense University, the University of California, the University of Hong Kong, and many others. The spatial and mapping configuration of Active Worlds is also impressive, boasting more than "1000 3D virtual reality worlds."

Interestingly, the most popular worlds are those which display mythical or fantastic elements: "Mars," "Metatropolis," "Atlantis," "Godzilla," "The 13th Floor," "Pollen World," "Fantasy World," "Castles Worlds," "Knights World," "Patagonia," "AD&DRPG" (Advanced Dungeons and Dragons Role Playing Game), "Ashmore," "Avalon," "Borg," "Destiny," "Kakariko," "Mutation," etc.

But is Active Worlds actually a workable cyberspace solution? According to Active World statistics, there are currently over 1.5 million individual users worldwide, making more than 1,000,000 hits to their universe per day, with more than 40,000 users having registered as "citizens." Sky maps of Alpha-World, the earliest and most famous world, are on display showing the population changes from 1996 to 2001 (after 2001, and in Active Worlds' own words, AlphaWorld maps became too large to be displayed online) . The total area of AlphaWorld covers about 400sq kilometers, and would take two hours for an avatar (the player's persona in cyberspace) to walk directly from one end to another.

Interaction between citizens (users who have paid their joining fees) or between citizens and tourists (users who have not paid fees and who are restricted to certain areas) is simple: once the Active World software is downloaded and installed, a graphical user interface (GUI) runs in a screen showing the area in front of the user, like in first-person shooters, and a communication area, like the one in chat rooms. Users move around with their avatar names hovering above their head. To communicate, users can click on other users and type the message in the chat area, or they can simply choose from a list of names and compose the message. Ralph Schroeder, Avon Huxor and Andy Smith conducted some insightful research on the geography and social interaction in Active Worlds. Their focus, though, was on spatial layout, transportation and mobility, and time. They accurately pinpoint the myth of the frontier that shaped the American society as one of the prime movers in the population boom of Active Worlds (at the time of their writing the article, in 2001, there were 500 worlds compared to more than 1000 now). The physical geography of AlphaWorld is a simple one: it is a flat plain of virtual land 429,038 x 429,038 km in size, 4.4% larger than California. Navigation is based on a Cartesian system with the center of AlphaWorld at coordinates 0,0, known as Ground Zero. Things function pretty much like in real life with, of course, all the liberties afforded by being disembodied in cyberspace. Distances can be quickly covered by flying. Citizens can build permanent residences after claiming virtual land according to Active Worlds regulations. A newspaper, "The New World Times," is issued; an Alpha World Police Department monitors irregularities such as "avabuse," or avatar abuse, mainly done through the medium of writing.[17] It is clear that even now, at the beginning of the twenty-first century—and more than twenty years after "Advent,"—myth and writing make up two of the most important pillars of successful cyberspace construction.

Interactive Fiction, in the meantime, was not going to lose ground to the graphical revolution that was slowly sweeping the market as processors grew in computing power and decreased in price. In 1979, students at MIT founded Infocom, the company destined to become synonymous with professional commercial IF. In 1980, "Zork: The Great Underground Empire" became the most famous IF game of all times, with an opening that soon became the stuff of legends:

> West of House. You are standing in an open field west of a white house, with a boarded front door.
>
> There is a small mailbox here.
>
> >

"Zork" was followed by other Infocom successes like "Arthur," "Border Zone," "Bureaucracy," "Deadline," "Enchanter," "Sorcerer," "Spellbreaker," "Lurking horror," "Planetfall," and "Suspended." Other companies soon followed in the wake of Infocom's success: Level 9, Scott Adams' Adventure International, Topologika, Magnetic Scrolls, Artic Adventures, Firebird, Infogrammes, etc. The years between 1982 and 1986 were the golden years of text adventures, yet it soon became clear that text-only games could not hold long in front of the more immersing graphical games unleashed on the market. Ever since the arrival of "Doom," "Quake," "Unreal," "Jedi Knight" and their sequels, IF went into a hibernation period, with most of the early gaming companies ceasing to publish text-based games. With graphically-intensive games such as "Morrowind," "Gothic" I and II (the third episode is scheduled to come out in late 2006) and "Oblivion," where players are let loose in an environment where *they* decide what to do and what quests to follow and whether *they* will stay in one game location as long as they wish or not, the "dynamic" nature of gaming has, with the addition of luscious graphics, acquired new dimensions.[18]

Paradoxically, however, the boom in graphical games produced a counter-culture which yearned for a more purist approach to gaming and which valued the imagination boost provided by text-only adventures where players actually *write* their actions and movements and receive *written* feedback on them. Cyberspace had become so much like reality that it lost its appeal. Users were expected to make a few mouse moves, click a few times, and the job was done. Photo-realistic renditions of users, earlier an asset, now became stale and unattractive. The magic was leaking somewhere, and the culprit was probably too much "eye-candy" and too much realism. If cyberspace were to became too realistic, then it would cease to be cyberspace and would be another real-life medium like television, only more interactive. But cyberspace had so much potential that such a fate has been, so far, averted, witness, among other things, a resurgence of interest in IF. Indeed, it is interesting to notice that, alongside giant strides on the graphical scene, a parallel boom can be witnessed in the opposite camp, that of text-only interactive fiction. Since 1995, a yearly IF competition, engineered by Gerry Kevin Wilson, has been gaining momentum: 12 IF games were entered in 1995, 26 in 1996, 34 in 1997, 27 in 1998, 37 in 1999, 53 in 2000, 51 in 2001, 38 in 2002, 30 in 2003, 36 in 2004, 36 in 2005, and 43 in 2006 (the results of the 2006 competition should be out toward the end of that year).[19] Gems such as "Anchorhead," "Christminster," "Curses," "Edifice," "Galatea," "Photopia," and "Rameses," to name a few, have propelled IF to the highest standards of fiction writing, and have rejuvenated interest in a genre where imagination, myth, and writing reign without rivals.

Indeed, movement along ephemeral map locations is probably what IF users will spend most of their time doing. As Lev Manovich observes in "The Aesthetics of Virtual Worlds," the new technologies are taking cybernauts back to "ancient forms of narrative" where the hero's movements in space define the plot.[20] What Manovich comes very close to but does not indicate is that ancient forms of narrative were built on the twin elements of myth and storytelling, the recurring pair which, as I am trying to show throughout in this book, combine to construct cyberspace and provide a framework for mapping it. It is safe to pronounce that most, if not all, of the above representations of cyberspace, from D&D to MUDs to IFs, can be grouped under the term of "fiction," very basically defined as "the class of literature comprising works of imaginative narration, esp. in prose form."[21] Active Worlds fits the definition well: although it is based on reality, it is a world fully created from the imagination, not presented as fact, and dependent for its existence and good functioning on writing and reading; it can thus be called literature in the loose sense of the word.

The development of the computer industry and the concomitant need for anchoring the cybernauts' bearings have been paralleled by the development of new literary genres that specifically deal with the possibilities inherent in cyberspace. In fact, it should come as no surprise, after the above, that fiction is the moving force behind many of the current concepts of cyberspace. Indeed, Gibson's *Neuromancer* and Neal Stephenson's *Snow Crash* have, almost all by themselves, constructed the cyberspace scene and have become cult classics. Dodge and Kitchin say:

> Cyberpunk recognized and explored our new post-modern condition through a literary vehicle that is itself decidedly post-modern...[Gibson and Stephenson] have been particularly influential in shaping the development, visual interface and spatial organization of cyberspace, and in articulating new geographic imaginations of emerging spaces such as the Internet. Indeed, it is now claimed by some that recent developments in both computing and society can be seen as an attempt to put their fictional visions into practice.[22]

The word "novel" comes from the Latin *nōvus*, meaning "new,"[23] and Gibson's *Neuromancer* is, indeed, a "new" "romance," for, if we look up the definition of "romance" we find that it is "a narrative depicting heroic or marvelous achievements, colorful events or scenes, chivalrous devotion, unusual or even supernatural experiences, or other matters of a kind to appeal to the imagination."[24] *Neuromancer* is almost all of the above. It is, of course, a narrative which depicts the heroic *and* marvelous achievements of a hero, Case, who, amidst many colorful events and more fantastic scenes, chivalrously devotes himself to the rescue of two women, one of them dead and spirited to the world of the matrix. In an Orpheus-like sacrifice, Case "jacks" into the matrix and encounters his lost love. The events are, to say the least, unusual and supernatural, and the end result is definitely appealing to the imagination. If one adds the term "new" to Gibson's "romance," a new literary genre, the "cyberpunk" novel, has indeed emerged from his novel and continues, albeit in a different form, to the present day.[25] Jameson, talking about attempts to think "the impossible totality of the contemporary world system," characterizes Gibson's novel as "a new type of science fiction, called *cyberpunk*," an "exceptional literary realization within a predominantly visual or aural postmodern production" expressing nothing less than "global paranoia itself."[26]

What theorists of cyberspace owe Gibson is immense. It was probably *Neuromancer* which expressed, for the first time, the joy and exhilaration of being in cyberspace in contrast to real life: "In the bars he'd frequented as a cowboy hotshot, the elite stance involved a certain relaxed contempt for the flesh. The body was meat. Case fell into the prison of his own flesh."[27] The way cyberspace is pictured might have come from descriptions like the following: "Faint kaleidoscopic angles centered in to a silver-black focal point...If he looked directly at that null point, no outline would form,"[28] and Case's cyber-fight with the AI defense system is an encounter of epic proportions delivered with a prose that sounds like poetry and a description where synesthesia blurs the boundaries of the senses: "The roof of his mouth cleaved painlessly, admitting rootlets that whipped around his tongue, hungry for the taste of blue, to feed the crystal forests of his eyes, forests that pressed against the green dome, pressed and were hindered, and spread, growing down."[29] A kind of epiphany awaits Case as he enters into the heart of cyberspace. In almost mystical overtones, he surrenders to the crushing emptiness and realizes that cyberspace, just like a hologram, contains the sum of everything in every parcel of it. Omniscience, the prerogative of God, is granted to the matrix "cowboy":

> He knew the number of grains of sand in the construct of the beach (a number coded in a mathematical system that existed nowhere outside the mind that was Neuromancer)...He knew the number of brass teeth in the left half of the open zipper of the salt-crusted leather jacket that Linda Lee wore as she trudged along the sunset beach, swinging a stick of driftwood in her hand (two hundred and two).[30]

Gibson, in *Mona Lisa Overdrive*, toys with this idea of god-in-cyberspace, leaving the reader to decide whether the matrix has a god which existed before it or whether humans, through the matrix, gave it a god:

> 'The mythform is usually encountered in one of two modes. One mode assumes that the cyberspace matrix is inhabited, or perhaps visited, by entities whose characteristics correspond with the primary mythform of a "hidden people". The other involves assumptions of omniscience, omnipotence, and incomprehensibility on the part of the matrix itself."
>
> 'That the matrix is God?'
>
> 'In a manner of speaking, although it would be more accurate, in terms of the mythform, to say that the matrix *has* a God, since this being's omniscience and omnipotence are assumed to be limited to the matrix.'
>
> 'If it has limits, it isn't omnipotent.'
>
> 'Exactly...Cyberspace exists, insofar as it can be said to exist, by virtue of human agency.'[31]

When Case, at the end of the novel, thinks that he has lost Linda forever, he suddenly discovers, in cyberspace, the truth of the matter:

> And one October night, punching himself past the scarlet tiers of the Eastern Seaboard Fission Authority, he saw three figures, tiny, impossible, who stood at the very edge of one of the vast steps of data. Small as they were, he could make out the boy's grin, his pink gums, the glitter of the long gray eyes that had been Riviera's. Linda still wore his jacket; she waved, as he passed. But the third figure, close behind her, arm across her shoulders, was himself.[32]

His earlier trip to the matrix and his encounter with Linda had left a trace on the "vast steps of data." Linda was not dead, after all, and his visit to her left not only a mark but his whole self. The old dream of parallel lives, of missed opportunities being granted anew and, most importantly, the eternal dream of immortality, are fulfilled. There, in cyberspace, everything is possible and nothing ever disappears. Memory, forever retained in data banks, is the great preserver. Compared to this, reality is only a pale shadow of this grand utopian world called cyberspace.

Neuromancer is, from the excerpts above, what every attempt at describing cyberspace boils down to: the battle between the flesh and the spirit, the artistic purity of lines, the mystical synesthesia or the drug-like confusion of sense, the mystically ethereal weightlessness, the feeling of omniscience, and the illusion of immortality. Theology, art, poetry, mysticism, power, and the ontological tragedy of being, all of these vie in *Neuromancer* to produce a discourse which will form the backbone of cyberspace.

Published in 1992, Stephenson's *Snow Crash* takes Gibson's *Neuromancer* one step further and adds a much-needed dose of humor to make cyberspace more palatable to the mainstream user. The hero of the novel, "Hiro

Protagonist," is described as "[l]ast of the freelance hackers, Greatest sword fighter in the world…Specializing in software-related intel (music, movies & microcode)."[33] The pun on Hiro's name is, of course, a realization that writing can offer degrees of play that are not allowed in other modes, as Derrida clearly showed with his coining of "différance" to rhyme with "difference." Hiro's Japanese links allow him to "hack" his way out of difficult situations, both in real life and in virtual reality, both as a katana master and a software guru.

Hiro's job, simply put, is to get information, any kind of information, store it, and make it available to whoever wants it later, for, in the world of *Snow Crash*, information is vital. As information is a commodity that is actively sought and dearly paid, cyberspace is not Gibson's elitist and ultra-sophisticated construct but a place where everybody can go. This place is accessed by jacking into the computer and donning special goggles:

> The resulting image hangs in space in front of Hiro's view of Reality. By drawing a slightly different image in front of each eye, the image can be made three-dimensional. By changing the image seventy-two times a second, it can be made to move. By drawing the moving three-dimensional image at a resolution of 2K pixels on a side, it can be as sharp as the eye can perceive, and by pumping stereo digital sound through the little earphones, the moving 3-D pictures can have a perfectly realistic soundtrack.[34]

In contrast to Gibson's matrix, Stephenson's 3-D world is, even to the layperson, immediately translatable into a tangible technology, with parts and terminology known to all.[35] Stephenson goes to great lengths to explain the differences between this virtual construct, called the Metaverse, and real life:

> So Hiro's not actually here at all. He's in a computer-generated universe that his computer is drawing onto his goggles and pumping into his earphones. In the lingo, this imaginary place is know as the Metaverse. Hiro spends a lot of time in the Metaverse. It beats the shit out of the U-Stor-It.[36]

Compared to the dismal reality of Hiro's real life accommodation, the Metaverse is heaven. In fact, much of what has already been said about Active Worlds can be found in the description and the functioning of the Metaverse, almost down to the rules laid out for land acquisition, building, and human interaction, and down to the liberties cyberspace can grant, including "free-combat zones where people can go to hunt and kill each other."[37]

Of course, all of the Metaverse's liberties with the physical and biological constraints of reality are only a programmer's show, the writing of a piece of incredibly complex code, but a piece of writing nonetheless. Stephenson, in the midst of a relaxed prose, is keen on reminding this fact to his readers:

> The number 65,536 is an awkward figure to everyone except a hacker, who recognizes it more readily than his own mother's date of birth: It happens to be a power of 2—2^{16} power to be exact—and even the exponent 16 is equal to 2^4, and 4 is equal to 2^2. Along with 256; 32,768; and 2,147,483,648; 65,536 is one of the foundation stones of the hacker universe, in which 2 is the only really important number because that's how many digits a computer can recognize. One of those digits is 0, and the other is 1.[38]

In the Metaverse, avatars are only pieces of software:

> They are the audiovisual bodies that people use to communicate with each other in the Metaverse... Your avatar can look any way you want it to, up to the limitations of your equipment. If you're ugly, you can make your avatar beautiful. If you've just gotten out of bed, your avatar can still be wearing beautiful clothes and professionally applied makeup. You can look like a gorilla or a dragon or a giant talking penis in the Metaverse.[39]

As events unfold in the novel, Hiro, both as avatar and as real physical person, has to counteract the evil represented by Raven in and out of the Metaverse, provoking interesting questions about the nature of what we call reality and what we recognize now as cyberspace.

But things are never simple in cyberspace. Raven is the chief instrument in bringing an information virus that affects hackers through the Metaverse: cyberspace is not only a simulation, it is most importantly a portal through which information, the essential element in the universe, can circulate. As such, the battle is fought in and out of the Metaverse, in and out of the written code, *against* a writing which wants to *write off* the data banks of those who specialize in this writing, namely, hackers. A *counter-writing*, this virus, called Snow Crash in the novel, parasites the writing of software and, by the same token, the writing of the Metaverse itself.

Snow Crash shows, maybe in a more lucid way than *Neuromancer*, that cyberspace—the Metaverse—is not necessarily a fake rendition of reality, and is maybe not *the* ultimate reality behind our everyday physical dimension. But the lack of distinction between the two worlds poses interesting questions about the actual reality of both. In an imaginative *tour de force*, Stephenson has a character called Ng wired to the Metaverse while simultaneously living, and occasionally driving, in real life, a tank-like van. Since Ng's real body is wired shut, he can only control his van *through* the Metaverse, from multiple monitors set in his cyberspace home, a French colonial villa in prewar Vietnam. In this absolute reversal, Ng's physical body is almost non-existent, a cumbersome and heavy tool controlled almost exclusively from the Metaverse through cameras relaying information to cyber-monitors.[40] Can the representation of the body, then, be only a medium through which information circulates and is stored, whether in real life or in cyberspace?

NOTES

1 William Gibson, *Virtual Light* (London: Penguin, 1994), 89–90.

2 The ramifications of such writing processes will be made clear as this investigation proceeds.

3 Even at the time of writing, countless numbers of people of all ages are playing "rogue" or "rogue-like" games like "NetHack," "Moria," "Adom," "Angband," "Alphaman," "Kharne," "Ragnarok," "Saladir," "Zangband," and others too numerous to mention where, on a DOS-like screen, heroes fight monsters in diverse environments, all represented as ASCII (American Standard Code for Information Interchange) characters. Graphic renderings with sound effect and music have been recently added, but the appeal of the game has quickly suffered as a consequence.

4 Adapted from Mathilde Maraninchi, *Donjons et Dragons: Le Jeu de rôle et de stratégie de la nouvelle génération* (Paris: Solar, 1982), 9–10.

5 Ibid., 11.

6 Ibid., 11.

7 Ibid., 61.

8 *Dungeon Master's Guide: Core Rulebook II v.3.5* (Renton: Wizards of the Coast, 2003), 15.

9 Julian Dibbell's *My Tiny Life: Crime and Passion in a Virtual World* (NY: Henry Holt, 1999), and Graham Nelson's *The Inform Designer's Manual*, 4th edition (St. Charles: The Interactive Fiction Library, 2001), online at http://inform-fiction.org/manual/ [Last accessed Oct. 12, 2006], especially his chapter 46, 342–63, of the PDF manual, entitled "A Short History of Interactive Fiction," contain interesting details on the history of virtual worlds and on the concept of mapping, and helped me edge my way, in some places, through the maze of companies and platforms which sprang up in the early days of computer gaming. Since it is not the purpose of this research to give a full history of the development of cyber-gaming–there are better books on the subject like the ones cited above–I have only followed the cybermapping trail. Other sources come from my personal collection of games, both table-top and digital.

10 Nelson, 344.

11 Nelson, 345.

12 Online at ftp://ftp.gmd.de/if-archive, at http://www.ifarchive.org/, and at other mirrors.

13 Mark J. P. Wolf, "Inventing Space: Toward a Taxonomy of On- and Off-Screen Space in Video Games," *Film Quarterly* 51.1 (Autumn 1997), 11–23, 13.

14 Michael Ostwald, "Virtual Urban Futures," in Bell and Kenney, *Cybercultures*, 658–75, 670.

15 The company's name is spelled "Activeworlds," and the simulated realms "Active Worlds."

16 This and following references can be found online at http://www.activeworlds.com [Last accessed Oct. 12, 2006].

17 Ralph Schroeder, Avon Huxor and Andy Smith, "Activeworlds: Geography and Social Interaction in Virtual Reality," *Futures* 33.7 (Sep. 2001), 569–87.

18 Two good chronologies of the development of the Internet can be found in Dery, *Escape*, 4–8, and in Dodge and Kitchin, *Mapping*, 6–12.

19 See http://www.ifcomp.org [Last accessed Oct. 12, 2006] for the latest competition news and archives.

20 Lev Manovich, "The Aesthetics of Virtual Worlds: Report from Los Angeles," in *Digital Delirium*, Arthur and Marilouise Kroker, eds. (Montréal: New World Perspectives, 2001), 288–300, 290–91.

21 *Webster's*, 527.

22 Dodge and Kitchin, *Atlas*, 229.

23 Bernard Auzanneau and Yves Avril, *Dictionnaire latin de poche* (Paris: Le Livre de poche, 2000), 405.

24 *Webster's*, 1242.

25 See Bruce Sterling's *Mirrorshades: The Cyberpunk Anthology* (NY: Arbor House, 1986).

26 Jameson, *Postmodernism*, 38.

27 Gibson, *Neuromancer*, 12.

28 Ibid., 216.

29 Ibid., 304.

30 Ibid., 304–305.

31 Gibson, *Mona Lisa*, 138.

32 Gibson, *Neuromancer*, 317.

33 Neal Stephenson, *Snow Crash* (London: Penguin Books, 1993), 17.

34 Ibid., 22.

35 True, Stephenson had the advantage of a technology which, since Gibson's *Neuromancer*, had not only grown exponentially, but had also become practically—and more intuitively—available to a wider population.

36 Stephenson, *Snow Crash*, 22.

37 Ibid., 23.

38 Ibid., 23.

39 Ibid., 34. See also John C. Briggs, "Virtual Reality is getting Real: Prepare to Meet your Clone," *The Futurist* 36.3 (May-Jun. 2002), 34–41.

40 Stephenson, *Snow Crash*, 206–12.

CHAPTER THREE

New Maps for a New Body

> Disdain the flesh: blood and bones and network, a twisted skein of nerves, veins, arteries.
>
> Marcus Aurelius, *Meditations*[1]

> If, today, there can be such an intense fascination with the fate of the body, might this not be because the body no longer exists?
>
> Arthur and Marilouise Kroker, *Body Invaders*[2]

Humanity's old dream to go beyond the limitations of the body finds in cyberspace an interesting testing ground: no longer the prisoner of an unreliable and vexing body destined to perish, the cyberbody promises access to immortality. Arthur and Marilouise Kroker ask the following: "Why then be sad as the body is unplugged from the planet? What is this if not the more ancient philosophical movement of immanence to transcendence as the body is on its way to being exteriorized again?"[3] Exteriorized to be reborn in other shapes, in other combinations, in other configurations. To Dyson, cybernauts are not in the present, for they are entering a part of the future; they are not humans, for they are cyborgs, half-beings half-machines; they are not on the earth, for they have entered into a digital realm; and they are not in their bodies anymore, for they are approaching what can be seen as pure mind. The new spaces where humans are treading are "apocalyptic," "nihilistic," "impossible," and presuppose "the end of organic life."[4] Lévy talks of the new body in cyberspace as being already "other," as already exchanging identities with the other bodies around it:

> We are at the same time here and there thanks to the techniques of communication and telepresence. Medical imaging has made our organic interiority transparent. Grafts and prostheses are mixing us to others and to artefacts...We are altering our

> individual metabolisms with drugs...Reproduction, immunity against diseases, the regulation of emotions, all these performances hitherto private have become public capacities, exchangeable, externalized.[5]

This new body, which Lévy calls the "hyperbody," is a multiple body the frontiers or limits of which have become blurred. Each new technology is adding like a new kind of skin to the actual visible skin; bodies are becoming disseminated toward the outside, and each individual body is becoming part and parcel of an immense hyperbody both hybridized and globalized. Humanity's hyberbody "extends its chimerical tissues between the epidermises, between the spaces, beyond the frontiers and the oceans, from one shore to the other of the river of life."[6] On the verge of becoming etherealized, the virtual body—the "hyberbody,"—becomes, to Lévy, pure speed, forever surging upward, a "glorious body" akin to that of the free-faller and the surfer.[7] Far from being a "disincarnation," the passage from the physical to the virtual is seen as a "reinvention, a reincarnation, a multiplication, a vectorization, a heterogenesis of the human,"[8] Like Mikhail Bakhtin's heteroglossia, the centrifugal effect of the new technologies is multiplying the body's voices in kaleidoscopic fashion. As such, the human body is also, like the computers which heralded the age of the virtual, the site of hacking practices, the locus of a frenzied obsession with changing, reworking, and re-programming the human body in order to make it work, as a program, better, faster, with fewer of the bugs it originally came with (one is tempted to say *shipped with*). To Gareth Branwyn, the body is indeed becoming a hack site, a "nexus where humanity and technology are forging new and powerful relationships."[9]

To others, the presence of the body cannot be cancelled and driven out of the cyberspace equation: we experience cyberspace, after all, because we have a very physical brain and physical senses without which we would be dead, lifeless bodies. Karen A. Franck voices this sobering reality of the physicality of the body in virtual reality:

> My physical body will occupy the virtual and physical worlds simultaneously; actions I take will have consequences, albeit different ones, in both worlds. As in the physical world, so in the virtual: perception will be active, depending upon actual or anticipated physical movements.[10]

Lawrence Lessig, in "The Zones of Cyberspace," sees both realms as places:

> Cyberspace is a place. People live there. They experience all the sorts of things that they experience in real space, there. For some, they experience more...While they are in that place, cyberspace, they are also here. They are at a terminal screen, eating chips, ignoring the phone. They are downstairs on the computer, late at night, while

their husbands are asleep.[11]

The antipodes of pure mind and pure body, of pure ethereality and of pure physicality, this still raises the question of bearings: whether cybernauts are free-floating, desincarnated entities, or bodies firmly anchored to a physical body and to a physical location, the problem of mapping is unavoidable. At the ISEA2000 conference, Lucia Leão raised the following questions: "[C]an we map the cyberspace? What kinds of maps are being created? Do these maps have any use? Do they rescue their old function, which was to help the navigator?" Leão then proceeds to give an introduction to cartography from Ptolemy to the labyrinth theme and its variants and then attempts a classification of cyberspace maps, citing "infrastructure maps," "traceroutes maps," "websites maps," "surf maps," "internet visualization maps," and "conceptual or topographical maps," ending with reflections on artists and maps.[12] For all the useful information presented, however, Leão fails to answer her own questions, stopping short of really exploring the affinities obviously present between cyberspace and myth.

But why is talk about cybermapping so difficult, or why does the issue evade any further exploration and slips, like quicksilver, the moment one tries to catch it? Is cyberspace, after all, so drastically different a dimension that language is bound to falter as soon as it tries to picture this *other* realm? Michel Serres begins his book *Atlas* with the following questions: "Without a plan, how to visit the city? Here we are, lost in the mountains or at sea, sometimes even on the road, without a guide. Where are we and what to do? Yes, where to pass by and where to go?"[13] Short of a specific plan for the city, for our city is virtual and multiple, we will strive to devise a *practice* and a *strategy* of mapping cyberspace.

But first, how badly do we need a map? Can we keep on switching from one reality to another, taking for reference point our everyday real-life bearings? Manovich believes that virtual worlds are accessed through constant, repetitive shifts between illusion and suspense, or between their own illusory spaces and real space. From a Brechtian angle, distance is essential as we are constantly reminded of the artificiality and constructedness of virtual worlds: we ceaselessly shift between our screens and the world around us. But even Manovich is aware of the ephemerality of this view, wondering whether cyberspace will remain the construction site we know now or whether it will engulf everything around us.

Indeed, what will happen when there will be no *other* space to turn our sight to, when all around will be only cyberspace? Are we now living in the twilight zone where we can almost seamlessly slide from one reality to another, unaware of the challenges ahead? Are we the last generation to enjoy the ability to return to real life and to our real physical body? Baudrillard thinks that simulation, unlike the mechanical prosthetic appendages of the previous technologies which needed the immediate feedback of the body, is capable of wrenching us from the physical for good:

> [W]hen one reaches a point of no return (deadend) in simulation, that is to say when the prosthesis goes deeper, is interiorized in, infiltrates the anonymous and micro-molecular heart of the body, as soon as it is imposed on the body itself as the "original" model, burning all the previous symbolic circuits, the only possible body the immutable repetition of the prosthesis, then it is the end of the body, of its history, and of its vicissitudes. The individual is no longer anything but a cancerous metastasis of its base formula.[14]

To Baudrillard, when geographic and spatial exploration are brought to an end by the disappearance of virgin territories, the principle of reality itself disappears; when imagination has nowhere to fly to, when the map we have currently drawn is covering the whole earth, when satellites have swept every single inch of our planet, reality is deprived of its necessary counterpart, imagination, and ceases to exist as well. Talking about the space race, Baudrillard says that it "constitutes an irreversible crossing toward the loss of the terrestrial referential."[15] Will cyberspace, once firmly established, also constitute an irreversible crossing toward the loss of the reality referential, or will it provide another kind of reality?

Paul Virilio, however, is more scathing in his attacks on the looming virtual landscape and heralds the end of movement as we know it and the advent of a hegemony of time:

> To pilot space, CYBERSPACE, like one used to pilot an automotive vehicle, here is indeed the great aesthetic mutation of the techniques of INFORMATION. To transfer to the near environment the control which was hitherto being exercised on the "object," the means of movement, and this thanks to the acquisition of a "fractal" dimension, not of space but of time; of a *real time* which now permits to virtualize the proximity of an individual through a procedure that enslaves movement, here is really the most stupefying utilization of interactivity.[16]

As the movable real space of cybernauts shrinks, humans lose the use of locomotion, and Virilio presents the frightening image of what might happen when, equipped with the modern prostheses, they finally become "invalid," bringing to them the world instead of going toward it. Similar to a "squirrel in its cage," we helplessly witness the "mobile advance of things" around us.[17] How will mapping be of any use when, still according to Virilio, virtual space will be nothing like space but only a software program? A kind of reversal, a shrinking of space will take place:

> Therefore, four centuries after the invention of Galileo's telescope and thanks to the prowess of tele-astronautics, *the astronaut will travel from his room*, calling to himself stars controlled less by the effects of gravitational attraction than by those of the reality generator.[18]

But Virilio does not lose sight, amidst these rather apocalyptic predictions, of the question of cybermapping, to him still an almost insurmountable problem, what he calls "the precise physical localization of the virtual object," and adds:

> "Delocalization" in turn producing an uncertainty as to the place of effective action, *prepositioning* becomes impossible, thus putting into question the principle of *anticipation*. The WHERE? abandoning its priority over the WHEN? and the HOW? there remains a doubt, less about the efficacy of the verisimilitude of "virtual reality" than about the nature of its localization, and thus on the actual possibilities of control of the virtual environment.[19]

Virtual reality, because it delocalizes the physical subject, is not the simplistic navigation in cyberspace; it is in fact the progressive "AMPLIFICATION OF THE OPTICAL THICKNESS of real world appearances,"[20] a thickening of reality in order to give space to what is called globalization, a duplication of the reality of the world.

But whether we agree with Virilio or not, the fact remains that cyberspace is not going to disappear; Neil Spiller, addressing Virilio's vehement attacks, remarks that cyberspace "cannot be uninvented," and that it is now a gradually ubiquitous feature of our lives. More, Spiller chooses to look at ways in which this delocalization so feared by Virilio can be put to positive uses. Spiller believes that the mere existence of cyberspace "makes us address what it means to be human," and adds that it "expands our facility to learn, to connect ideas and to talk and meet people."[21]

Lévy, again, takes up the challenge posed by deterritorialization and builds his theory of collective intelligence precisely on this point: social links are better built on the relationship to knowledge, and this relationship can best extend and expand in a "deterritorialized civility," the merger between the power of contemporary technology and the most intimate of subjectivities.[22] To the deterritorialization of economic, human, and informational currents, Lévy is proposing to answer with a deterritorialization of humanization itself and specifically answers Baudrillard's "kind of universal disappearance" and Virilio's "terrifying implosion of space-time":

> This book [*Qu'est-ce que le Virtuel?*] defends a different hypothesis, not catastrophist: among the cultural evolutions working at the turn of this third millennium—and despite their undeniably somber or terrible aspects—is being expressed a pursuit of *hominization*."[23]

Hominization can be an evolutionary process whereby humans can, if need be, shed their bodily envelope and freely roam in realms of pure mind and pure interactivity.

As is evident from the above, positioning in cyberspace is not a mere exercise in either theory or cartography. It is an essential element with far-reaching ontological repercussions: if positioning is indeed blurred, prepositioning is impossible, and anticipation is halted. If anticipation is put to a stop, is the cybernaut destined to blindly follow the path drawn by software programmers? In a place where bearings are unmoorable, control, if any, has to be delegated to somebody else.

Foucauldian critics might here be tempted to argue that control has *always* been in the hands of somebody else anyway, and that cyberspace is just another dimension where control shifts from the physical to the virtual. Of course, in cyberspace, Bentham's/Foucault's panopticon is a dream come true and virtual reality is the surveillance hunting grounds *par excellence*. Michel de Certeau's seminal book, *The Practice of Everyday Life*, was meant, among other things, to counter this Foucauldian tendency and now, more than twenty years after its publication, the pertinent questions it raised are still valid. To de Certeau, individuals can—and indeed, continuously do—thwart methods of control imposed by power centers by "ways of operating" and reappropriating "the space organized by techniques of sociocultural production," sometimes clandestinely through the "dispersed, tactical, and make-shift creativity of groups or individuals already caught in the nets of 'discipline'."[24] De Certeau's aim in *The Practice of Everyday Life* is to show that, notwithstanding the mind-bogglingly efficient apparatus put in place by centers of power, individual users, on the micro-level of everyday life and actions, do in fact stand a chance to *write* their own lives as narratives through a multitude of tactics such as walking in the city, using language, and other actions located mainly in a peculiar strategy of space. De Certeau's micro-level of resistance, as I will show later in more detail, can be seen here also as an answer to Virilio's end-of-days scenario.

What is important is the way de Certeau sees space and maps in the context of story-making or the writing of narratives: everyday, stories "traverse and organize places; they select and link them together; they make sentences and itineraries out of them. They are spatial trajectories."[25] If Virilio does not see any resistance roles in the individual except as an invalid immobilized in front of virtual reality, de Certeau is aware that as long as users construct narratives, they are in fact organizing space, defining boundaries, indeed *positioning* and thus *prepositioning* themselves and *anticipating* as well. To de Certeau, "[e]very story is a travel story—a spatial practice."[26] Furthermore, de

Certeau makes a crucial distinction between space and place, and what catches our attention is that Virilio's *space* is indeed nothing more than a sterile and passive *place* where users are potential prisoners. A place is an order where things are distributed, where things are neatly classified, where no two things occupy the same place; it is distinct and stable. Being in a place is "just being there," inert and lifeless as an object. Space, on the contrary, is dynamic, it is the locus of vectors of direction, velocities and time variables, where people and things intersect and dynamically interact. Being in space is *practicing* a place, *operating* in it and through it, and sometimes *against* it. A street, for example, is constructed geometrically, as a place, but it becomes a space the moment pedestrians walk on it; a text is a place waiting to be practiced through the act of reading. To de Certeau, everyday users construct stories on and about the places they are living in and transform them into spaces.[27]

Spaces and places are linked by de Certeau to tours and maps: in a study conducted in 1975 by C. Linde and W. Labov in New York, users are asked to describe their apartments.[28] Taking this study as an example, de Certeau points out that two ways of description are used: the tour and the map. The tour is an active, operational narrative which says that "if you turn left, you will see this and that." On the contrary, the map is a static localization of the kind "the bedroom is to the left of the kitchen." It is obvious to de Certeau that the tour is linked to space in terms of operation and is really a *speech act*, whereas the map is linked to place and does nothing. A map is only seeing, it is a tableau; space is acting and movement.[29] Cybernauts will quickly recognize their own presence in cyberspace as belonging to the spatial type: the most common example of speech acts, of narratives in space, is the universal injunction: "click on this link, and you will be taken to this or that site" or "type your name and you will be registered." Hardly a lot of interactivity, agreed, but the point is that, contrary to what Virilio wants to portray, cybernauts, like their real-life counterparts the pedestrians, use tactics whereby their location in a place, however intangible, however "delocalized" it is, is immediately transformed into a proairetic space linked to a narrative, no matter how short or how insignificant it appears to be.

Yet even de Certeau is either unwilling to take his own theory further, or is unaware of the potentiality present in terms of cyberspace mapping. Falling under the illusion that it is only in real place that ways of resistance (space) can be applied, he bemoans the fact that the map, since the "birth of the modern scientific discourse," has been slowly moving away from its initial tour-like and space-writing quality, and the end of the atlas as tour is deplored:

> The map, a totalizing stage on which elements of diverse origin are brought together to form the tableau of a "state" of geographical knowledge, pushes away into its

prehistory or into its posterity, as if into the wings, the operations of which it is the result or the necessary condition. It remains alone on the stage. The tour describers have disappeared.[30]

Yet de Certeau is aware that users are, in the final analysis, *always* able to transform places into space, static maps into tours. Still, are we the "posterity" who will produce anew the tour-like quality of cyberspace through our re-writing of spatial narratives? As de Certeau points out, users rely on history and memory to construct stories that will re-colonize places and re-spatialize them: "As operations on places, stories also play the everyday role of a mobile and magisterial tribunal in cases concerning their delimitation."[31] This means that story-telling marks out boundaries, actually *localizing* what is hitherto simply a place or, to answer Virilio, what the current threat is, that of "delocalization." The user is indeed a *bricoleur* who uses the available means at hand in order to construct a space that is forged by memories of past actions, events, and figures. In cyberspace terms, hackers are *de facto* bricoleurs who continuously construct a space out of the already-there places defined by rules and regulations.[32]

It is to Barthes and Derrida that I will turn for another interesting problematization of the issue at hand, away from apocalyptic scenarios that detract from dealing with what is probably an unavoidable shift in the ways we perceive space in and out of reality. Barthes' statement quoted above, "[i]t is not the 'person' of the other which is necessary to me, it is space: the possibility of a dialectic of desire, of an *unpredictability* of jouissance,"[33] can be read with the de Certeau distinction in mind. The concepts of fissure and schizophrenia are essential elements with Barthes. Every writer is at the middle point between madness and sanity, between abnormality and normality, between what is not and what is, between absence and presence. Barthes' famous statement: "Any writer will thus say: *mad I cannot be, sane I deign not to be, neurotic I am*"[34] can be fruitfully applied to the search for new maps for the new body. The fissure which exists—and which is lamented by so many—between real life and cyberspace is an essential, almost inherent component of things. Without it, the *seduction* of either will be impossible. Talking about the Marquis de Sade's *écriture*, Barthes masterfully writes:

Sade: the pleasure of reading obviously comes from certain ruptures (or from certain collisions): antipathetical codes (the noble and the trivial, for example) enter in contact…As the theory of the text says: the language is redistributed. Indeed *this redistribution is always made by cutting*. Two edges are traced: one good edge, conforming, plagiaristic (it is a matter of copying the language in its canonical state, as it was fixed by the school, by good usage, by literature, by culture), and *another edge*, mobile, empty (ready to take any contours), which is never but the locus of its own effect: there where the death of the language is glimpsed.[35]

The attraction of cyberspace and the pleasure obviously derived by cybernauts come, in Barthean terms, from the constant ruptures between the two worlds, from seeing, at the same time, the two edges of reality and virtuality coming so close together, rubbing sides. The first edge, the "good" one, conformist, plagiaristic since it copies and re-copies itself, is real life, the model by which other worlds are judged, the canon of acceptability; the other edge, mobile and empty, bad and dangerous to some, is virtual reality, the first real competitor to real life in the history of humanity. But what is interesting for Barthes is the fact that neither real life—what he calls in a different context "culture"—nor cyberspace—its destruction—is the locus of attraction. It is the continuous moving from one to the other which seduces us and, what is more, which carries signification:

> These two edges, *the compromise they put to play*, are necessary. Neither culture nor its destruction is erotic, it is the crack of the one and the other which is. The pleasure of the text is like that untenable instant, impossible, purely *Romanesque*, which the libertine tastes at the end of a bold move, cutting the rope which hangs him, at the very moment of his pleasure.[36]

As such, cyberspace is truly a product of modernity and the tangible sequel or by-product of postmodern and post-structuralist theories. Barthes associates modernity with the duplicity present whenever two edges compete for supremacy:

> The subversive edge might appear to be privileged because it is the edge of violence; but it is not violence which impresses pleasure; destruction does not interest it; what it wants is the place of a loss, it is the fissure, the cut, the deflation, the *fading* which grabs the subject in the heart of jouissance.[37]

Cyberspace is the product of the last half of the twentieth century; it appears to many as a subversive agent which threatens to destroy our culture by the sheer violence of its immersing nature, its lack of compromise with reality and its awesome threat to the body. Yet it is not this violence to the body and to reality which keeps it coming and seizing cybernauts, it is the "fading," the line in-between, the twilight zone, the place(s) where loss is about to occur but which never does, the suspense, the uncertainty of the game being played.

It is worthwhile noting that de Certeau and Barthes, the first with his notion of space as a narrative practice, the second with his notion of the pleasure of the text, ascribe to writing a prominent role. Barthes makes another useful distinction in his seminal *S/Z*, that between *readerly* and *writerly* texts. The distinction is crucial in understanding the theory behind cyberspace mapping. De Certeau's binaries of place/space, map/tour, seeing/acting, and tableau/movement can make Barthes' readerly/writerly pair more appropriate in the context of cyberspace mapping. If real life is a place, a map, an inert tableau, then the user is in passive mode:

> This reader is thereby plunged into a kind of idleness—he is intransitive; he is, in short, *serious*: instead of functioning himself, instead of gaining access to the magic of the signifier, to the pleasure of writing, he is left with no more than the poor freedom either to accept or reject the text: reading is nothing more than a *referendum*...We call any readerly text a classic text.[38]

But the question is: is real life a "classic text"? Are we overly "serious" and obsessed with the mania of searching for signifieds at all cost? Is our being in real life nothing more than a "referendum"? One of cyberspace's undeniable virtues is to force us to problematize our views of classical reality.

Uncannily, Barthes' description of writerly texts almost reads like a contemporary account of cyberspace:

> [T]he writerly text is not a thing, we would have a hard time finding it in a bookstore. Further, its model being a productive (and no longer a representative) one, it demolishes any criticism which, once produced, would mix with it: to re-write the writerly text would consist only in disseminating it, in dispersing it within the field of infinite difference.[39]

Indeed, *where* is cyberspace? Serres' "Where are we and what to do? Yes, where to pass by and where to go?" quoted above rings throughout cyberspace; we have come across cyberspace *qua* simulation by accident, fleetingly. It is not a thing which one can put a finger on.

Our maps of cyberspace cannot be unitary or unifying, hence my attempt to stay clear from such endeavors; our maps, born from language, expressed in language, a writerly production which defies attempts at place-like localizations, are always, and forever, *plural*. Barthes writes the following which can be read as a description of the present Internet:

> To interpret a text is not to give it a (more or less justified, more or less free) meaning, but on the contrary to appreciate what *plural* constitutes it...In this ideal text, the networks are many and interact, without any one of them being able to surpass the rest; this text is a galaxy of signifiers, not a structure of signifieds; it has no beginning; it is reversible; we gain access to it by several entrances, none of which can be authoritatively declared to be the main one; the codes it mobilizes extend *as far as the eye can reach*, they are indeterminable.[40]

In other words, to map cyberspace (to "interpret a text") is not to give it a stable signifying status but, on the contrary, to come up with a framework which will take into account its inherent *plurality*, thereby allowing the many networks to interact freely in a "galaxy of signifiers." Serres' question "Where are we and what to do? Yes, where to pass by and where to go?" hence acquires yet another meaning, and he finally answers—albeit indirectly—his questions by rapturously declaring:

> This burning dance of moving foliage, these quick tongues, bi-forked, moving, of flames high and low, this map, unstable and stable, written on incandescent layers, how to name it?...The golden bough, with which we cross real earth and virtual spaces, heaven or hell, without getting lost? The intuition which begins or the fire which destroys? The column of fire which guides in the desert? The burning bush on the top of the mountain? Or the fire of the Spirit, in the morning of the Pentecost, about which it is written that those who receive it will speak in tongues.[41]

Once again, Serres' use of myth (James Frazer's *Golden Bough* and the Biblical allusions) is striking in the context of such a contemporary topic as cyberspace, and is yet another pointer toward the relationship between cybermapping, writing, and myth.

Barthes' concept of the productive play with the text is echoed, though differently, by Derrida. To the latter, binary systems always revolve, in western thought, around the perception that one component in the pair is preferable to the other, one held as the center and the other relegated to the margin. The center has been thought of as the stable unity which is able to keep the whole system in order. Without it, chaos would ensue. In Barthean terms, the center has taken the role of a readerly outlook and has limited attempts at writerly production. Derrida is aware of the stifling nature of the concept of center and its effect on structure:

> [S]tructure...has always been neutralized or reduced, and this by a process of giving it a center or of referring it to a point of presence, a fixed origin. The function of this center was not only to orient, balance, and organize the structure—one cannot in fact conceive of an unorganized structure—but above all to make sure that the organizing principle of the structure would limit what we might call the *play* of the structure.[42]

In other words, the structure of our mapping methodology began, as de Certeau points out, as a narrative game where maps, though not accurate by modern standards, were nonetheless useful as they told stories of events, of myths, and of heroes. The Columns of Hercules marked the end of the known world, sirens were thought to inhabit specific seas, and later leviathans roamed the deep, wreaking havoc on boats and ships. As the tour died out, the map took over the structure and a firm center was established. The function of the center, as Derrida says above, was to organize a body of hitherto un-mappable elements, or of elements which could not, in a culture where certainty is to be the basis of all things, fit in the overall picture. An accurate map it is indeed, but only a readerly one where personal or communal narratives are barred from entry. In such a map, the free play of the structure is limited and cannot account for aberrant maps such as those of cyberspace.

This is probably the reason why attempts at cybermapping have only succeeded in producing ephemeral and/or aesthetically-pleasing drawings, and no concrete theory or framework. Drawings are safe in the sense that they do not threaten the center of our mapping methodologies which rely on observable, stable, and quantifiable categories. It is sad that what began as sincere attempts at mapping cyberspace is now relegated to the world of art and hung at museums, simply because these attempts potentially threaten the essence of western thought, namely, presence, under whatever guise it has appeared in history. Derrida says:

> [A]ll the names related to fundamentals, to principles, or to the center have always designated an invariable presence—*eidos, archē, telos, energeia, ousia* (essence, existence, substance, subject) *alētheia*, transcendentality, consciousness, God, man, and so forth.[43]

It is interesting to note that all the above names are threatened, in one way or another, by cyberspace: presence, mainly, is the one term which is invariably used to counter the "absence" of cyberspace, for the latter is thought of as "unreal," "virtual," "fake," a "simulation," etc; cyberspace has no real essence, for it is only a software program; it has no substance except in our imagination; we as humans lose our specific subjectivity, and identities are effortlessly switched, the biggest fear being a total loss of individuality in the apocalyptic vision of an all-containing giant brain; finally it is the essence itself of God which is threatened by cyberspace for He is the one who creates worlds and who are we mortals to play His game? The presence of an ultimate signified which could, in a universe thought to be at the mercy of chaos and uncertainty, be referred to is essential. This presence, whether God or Reality, has necessitated the notion of center which has probably been the single most important concept of Western philosophy, and when Derrida attacked the hegemony of the center, he also disrupted Western culture's notion of reality. What cyberspace is allowing us now, *practically*, to do, is to apply deconstructive criticism on the ways in which we view reality. What were hitherto theoretical forays accessible only to the academic elite is now openly offering itself to the gaze and practice of millions of cybernauts. Derrida hails the *break* in the following words:

> Henceforth, it was necessary to begin thinking that there was no center, that the center could not be thought in the form of a present-being, that the center had no natural site, that was not a fixed locus but a function, a sort of nonlocus in which an infinite number of sign-substitutions came into play.[44]

The center of cyberspace has "no natural site," and as space it is, in the same way as de Certeau points out, a "nonlocus" where an infinite and ever-growing number of signifiers compete with one another. Again, it is through narrative, through language, that the center is de-centered and structure is permitted, after a long absence, to freely express itself and dance the dance of ludicity:

> This was the moment when language invaded the universal problematic, the moment when, in the absence of a center or origin, everything became discourse...that is to say, a system in which the central signified, the original or transcendental signified, is never absolutely present outside a system of differences.[45]

In other words, the new system *contains* the ultimate signified inside of it, i.e., cyberspace *contains* within itself real life, the latter, as central signified for thousands of years, "never absolutely present" outside the system. When the transcendental signified is securely brought back from *outside* to the *inside* of the equation, the structure can once more allow itself to be produced dynamically and in a writerly manner as a discourse which orbits not around meaning but around signification, i.e., as a discourse which is not obsessed anymore by a search for signifieds and stable binary structures located on a Cartesian grid, but which is content to witness the play of signifiers in a de-centered continuum. Indeed, as Derrida magisterially says: "The absence of the transcendental signified extends the domain and the play of signification infinitely."[46]

We can now put in a better context Barthes' statement quoted above that the writerly "demolishes any criticism," for if the absence of the transcendental signified infinitely extends the play of signification, it is clear that any attempts at *actually* mapping cyberspace, at trying to pinpoint the topography of a system which has caused a fundamental rupture in western culture itself, are bound to fall short of the mark. At best, the results will be relegated to the museum of oddities. And this is the main reason why this study is only looking *toward* a theory of cybermapping, and not *at* it, for it is only through a gaze that averts itself and avoids looking directly at the object that *more*, not less, can be seen. Derrida's comments on the Internet as an averted gaze which sees more than it appears to is very appropriate. In an interview in August 1996, he said:

> The computer installs a new place: one is there more easily projected toward the exterior, toward the spectacle, toward the face of the written thus snatched from the presumed intimacy of writing, following a trajectory of extraneousness...in this new experience of specular reflection, there is more outside and there is no outside anymore...Think of the "addiction" of those who travel, day and night, in this *WWW*. They can no longer do without these journeys across the world by sailing—and without the sail/veil which crosses them or freezes them in its turn.[47]

A system where the map, the mapper, and the act of mapping are confounded, where the infinity of spaces, instead of conjuring up images of apocalypse, enlarges our consciousness and our vision of reality and virtuality alike.

The above echo not only Gibson's depiction of cyberspace as "the infinite neuroelectronic void of the matrix,"[48] but also Deleuze and Guattari's *Mille Plateaux* and their concept of the rhizome. The famous opening lines of the introduction to *Mille Plateaux*, quoted previously, summarizes the way in which plurality and multiplicity are dealt with, and it is interesting to see how Deleuze and Guattari apply their theory of the rhizome to mapping. To begin with, *Mille Plateaux* tries, with the rhizome, to steer clear of binary oppositions, those of the "tree" model, and of pseudo-multiplicities, those of the "root" model, itself a hidden version of the first. The third model, the "rhizome," offers solutions that parallel those presented by Barthes, Derrida, de Certeau and Serres, and affords new vistas for a theory of cyberspace mapping. The first and second principles of the rhizome read, here again, like a description of Internet hypertextuality, for in order to fulfill the demands of connection and heterogeneity, "any point of a rhizome can be connected to any other point, and indeed must be so," and a rhizome "can be cut, broken at any point," and "takes over following this or that line of itself and other lines as well."[49]

As far as rhizomatic mapping is concerned, *Mille Plateaux* makes clear the distinction between cartography and decalcomania. The *decal* is a mere imitation which aims at keeping the status quo before the *coupure* mentioned previously, having the model of the tree at its center:

> All the logic of the tree is a logic of the decal and of reproduction...It consists in decaling something given as already done, from a structure which surcodes or from an axis which supports. The tree articulates and hierarchizes decals, the decals are like the leaves of a tree.[50]

The tree model works like Nietzsche's Apollo veil in *The Birth of Tragedy*: it nourishes itself from illusions as to the nature of the world and of reality, attempting to close the eyes to the violence and ultimate uncertainty of raw life. The rhizome, on the other hand, can be likened to Nietzsche's Dionysian furor as both involve an energy which is the opposite of a mere Apollonian reproduction of reality:

> Very different is the rhizome, *map and not decal.* To make a map, and not a decal...The map is conducive to the connection of fields, to the de-blocking of bodies without organs, to their maximal opening on a plane of consistency. The map is itself part of the rhizome. It is open, it is connectible in all its dimensions, it can be taken apart, it is reversible and susceptible to constantly receiving modifications. It can be torn, thrown over; it can adapt to all kinds of montages, can be put into effect by an

individual, a group, a social formation.[51]

Cyberspace is indeed a realm with multiple entrances, never the same, constantly changing and morphing into one another. The map is a writerly production, the decal a readerly one: "The map is performance, the decal always brings one back to a so-called 'competence'." The map, a Dionysian manifestation, cannot be stopped in its flow. Only the decal can do so. What is needed is to go through the inverse operation, that of linking the decals to the map and of bringing back the roots or the trees to the rhizomes.[52] In other words, if the rhizome is cyberspace and the trees and roots are real life, what can be done is to link back the decal to the map, i.e., to bring back real life to cyberspace, and to realize that cyberspace, as origin of desire, as Dionysian realm, as the multi-entrance rhizomatic mode, can be the real map which our reality pitifully decals.

In the same context, Deleuze and Guattari introduce the distinction between *smooth* and *striated* spaces, the first as nomadic, the second as sedentary; the first as war machine, the second as state apparatus. Smooth space is of a Dionysian nature, forever in movement, wild and unaccountable; striated space is the Apollonian order, the satisfaction of having laid out rules which explain otherwise uncontrollable phenomena. For our argument, it is immediately clear that smooth space is cyberspace/virtual reality, and that striated space is real life. Although the two spaces are distinct, there are times when, as with everything else, clear-cut boundaries disappear and, what is more, sometimes even the distinction is blurred. Deleuze and Guattari write that "the two spaces exist only through their mixing with one another: smooth space is ceaselessly translated and crossed by striated space; striated space is constantly reversed, taken back to smooth space."[53] The same concerns animate this study. Is cyberspace one fully autonomous mode which can be either wholeheartedly adopted or vehemently attacked as sham and illusion? Can cyberspace be thrown back to oblivion, as if nothing had happened? If not, and cyberspace is taken to represent another kind of existential status, where can we draw the limits between this mode and the mode we have lived in so far? Is everyday life crossed by cyberspace as much as cyberspace is crossed by everyday life? Deleuze and Guattari propose, in *Mille Plateaux*, different models which can help in disentangling some of the above conundrums, such as the technological, the musical, the maritime, and the mathematical ones. The maritime model is of interest here since cyberspace, in many ways, offers in its present stage analogies with the sea (we speak of "surfing" the Net) as far as representational and cartographic issues are concerned. Deleuze and Guattari identify the maritime spaces with, expectedly, smooth spaces, where the points, characteristic of striated spaces (points help anchoring and ordering our bearings), are replaced by trajectories:

> In smooth space, the line is thus a vector, a direction and not a dimension or a metrical determination. It is a space constructed by local operations with changes of direction. These direction changes can be caused by the nature of the itinerary itself...but then can also be more caused by the variability of the goal or point to be reached.[54]

The analogy with the Internet is clear: when we "surf" the Net we do not move from one point to another in a pre-determined manner. The space we construct while we are in cyberspace is governed by the laws of uncertainty and surprise. Searches deviate, sometimes fantastically, from their initial starting point; pages are visited through hyperlinks posted on other pages; options and ideas spring up phantasmagorically as more and more links are followed. As in a sea voyage, surfing the Internet is to fall prey to the unpredictability of the medium itself. And as the sea was both the most difficult space to map and the space which needed mapping most, so is cyberspace. And as cyberspace is now a special problem that *has* to be dealt with, so was the sea until the year 1440, which figures as the title of a chapter in *Mille Plateaux*, "1440 – The Smooth and the Striated." 1440 marks the year of the definitive striation through the twin concepts of the point and the map:

> [T]he sea is the smooth space *par excellence*, and yet it is the one that has, from the earliest times, found itself confronted to the exigencies of a gradually stricter striating process...Maritime space has been striated in function of two acquisitions, astronomical and geographical: *the point*, obtained by a number of calculations from an exact observation of the stars and the sun; *the map*, which crosses the meridians and the parallels, the longitudes and the latitudes, thus criss-crossing the known or unknown regions.[55]

But then, after this striating process, the sea—and, by the same reasoning, cyberspace—slowly regains its smooth nature, as it becomes the haven of nuclear submarines and spy satellites and as such controls, "in the strangest of reversals," the striated land. If cyberspace, the "smoothest" of all spaces so far, acquires bearings, *points*, and a *map*, and is eventually striated, criss-crossed by lines which would determine positions and dimensions instead of directions and vectors, will it become, by the same paradox, the most awesome power known to human civilization? As opposed to Virilio's fear of "delocalization," "prepositioning," and "anticipation," Deleuze and Guattari propose a new definition of "deterritorialization"—the term is taken from Virilio—as being the major feature of smooth spaces; indeed, the smooth "always possesses a force of deterritorialization superior to the striated." Deterritorialization is the movement by which one leaves the territory, leaving the beaten track for nomadic existence again.[56]

Bell, in his introduction to *The CyberCultures Reader*, also chooses to use the term rhizomatic to describe the "infinite, uncentred, root-like structure" of cyberspace, whether it is apprehended cartographically or schematically.[57] Mark Nunes, likewise, adopts the Deleuze and Guattari scheme in the context of virtual topographies but states an obvious Foucauldian principle when he says that the concept of striated spaces and grids is a function of all centers of power, not only of totalitarian ones, as it stems from the universal desire to render the world "comprehensible and controllable."[58] In the same vein, Spiller goes as far as recognizing that the concept of the rhizome as a "non-hierarchical system that is uncentred and without definable control" has been adopted as model by cyberculture: the moment computers are linked together, the movement of information flows in all kinds of ways in a rhizomatic system which is "in continuous motion, and forever changing, connecting and realigning."[59] Lévy cuts to the heart of the problem when he says that the "Space of knowledge," meaning cyberspace, "does not exist." It is a "u-topia, a non-place," nowhere realized yet already virtual, waiting to be born. In terms similar to those used by Deleuze and Guattari, Lévy elaborates on this non-place: "It is already present, but hidden, dispersed, unidentifiable, mixed, shooting rhizomes here and there; it emerges like stains, in dashed lines, as filigrane; it blinks without having yet built its autonomy, its irreversibility."[60]

Yet not everybody is ready to accept metaphorical descriptions like the above. Guy C. Jules Van Belle and Ronald Soetaert, in their "Breakdown into the Virtual User-Involved Design and Learning," mercilessly attack Deleuze and Guattari—and would probably attack Baudrillard, Virilio, de Certeau, Barthes, Serres and Derrida—for willful obscurantism and "abstract rhetoric to explain nothing other than what others were talking about much more clearly and influentially, some 20 years before."[61] While the post-structuralist hegemony of the last twenty years is being more aggressively challenged in ways that merit serious consideration,[62] two things are worth noting when such attacks occur: first, researchers like Jules and Soetaert are desperately in need of *tangible* results and have become impatient with theories about a cyberspace which has been around for more than two decades; second, serious theorists are loathe to indulge in facile and simplistic descriptions and are aware that *models* and *frameworks*, such as the simulacrum, delocalization, maps and tours, place and space, writerly and readerly, centers and decentering, and rhizomes are only pointers toward future attempts at cybermapping. An example of over-enthusiastic claims and simplistic uses of theoretical terminology is Barbara Kennedy's euphoric view of her own book as a unique choreography in cyberspace:

> We invite the reader to taste, feel and move with the words, the tones, the images and rhythms of this introduction, equipped to then feel some experimental flights between, across and through the interstitial spaces within the book. Those not brave enough to fly alone, preferring the more sedate pages of a linear, 'logically' framed book (such loss of *jouissance*!) will be helped by the User's Guide.[63]

What Bell and Kennedy are not able—or not willing—to see is the facile usurpation of a theoretical discourse in order to describe the otherwise mundane act of choosing to read a collection of essays either in order or randomly. "Brave" readers will move from one essay to another with no specific order and will see the "interstitial spaces," whereas the "not brave enough" will read sequentially, like a herd of docile animals, as if reading has ever been anything else than a reading for *jouissance*. Clearly, cyberspace is more than such easy binary oppositions.

On the one hand, vulgarizations of cyberspace in the form of artistic maps and comments thereon offer nothing new to the serious investigator; on the other hand, "abstract rhetoric" and facile approximations exasperate everyday users who are eager to know their whereabouts in cyberspace. The question, therefore, is not only whether we can map cyberspace or not, whether the hitherto "smooth" can be "striated," "localized," and/or "produced" by its users; it is also whether a theory of cybermapping can accommodate our double urge to understand and to use, to be at the same time fascinated by the wonderful vistas opened by cyberspace and to boldly use this knowledge to achieve tangible results. This conundrum can be eased if one approaches cybermapping both metaphorically and practically, both through, specifically, the metaphor of myth and the practice of writing on a city-like model.

Our map, then, will be at one and the same time a mythical writing of the virtual city we have called cyberspace. The project is new but the means have been used before. Italo Calvino, in *Invisible Cities*, has Marco Polo initiate the great Kublai Khan into the secrets of mythical mapping through language:

> Returning from the missions on which Kublai sent him, the ingenious foreigner improvised pantomimes that the sovereign had to interpret: one city was depicted by the leap of a fish escaping the cormorant's beak to fall into the net; another city by a naked man running through fire unscorched; a third by a skull, its teeth green with mold, clenching a round, white pearl. The Great Khan deciphered the signs, but the connection between them and the places visited remained uncertain...But, obscure or obvious as it might be, everything Marco displayed had the power of emblems, which, once seen, cannot be forgotten or confused.[64]

Will we be able to ascertain our bearings in cyberspace? Will a map based on the *writing of a mythical city-like landscape* quench our thirst for localization and appease our frustration? Maybe, but cyberspace is unlike any other space we have visited so far, and we might end up discovering that we are and have always been a mythical writing ourselves. The seduction of cybermapping can well be summarized by the following exchange, again, between Kublai Khan and Marco Polo:

> "On the day when I know all the emblems," he [Kublai] asked Marco, "shall I be able to possess my empire, at last?"
>
> And the Venetian answered: "Sire, do not believe it. On that day you will be an emblem among emblems."[65]

With this fascinating prospect ahead of us, let us proceed to investigate the "emblems" provided by myth in the search for ways to map cyberspace.

NOTES

1 Marcus Aurelius, *Meditations* (London: David Campbell Publishers, 1992), 7.

2 Arthur and Marilouise Kroker, "Theses on the Disappearing Body in the Hyper-Modern Condition," in *Body Invaders: Panic Sex in America*, Arthur and Marilouise Kroker, eds. (Montréal: New World Perspectives, CultureText Series, 2001), 20.

3 Ibid., 31.

4 Dyson, "Space," 41–42.

5 Lévy, *Virtuel*, 25.

6 Ibid., 29.

7 Ibid., 30.

8 Ibid., 31.

9 Gareth Branwyn, "The Desire to Be Wired," in Beckmann, *Virtual Dimension*, 323–32, 325.

10 Karen A. Franck, "When I Enter Virtual Reality, What Body Will I Leave Behind?" in *Cyber_Reader: Critical Writings for the Digital Era*, Neil Spiller, ed. (London: Phaidon, 2002), 240–45, 240.

11 Lawrence Lessig, "The Zones of Cyberspace," *Stanford Law Review* 48.5 (May 1996), 1403–11, 1403.

12 Lucia Leão, "New Labyrinths and Maps: The Challenges of Cyberspace's Art," *Tenth International Symposium on Electronic Art (ISEA)*, Paris, France (Dec. 7–10, 2000), proceedings online at http://www.isea2000.com/ [Last accessed Oct. 12, 2006].

13 Michel Serres, *Atlas* (Paris: Flammarion, 1996), 11.

14 Baudrillard, *Simulacra*, 100.

15 Ibid., 123–24.

16 Paul Virilio, *L'Art du moteur* (Paris, Galilée, 1993), 185–86.

17 Ibid., 192–93.

18 Ibid., 195.

19 Ibid., 196–97.

20 Paul Virilio, *La Bombe informatique* (Paris: Galilée, 1998), 24–25.

21 Spiller, *Cyber_Reader*, 19.

22 Lévy, *Intelligence*, 26–27.

23 Lévy, *Virtuel*, 9.

24 Michel de Certeau, *The Practice of Everyday Life* (Berkeley: University of California Press, 1988), xiv–xv.

25 Ibid., 115.

26 Ibid., 115.

27 Ibid., 117–18.

28 Charlotte Linde and William Labov, "Spatial Networks as a Site for the Study of Language and Thought" *Language* 51 (1975), 924–39.

29 De Certeau, *Practice*, 118–20.

30 Ibid., 121.

31 Ibid., 122.

32 When using the term "hacker" I am always making the distinction between "hacking" and "cracking," the former being the noteworthy endeavor to continuously try and make software work better, the latter being the spurious defacing/stealing of other users' property.

33 Barthes, *Plaisir*, 11.

34 Ibid., 13.

35 Ibid., 14–15.

36 Ibid., 15.

37 Ibid., 15.

38 Roland Barthes, *S/Z* (Oxford: Blackwell, 1996), 4.

39 Ibid., 5.

40 Ibid., 5–6.

41 Serres, *Atlas*, 279.

42 Derrida, *Writing*, 278.

43 Ibid., 279–80.

44 Ibid., 280.

45 Ibid., 280.

46 Ibid., 280.

47 Jacques Derrida, *Papier machine: Le ruban de machine à écrire et autres réponses* (Paris: Galilée, 2001), 161. The original French of this quote is, unfortunately, untranslatable: Derrida is, as usual, playing on the meaning of "voile" which is at the same time the tissue, the sail, and the veil; at once the text and the net of the World Wide Web, the cybernauts' sail, and the veil which hides them from real life.

48 Gibson, *Neuromancer*, 139.

49 Deleuze and Guattari, *Mille Plateaux*, 13, 16.

50 Ibid., 20.

51 Ibid., 20.

52 Ibid., 20, 22.

53 Ibid., 592, 593.

54 Ibid., 597–98.

55 Ibid., 598.

56 Ibid., 599. See, further down, Hakim Bey's recent disavowal of the Internet as a potential smooth space after what he thinks is the centers of power's full control and thus striation of this last bastion of free thinking.

57 David Bell, "Introduction I – Cybercultures Reader: A User's Guide," in Bell and Kennedy, *Cybercultures*, 1–12, 2.

58 Mark Nunes, "Virtual Topographies: Smooth and Striated Cyberspace," in Ryan, *Cyberspace Textuality*, 61–77, 63.

59 Spiller, *Cyber_Reader*, 13.

60 Lévy, *Intelligence*, 137.

61 Guy C. Jules Van Belle and Ronald Soetaert, "Breakdown into the Virtual User-Involved Design and Learning," *Journal of Technology and Teacher Education* 9.1 (Spring 2001), 31–42 , 34.

62 What has been known as "The Sokal Affair," the famous academic hoax perpetrated by New York University physicist Alan D. Sokal with his article "Transgressing the Boundaries: Toward a Transformative Hermeneutics of Quantum Gravity," *Social Text* 46/47 (Spring-Summer 1996), 217–52, and composed of a whooping twelve pages of notes and ten pages of references, serves as a historical example of a successful attack on the excesses of post-structuralism. Sokal later wrote a book in 1997 with Louvain University theoretical physicist Jean Bricmont entitled *Impostures Intellectuelles* (Paris: Odile Jacob) where both authors take up the issue of post-structuralist stars—such as Lacan, Kristeva, Irigaray, Latour, Baudrillard, Deleuze, Guattari, and Virilio—acting as impostors.

63 Barbara Kennedy, "Introduction II – The 'Virtual Machine' and New Becomings in Pre-Millennial Culture," in Bell and Kennedy, *Cybercultures*, 13–21, 16.

64 Italo Calvino, *Invisible Cities* (London: Vintage, 1997), 21–22.

65 Ibid., 22–23.

CHAPTER FOUR

Cyberspace as Myth

Ariadne's thread is a line that traces out the corridors of a labyrinth that is already a kind of writing.

J. Hillis Miller, *Ariadne's Thread: Story Lines*[1]

Part sacred space, part ethereal region, part digital fact, cyberspace involves a regional geography perhaps best captured in a koan: What is the place where everyone is but nobody lives?

Paul F. Starrs, *The Sacred, the Regional, and the Digital*[2]

We stand awkward between the earthloving beast and the cool, hot electronic angel. We will feel the dirt in our blood and the sun in our eyes even after they're gone or just memories. Even after we'll have no blood and no flesh eyes. Dirt and sun made us. We won't forget.

Greg Bear, *Queen of Angels*[3]

Jacques Gaillot, bishop of Evreux, France, since 1982, is called back to the Vatican in 1995 and dispossessed of his French diocese. He is given instead the diocese of Partenia, in Algeria. But Partenia is not on the map since the fifth century and actually lies under the sand. Bishop Gaillot, far from giving up, is helped in 1996 by Léo Scheer, Baudrillard's friend and colleague, who swiftly endows him with another virtual diocese, this time on the Internet. As Starrs notes: "Although there might be no living patron resident within the geographical confines of Partenia, on the World Wide Web Partenia had become a virtual diocese, with Gaillot ministering to any and all who tapped the hypertext link."[4] Scheer said later: "Instead of a metaphysical idea of a bishop, attached to a real place, we would have a metaphysical idea of a place, attached to a real bishop," adding: "The mind of God is imitated by the virtual structure of the Internet, where the difference between physical actuality and real existence has at last been breached."[5] Starrs explains:

> Surely "God," if you happen to subscribe to such a notion, can be ascribed more than a few trappings of cyberspace—trafficking in mysterious ways; operating at highly variable bandwidths; remaining nearly impossible for most to see; posting rules and engaging in operations that remain more than a little Delphic; vast in reach but evanescent in form; evolving quickly, in many guises, in sundry places, with each claiming the True Faith; administered on earth by an exotic priesthood of acolytes; difficult to map or locate, and essentially elusive.[6]

Margaret Wertheim, in "The Medieval Return of Cyberspace," draws interesting parallels between cyberspace and the medieval vision of physical vs. spiritual realities. The analogies are helpful in that they call to attention the possibility of cyberspace being the actualization of existing ideas that have evolved with humanity. To Wertheim, the seventeenth century has waved away centuries of medieval metaphysics and replaced them with a materialistic view of the universe. Whereas the medieval worldview saw the "soul" as the only reality in an illusory physical world, materialism has reverted this view and made the tangible world the only standard by which to comprehend the universe. Wertheim interestingly shows that, with the advent of the new technologies, the situation has been reversed again: cyberspace is seen as a return to a metaphysics of otherworldliness. She says: "Who could have foreseen that the electronic gates of the silicon chip would become a metaphysical gateway, punching a porthole in the bedrock of materialism?" The soul, kept out of the equation for three centuries, has "once again found a space that it might call its own."[7] The progress made by science has only estranged us, Wertheim says, from our innermost soul and has, in a reversal of priorities, hurled people *away* from science and *into* the reaches of cyberspace.[8] While Paul Levinson, in his *Real Space*, bemoans the fact that cyberspace is an illusory construct which has diverted us from further exploring the "real space" of our planet and that of others in our solar system, Wertheim takes the opposite view that, while prospects of life on other planets are still far-fetched dreams, the real life is now taking place, everyday, in cyberspace, a "silicon facilitated Cambrian explosion of genus and species limited only by the human imagination."[9] Wertheim's stand brings a refreshing meditation on the function of cyberspace in a twenty-first century plagued by materialism and offers a much-needed defense of cyberspace as *not* the ultimate technological monster which will gobble reality and leave humanity at the mercy of AIs, but on the contrary as a gate through which our humanity can soar again unfettered.

Benedikt, like Wertheim, re-situates cyberspace in its relationship with the most essential needs of humans. Going further back than just the medieval age, Benedikt sees the old mythological themes present in almost all societies as playing a vital part in late twentieth-century technologically-advanced cultures. He notes that it is not a coincidence that the new technologies are the preferred grounds of young people who have been fed on a diet of science fiction, comic books, and computer games. The new technologies are filled with myth, magic, and lore and provide the younger generation with ways to reinscribe themselves in the wider picture of the universe.[10] The seduction of cyberspace comes in part from the relative ease with which cybernauts can immerse themselves into states of being, into worlds and realms of fantasy and fiction hitherto restricted to the initiated few. As such, cyberspace is not to be equated only with the mere triviality of computer gaming:

> [C]yberspace's inherent immateriality and malleability of content provides the most tempting stage for the acting out of mythic realities, realities once 'confined' to drug-enhanced ritual, to theatre, painting, books and to such media that are always, in themselves, somehow less than what they reach for, mere gateways. Cyberspace can be seen as an extension, some might say an inevitable extension, of our age-old capacity and need to dwell in fiction, to dwell empowered or enlightened on other, mythic planes, if only periodically, as well as this earthly one.[11]

To Benedikt, the need for myth in our technologically advanced societies takes the shape of an uncanny mixture between the demands of a materialistic culture, based on reason and business, and the age-old need to self-expression and art. These two modes of being are best united, precisely, in cyberspace, which becomes thus the "mytho-logic" place *par excellence*.[12]

Dery goes further than that and presents the idea, shared by cyber-hippies, technopagans, and New Agers, that the machine, at this stage of its development, is slowly acquiring a soul, and that dormant myth has been relocated in the new realm of cyberspace.[13] The young generation, pushed by science to relinquish the spiritual, is fighting back: "With rationalism and materialism encroaching on all sides, those who feel impoverished by the withering away of the Spiritual have adopted the strategy, consciously or not, of legitimating spiritual beliefs in scientific terms."[14] Computers, in an abrupt reversal of values, are seen by technophiles as gods, and computer programmers, since they mediate between cyberspace and the realm of physical reality, are seen as priests.[15] The late twentieth-century need for magic is so strong that the terminology of computer programming evinces the interaction between magic and science: hackers are variously known as "gurus," "ninjas," or "wizards"; computer hardware borrows terms such as "voodoo," "mystique," "trident," or "Hercules."

Miller sees the new technologies as being able to bridge the gap between the past, the present, and the future, and that between the here and the there, almost magically:

> [M]odern communications technologies, from trick photography, to the telephone, to cinema, to radio, to television, to recordings on disks, tapes, or CDs, to the computer connected to the Internet, fulfill in reality old dreams of magic communication, at a temporal or spatial distance, with the living or with the dead. I can, any time I like, hear Glenn Gould play Bach's *Goldberg Variations* with fingers long since turned to dust. I can even hear Alfred Lord Tennyson reciting his poems. Talk about raising ghosts!"[16]

Since myth is taken to be so vital a part of cyberspace construction, it is appropriate to begin with a basic definition of myth which will be refined as we move along. *Webster's Dictionary* offers the following definitions:

> 1. a traditional or legendary story, usually concerning some superhuman being or some alleged person or event, with or without a determinable basis of fact or a natural explanation, esp., a traditional or legendary story that is concerned with deities or demigods and the creation of the world and its inhabitants.
>
> 2. stories or matter of this kind: *in the realm of myth.*
>
> 3. any invented story, idea, or concept: *His rationalizations of his failings are pure myth.*
>
> 4. an imaginary or fictitious thing or person.

The etymology given is also highly interesting: "myth" comes from the Greek *mŷthos*, meaning "story," "word."[17]

What is striking is the resemblance between myth and simulation as both involve representations of things which do not have a counterpart in real life, and both can be fictitious and devoid of separate existence independently of the act of simulation or the act of myth-making. Cyberspace is seen as an "alleged" plane of existence without an apparent determinable basis in factual reality. It does have its peculiar denizens, its demigods, its stories of creation which have become, with time, the stuff of legend. The other striking feature, one which I will be exploring later, is the etymological relationship between myth and story-telling, myth and word, myth and *écriture*.

But back to the opposition between myth and reality. Mircea Eliade points out that in the language of the nineteenth century, myth was anything which was *not* reality, a semantic legacy from early Christianity's battles against paganism: anything which was not justified by the Bible was a "fable." But in so-called primitive societies, myth is the opposite of this Judeo-Christian view, as it expresses an absolute truth, a sacred story, a transhuman revelation:

> Being *real* and *sacred*, myth becomes *exemplary* and thus *repeatable*, for it serves as

> model, and thus as justification of all human actions. In other words, a myth is a *true story* which took place at the beginning of Time and which serves as model to human behavior. By *imitating* the exemplary actions of a god or a mythical hero, or simply by *telling* their adventures, the man of archaic societies detaches himself from profane time and magically rejoins the Great Time, the time of the sacred.[18]

Eliade cautiously attempts a definition of myth that can encompass discourse, creation, and the sacred:

> Myth narrates a sacred history; it relates an event that took place in primordial Time, the fabled time of the "beginnings." In other words, myth tells how, through the deeds of Supernatural Beings, a reality came into existence, be it the whole of reality, the Cosmos, or only a fragment of reality—an island, a species of plant, a particular kind of human behavior, an institution. Myth, then, is always an account of a "creation"; it relates how something was produced, began to *be*...It is this sudden breakthrough of the sacred that really *establishes* the World and makes it what it is today.[19]

Myth explains how "a reality came into existence," and the potential for using myth to construct the reality of cyberspace is very tempting; were it not for the "breakthrough of the sacred" into the everyday world, as Eliade suggests, reality would not be revitalized and apprehended in its totality. Myth thus works to give meaning to reality, just like cyberspace works to give meaning to physical reality, constructing it or, better, re-constructing it from that other side which has always been present but which is only now so pressingly available. One can see the affinities which can exist between cyberspace and Eliade's re-adjustment of the idea or practice of myth. As cyberspace is gaining in popularity and as theory is finding many of its pronouncements being almost *magically* justified in simulated worlds, cybernauts, like the so-called primitives of archaic societies, are allowing themselves to be increasingly detached from the "profane time" of real life and are finding themselves more and more fascinated by the perceived sacredness of cyberspace.

In a leap of speculative imagination, will there come a time when cyberspace will be the *model* which real life will have to imitate? One is reminded here of Eusapia, one of the cities Marco Polo describes to Kublai Khan in Calvino's *Invisible Cities*: the inhabitants of Eusapia, to make their passage to death smoother, have constructed an identical copy of their city and put it, obviously, underground. The twin city, as necropolis, is "crowded with big-game hunters, mezzosopranos, bankers, violinists, duchesses, generals—more than the living city ever contained." Yet, with the passing of time, the living notice that things are changing in the underground realm:

> [T]he dead make innovations in their city; not many, but surely the fruit of sober reflection, not passing whims. From one year to the next, they say, the Eusapia of the

> dead becomes unrecognizable. And the living, to keep up with them, also want to do everything that the hooded brothers tell them about the novelties of the dead. So the Eusapia of the living has taken to copying its underground copy.[20]

If cyberspace is, to some, an end-of-times apocalyptic realm, a dead city, dead to life and to reality, a necropolis, are we, as cybernauts, re-building our Eusapia and making it unrecognizable? The "hooded brothers," the fraternity which maintains the link between the two worlds, are our programmers and hackers. But Calvino's Eusapia is more than a fantastic meditation on life and death, for it delivers its *coup de grâce* at the end: "They say that this has not just now begun to happen: actually it was the dead who built the upper Eusapia, in the image of their city. They say that in the twin cities there is no longer any way of knowing who is alive and who is dead."[21] And the circle is complete as we go back to the *Webster's* definition of myth as "a traditional or legendary story that is concerned with deities or demigods and the creation of the world and its inhabitants," and Eliade's "a *true story* which took place at the beginning of Time and which serves as model to human behavior" acquires more interesting overtones. With the construction of our own Eusapia, our own twin city, are we *really* in real space or have we been, from the beginning, in cyberspace without knowing it?

McLuhan, quite interestingly, proposed a definition of myth which takes into account the dichotomous world we live in: "For myth *is* the instant vision of a complex process that ordinarily extends over a long period…We *live* mythically but continue to think fragmentarily and on single planes."[22] Mankind is unable, due to its short life-span, to comprehend and assimilate the long and complex processes that shape life and the universe. Myth, with its stories, heroes, monsters and magical realms, affords us to metaphorically glimpse such processes. The "single planes" we have so far lived in are not sufficient anymore: we *had* to construct our twin Eusapia in order to extend the reaches of our experience. Cyberspace *is* that other plane which can offer, as myth, this instant vision: invisible yet omnipresent in its capability to allow almost instant hyperlinking to any other cyber-place, intangible yet omnipotent in what it can potentially do, a mere piece of hardware, yet omniscient in the unlimited stores of information it can contain, process, and analyze. A highly seductive cyberspace it is, and even Virilio, the most outspoken voice of rebellion against the new technologies, is found to say:

> Curiously, telecommunications put properties of the divine into play in civil society: the ubiquity (to be all present together at the same time), instantaneity, immediacy, omnivoyance, omnipresence. Each of us is metamorphosed into a divine being, at once here and there, at the same time.[23]

Of course, Virilio prefers to see this kind of power as a purely negative and illusory acquisition that will transform human beings, through the ascendancy of the media, into a passive audience incapable of meditating on the events taking place around them.

One of Lévy's major premises, stated in the introduction to *Les Technologies de l'intelligence*, is the equation between, among other things, myth and technologies: "I will show that the usual categories of the philosophy of knowledge, like myth, science, theory, interpretation or objectivity are intimately dependent on the dated and situated historical usage of certain intellectual technologies."[24] We can reverse this statement and say that certain intellectual technologies, and here I mean cyberspace, are tightly dependent on myth: cyberspace is shaped by myth and, in return, produces mythical ethos peculiar to our age.

But let us begin with beginnings. Barlow, in 1996, issued his famous "Declaration of the Independence of Cyberspace," establishing a mythical land, the "home of Mind," which he sees as superseding the corrupt societies of the physical world. The utopian overtones are unmistakable:

> Governments of the Industrial World, you weary giants of flesh and steel, I come from Cyberspace, the new home of Mind...I declare the global social space we are building to be naturally independent of the tyrannies you seek to impose on us...It is an act of nature and it grows itself through our collective actions...Ours is a world that is both everywhere and nowhere, but it is not where bodies live. We are creating a world that all may enter without privilege or prejudice accorded by race, economic power, military force, or station of birth...We will create a civilization of the Mind in Cyberspace. May it be more humane and fair than the world your governments have made before.[25]

This place where the mind but not the body lives is, however, to be reached through a conscious journey, and cybernauts become the first travelers to that new realm. Indeed, as Dyson points out, the cybernaut is far from being a passive, time-wasting viewer glued in front of a screen. Contrary to cinema and television, where consent is turned down to a minimum and viewers are reduced to mere voyeurs, cyberspace creates "voyagers," entities who are journeying "into a space that is already there, pre-existent, with its own restrictions, its own 'reality'."[26]

Probably the most enthusiastic description of the cybernaut voyager ever written so far has to be ascribed to Timothy Leary's essay "The Cyberpunk: The Individual as Reality Pilot," published in 1991. The ex-Harvard university psychologist saw the "cyberpunk" as the re-embodiment, thanks to cyberspace, of a long-lost original character who is a cross between a genius, a freethinker, a pioneer, a maverick, and a pilot:

> Who is the cyberpunk?...Every stage of history has produced a name and an heroic legend for the strong, stubborn, creative individual who explores some future frontier, collects and brings back new information, and offers to guide the gene pool to the next stage.[27]

In a vein similar to Lévy's, Leary sees cyberspace as the harbinger of a new species of humans, what he calls "homo sapiens sapiens, cyberneticus." These new humans are the "Pilot People" who, in what looks like a home-grown version of Emersonian self-reliance, can pilot their way around "clearly and creatively, using quantum-electronic appliances and brain know-how," and thus become examples and models for others to emulate.[28] Although cyberpunks are fairly new, their prototypes have always existed and have always been, as they are now, hunted down:

> Self-assured singularities of the Cyber Breed have been called mavericks, ronin, freelancers, independents, self-starters, nonconformists, oddballs, troublemakers, kooks, visionaries, iconoclasts, insurgents...Religious organizations have always called them heretics...In the old days, even sensible normal people used to call them mad.[29]

The cyberpunks' strength—and threat to others—can be in part understood when one looks at the etymologies involved. Leary patiently explains that "cybernetics" comes from the Greek "kubernetes," meaning pilot, a word filled with "Greek traditions of independence and individual self-reliance" and which, Leary adds, is "derived from geography." As the word "kubernetes" moved to Latin, it was changed to "gubernetes," from "gubernare," to control, regulate, steer, and acquired quite a different connotation from its original one. What had been playful, imaginative piloting had become a means of control. From the Romans to Norbert Wiener's 1948 coining of the word "cybernetics," more than two thousand years of misunderstanding have elapsed. Leary's enthusiasm springs from the discovery that cyberspace has, finally, given humanity the chance to grasp again the true meaning of piloting. He says: "We are liberating the term, teasing it free from serfdom to represent the autopoetic, self-directed principle of organization which arises in the universe in many systems of widely varying sizes. In people, societies and atoms."[30] If cybernauts are typically caricatured as shabby, disheveled teenagers wasting their lives while "reality" is somewhere *out there, in the real world*, Leary sees them, on the contrary, as exemplifying the true spirit of adventure and daring:

> Pilots, those who navigate on the seven seas or in the sky, have to devise and execute course changes continually in response to the changing environment. They respond continually to feedback, information about the environment. Dynamic. Alert. Alive...The Hellenic concept of the individual navigating his/her own course was an

> island of humanism in a sea of totalitarian empires.[31]

Far from paralyzing humanity, as Virilio thinks, cyberspace is proving to be the new grounds where imagination, creativity, and free will are expressing themselves after the long night of materialism and oppression. Barlow, in "Crime and Puzzlement: In Advance of the Law on the Electronic Frontier," gave in 1990 this picture of cyberspace:

> Cyberspace, in its present condition, has a lot in common with the 19th Century West. It is vast, unmapped, culturally and legally ambiguous, verbally terse...hard to get around in, and up for grabs...It is, of course, a perfect breeding ground for both outlaws and new ideas about liberty.[32]

Barlow who, incidentally, co-founded in 1990 EFF, the Electronic Frontier Foundation,[33] has given above a perfect description of cyberspace as the new American frontier with all the myths and legends surrounding it. Others, like Schroeder, Huxor and Smith, use the frontier theme to explore ways in which Active Worlds was populated, and see the "tough" conditions prevalent at the birth of cyberspace as equivalent to those that shaped early American society. Kroker and Weinstein categorically say: "A frontier mentality rules the drive into cyber-space."[34] The struggle to people the new continent is perhaps unequaled in the history of human civilization and the large-scale movements from the 17th century onward, from the Old World to the New one for religious, spiritual, philanthropic, political, financial, territorial, and social reasons, represent one of the most impressive drives known to us. A similar drive is happening now in cyberspace: from Geocities' street-based maps of web pages to the terminology used in connection with building a site (site "under construction") to "domain" names to addresses, everything tends to replicate the rush for land-grabbing which possessed the early settlers of the new continent. Florian Röetzer says in this context:

> [A]fter the Cold War and programs like Star Wars are long over, a "new frontier" is born, the dream of an American people. "Go Cyberspace" replaces "Go West." Cyberspace is the latest American frontier. Hackers are celebrated in the same way as conquerors of new territories or outlaws were in the past, at least when they are finally integrated into the economic system after having sowed their wild oats in the new Wild West...The conquest of cyberspace follows the example set by the settlers, cowboys, heroes of the Wild West and soldiers who subjugated a continent that, in their eyes, didn't belong to anyone—pure colonialism.[35]

Fredrick Jackson Turner, in his often-quoted paper "The Significance of the Frontier in American History,"[36] addresses what can be today equally applied to cyberspace. To Turner, the history of America is the history of the colonization of the Great West, and the frontier, always receding westward, is the key to understanding the American mind and culture. Following these lines, we can also say with a fair amount of certainty that the history of the new technologies in general and of the Internet in particular is indeed the history of the colonization of cyberspace, and that the key to understanding the spirit of cyberspace can be found in humanity's drive to colonize new territories. Turner quotes the Italian economist Loria as saying that America holds the keys which Europe, the Old World, has for centuries sought in vain, and explains that the colonization of America can be seen as a microcosm of the evolution of human society from Indian "savagery" to civilization. Here Turner comes very close to McLuhan's definition of myth, cited previously, as "the instant vision of a complex process that ordinarily extends over a long period." Turner is thus implicitly giving the colonization of America, through the expansion of the frontier, a mythical quality: the instant vision of a complex process which has taken millennia for Europe to go through has, almost magically, been accomplished in the New World.

Following our analogy, we can say that cyberspace offers the key to the enigmas that were plaguing the "Old World," representing here real life. What took millennia to accomplish in real life can be done in a mere fraction of that time in cyberspace. Indeed, the technological and scientific progress witnessed since the second half of the twentieth century has moved in exponential leaps. Turner identifies three results of the colonization of the West: one, cosmopolitanism, two, independence from England, and three, the promotion of democracy in both worlds. These three results, uncannily, are duplicated in cyberspace: one, cosmopolitanism has become globalization where the Old World is one vast global village connected, instantaneously, to all of its parts like a giant hologram; two, independence from England has become increased independence from physical reality: the post office, the typewriter, paperwork, real-life banking, education, books, entertainment, games, are slowly becoming obsolete as they are replaced by their digital counterparts; and three, the promotion of democracy is seen as being fostered by the Internet as it provides ways of expressing resentment toward totalitarian regimes, of criticizing political practices, of communicating through secured channels, etc.[37] Turner also speaks about the character of the colonizers and points out that, while transforming the wilderness, they also imperceptibly leave behind their old traits and become peculiarly Americans, that is, they are characterized by coarseness, strength, acuteness, inquisitiveness, inventiveness, and are quick to find expedients, all features peculiar to prolonged existence at the frontier. One would almost read here a description of hackers who, living on the frontier, in cyberspace, match wits with the very software they have collaboratively created, always trying to find solutions to bugs, always trying to improve their own programs.

Turner becomes, for the purpose of this study, even more relevant when he writes that it is also the wilderness which masters the colonists, as it receives Europeans fully acquainted with the niceties of civilization and throws them, many times at the cost of their life, into canoes, hunting shirts, moccasins, log cabins, and replaces their advanced weapons with coarse and primitive ones. The New World, cyberspace-as-Eusapia, dispossesses us from our old habits, molds us, and though we think that *we are constructing a New World*, the opposite is also valid: *the New World is constructing us*, instilling into our minds routines which are specifically of the nature of cyberspace. We speak of "saving," "loading," "undoing," "editing," "printing," "backing up," "restoring," "deleting," "inserting," "clicking," "merging," "emailing," "formatting," and many others actions which, although they owe their origin to real-life actions, have become essentially digital terms coloring the way we see the real world. Turner also warns against the fears and jealousies of the Old World, and observes that what he calls the "East" has always feared the colonizers' progress westward and saw it as an unregulated advance which would jeopardize its own domination of the known world and, as such, saw it as its duty to check or at least guide it. Here again the similarities are striking: from Neo-Luddites to apocalyptic scenario-mongers, a whole industry has made it its duty to disparage cyberspace and to throw the discredit on its very ontological bases. Turner's "East" is here real life ultimately threatened by the explosive advance of the colonizers of cyberspace. But this is quite understandable, if not condonable: for the first time in the history of human civilization, a whole, nearly fully-equipped, almost universally accessible, cheap, with little physical dangers, and supremely attractive alternative to reality is offered. Real life's hitherto unshakable grip on its denizens, from religion to science, is about to receive blows that may endanger its very *raison d'être*.

Turner ends his paper in a quasi-prophetic manner: although the westward expansion has abated, yet the spirit of Americanness still prevails and the American energy is bound to continually demand wider fields in which to exercise its expansiveness and colonizing propensities. He closes by calling the end of the westward colonization the first period of American history. But little did Turner realize the accuracy of his predictions: more than five centuries after the discovery of America, cyberspace is once again offering lands—presumably really virgin, this time—to be colonized, this time not by Americans only, but by a global community of daring cybernauts. A new period of worldwide history began in the 1980s with the colonization of cyberspace, and the myth of the frontier is nowhere more apparent, nowhere quicker to gauge and assess, than now: realms hitherto unexplored, limited not by physical boundaries but by the imagination of its outward-looking colonizers, cyberspace is now on the brink of providing humanity, for the first time, with simultaneous multiple existential modes where only the limits of desire apply. Paul C. Adams, in a discussion of the different virtual-place metaphors associated with the new technologies, cites the electronic frontier as one of them, pointing out that Turner's frontier "has been transposed in science fiction movies and novels, particularly those in the subgenre called *cyberpunk*, into the cutting edge of high technology,"[38] and Arthur and Marilouise Kroker equate the American character with the mindbogglingly fast advances made by the new technologies:

> The basis of American identity is the will to technology. Only Americans have been courageous, or maniacal, enough to pay the price for the coming to be of virtual reality. They are Nietzsche's experimental subjects who transform themselves into nutcrackers of the soul, objects of conscience and body-vivisectioning. They can be observed from a distance by Asians, Europeans and Canadians with a mixture of adulation, scorn and feelings of cultural superiority, but not without a lingering sense of deep admiration and awe for these Kings and Queens of the virtual kingdom.[39]

Yet what Röetzer hints at above, when he describes both expansionist movements as "pure colonialism," must not be forgotten or cast aside as the rush to colonize cyberspace is sweeping the western culture. Ziauddin Sardar uses strong words to unmask the ideology behind a drive which would like to appear as a candid pastime miles away from physical reality. To Sardar, the race to colonize the Earth has not ended; on the contrary, cyberspace is just another excuse to continue the subjugation of the weak by the strong:

> The outer space is a domain best left, for the time being, to *Star Trek*. For the conquest to continue unabated, new terrestrial territories have to be found; and where they don't actually exist, they must be created. Enter, cyberspace…It [cyberspace] is a conscious reflection of the deepest desires, aspirations, experiential yearning and spiritual *Angst* of Western man…That it is a 'new frontier', a 'new continent', being reclaimed from some unknown wilderness by heroic figures not unlike Cristobal Colon, is quite evident from how the conquest of cyberspace is described by many of its champions. Analogies to colonization abound.[40]

Worse, cyberspace to Sardar is a devilish attempt to re-write history, to wipe out from the physical memory of humans the centuries of oppression by creating, as if *in vitro*, a new species which would not only turn a blind eye to the suffering caused by its less fortunate predecessor but one which would also see history as beginning anew, with everything that was before having been conveniently spirited away.[41]

But there is more to the frontier myth than just the rush of colonization. Stefan Zweig, in his *Amerigo*, relates how Vespucci's 1503 six-page pamphlet entitled *Mundus Novus* ensured its author an everlasting fame, despite the large body of controversy surrounding the legitimacy of naming the new continent after the Florentine merchant. According to what is described in the letter, the "New World" is a blessed land: toil is unknown, trees, rivers and seas give their product freely and abundantly, men live in total innocence and share all goods in common, including women. One single sentence, coupled with the title, made of this pamphlet the elixir for all the Western world's sorrows: "if paradise on earth exists somewhere, it must not lie too far from here."[42] To Zweig, a *Mundus Novus*, especially at that time, was hailed as the panacea to cure all ills. How similar are we to the inhabitants of Europe at the beginning of the sixteenth century? Is cyberspace another *Mundus Novus* that promises so much, as it did then, in the face of looming catastrophes threatening to obliterate humanity? Is cyberspace as *Mundus Novus* another paradise, not on earth, but in virtuality, since our planet has been so meticulously mapped that no human being can, for too long, hide?

Yet some have been disillusioned with the myth of cyberspace. Nirre, in the same article cited previously, is suspicious of the way the myth has gone from magic to fable, from promises of a better world to mundane concerns, from connecting to cyberspace and coming out in a fully virtualized body in a sophistication never seen before to an illusory manufactured simulation, from dreams of apotheosis and fantastic powers and phoenix-like awakenings to the loss of all expected charms. But perhaps Nirre and many others were expecting too much from cyberspace, and have over-inflated the myth to proportions where it was indistinguishable from pure fantasy, for if myth is a natural and essential attempt to understand the deeper forces at work in a society, fantasy is only the unbridled imagination let loose (*Webster's Dictionary* defines fantasy as "imagination, esp. when extravagant and unrestrained" and as "the forming of grotesque mental images"[43]). Cyberspace is definitely not the panacea that will cure humanity's ills, despairs, and depressions, just as the American frontier was not the end of all woes. François de Closets, at the turn of the third millennium, was writing: "In the year 2000, which, in those old days, represented the absolute future, the computer has been put back in its place: the best of our slaves, but certainly not our rival, even less our equal."[44] Cyberspace is neither hell nor heaven, it is neither the work of the devil nor the work of angels coming to deliver mankind from the fetters of the flesh; cyberspace is an alternative mode of existence which challenges our views of the world as we know it, forcing us to re-assess our notions regarding time and space. As Lévy simply and accurately says: " We have dreamed, and maybe sometimes reached, especially since the middle of the 1980s, a desirable software space open to explorations, to connections with the outside, and to singularizations." [45] No magical solutions, no out-of-body experiences await the serious cybernaut.

Lévy also enumerates the ways in which oral societies code their knowledge as myth and writes that representations of reality have to be richly interconnected; connections between them will use cause-and-effect relations; propositions will refer to concrete and familiar domains of knowledge which can be used on pre-established schemes; and finally these representations must have real bonds with problems of everyday life and be heavily and emotionally charged.[46] Myth, to Lévy, can be rich and emotionally charged without being fantastic, but it has to be, nonetheless, a social construct. Indeed, Roger Caillois, in his famous 1938 *Le Mythe et l'homme*, wrote:

> Myth…belongs by definition to the *collective*, it justifies, supports, and inspires the existence and the action of a community, a people, a group of craftsmen or a secret society. A concrete example of how to act and a *precedent*, in the judicial meaning of the word, in the vast domain of *sacred culpability*, myth becomes, to the eyes of the group, clothed with authority and coercive power.[47]

Cyberspace is a "collective" space *par excellence*. Without the cybernauts and the AIs which people it, cyberspace quickly loses its appeal and thus its *raison d'être*. The miracle of being able to connect to others beyond the limitations of physical distances, already heralded by the telephone, is magnified as cybernauts can connect to hundreds, even thousands, of other users simultaneously and exchange information otherwise un-exchangeable by other means.

The community that inhabits cyberspace is varied, but hackers probably deserve the right to be called the aboriginal inhabitants of this new world. A secret society they are, disguising themselves under shocking and not-so-shocking pseudonyms many of which owe to the world of mythology and magic. Barlow, in his early encounters with hackers, found that they had a set of ethics and that they were trying to protect the Internet and its architecture.[48] Hackers, like the knights of yore, took it upon themselves to protect the lands they deemed sacred. The sense of community is also present with "normal" everyday users, witness Dibbell's account of a "rape" in cyberspace when one user of LambdaMOO, a certain "Mr Bungle," appropriated the persona of another user and started sending obscene messages to the other users. The action, appropriately called a "voodoo doll," was immediately deemed of utmost gravity, and Mr Bungle was, after unanimous agreement, "toaded," i.e., his account was summarily canceled by the programmers of LambdaMOO, also appropriately called "wizards."[49] Caillois' description of myth, as we can see from Dibbell's account, is valid in cyberspace as well, if not in a better way.

Claude Lévi-Strauss' linking of myth with *bricolage* is, in this context, also relevant: Lévi-Strauss begins by refusing to equate the faculty of constructing myths with that of fabulation, saying that the former is "far from being, as has often been held, the product of man's 'myth-making faculty'," ascribing to it the role of preserving for coming generations the remains of methods and ways of observation and reflection, what De Certeau would call *ways of doing*. Myth is with Lévi-Strauss a "science of the concrete," restricted yet no less potent and genuine than what is called the exact natural sciences. The narratives of myths preserve results "secured ten thousand years earlier" which "still remain at the basis of our own civilization."[50] This science of the concrete as opposed to exact science, of myth as opposed to real life, what Lévi-Strauss calls "bricolage," can be equated with the colonizing movement of hackers in cyberspace. His description of the "bricoleurs" can effortlessly be seen as a description of hackers:

> [T]he 'bricoleur' is still someone who works with his hands and uses devious means compared to those of a craftsman. The characteristic feature of mythical thought is that it expresses itself by means of a heterogeneous repertoire which, even if extensive, is nevertheless limited. It has to use this repertoire, however, whatever the task in hand because it has nothing else at its disposal. Mythical thought is therefore a kind of intellectual 'bricolage'—which explains the relation which can be perceived between the two.[51]

Hackers are the myth-builders of cyberspace. Armed with their brains and their fecund imagination, they are bricoleurs who make do with whatever is available. As such, it is not strange to see a strong sense of community and bondage between hackers, and an ethics of sharing the tools of the trade. Myth is "intellectual bricolage" and cyberspace, if opposed to the "engineer" nature of the real world as a place where each thing receives a set position in time and space, is thus seen as a mythical plane of existence initially pieced together by hackers and thereafter continuously added to, bricolage-wise, by the millions of users who, with the means at hand, add a piece here and a piece there to the formidable edifice. Lévi-Strauss' engineer prefers a view of reality from the outside, from "beyond the constraints imposed by a particular state of civilization," while his bricoleur works from within the system, trying to use what is already available.[52] What Lévi-Strauss says about the "savage mind" and its relationship to myth and magic throws an interesting light on the reasons why cyberspace is fulfilling a primeval human need:

> [M]agical thought, that 'gigantic variation on the theme of the principle of Causality' as Hubert and Mauss called it…can be distinguished from science not so much by any ignorance or contempt of determinism but by a more imperious and uncompromising demand for it which can at the most be regarded as unreasonable and precipitated

> from the scientific point of view.[53]

What cybernauts are doing is not mere escapism from the harsh realities of everyday life: just as their "savage" counterparts, in so-called primitive societies, are able to apprehend reality *through* myth and magic, cybernauts are given the chance to re-think that same reality *through* the prism offered by cyberspace. The "imperious and uncompromising demand" for cyberspace stems from just that need.

That cyberspace does not have to coincide with reality, both in format and in content, is obvious. If it were otherwise, cyberspace would be redundant and would not command the attention it has been getting for years. Further, it is *precisely* because the map of cyberspace is *untransferrable* onto that of physical reality that it can survive and exert its optimum influence on reality. Borges' often-quoted passage on the fallacy of precise mapping provides an interesting analogy:

> In that Empire, the Art of Cartography attained such Perfection that the map of a single Province occupied the entirety of a City, and the map of the Empire, the entirety of a Province. In time, those Unconscionable Maps no longer satisfied, and the Cartographers Guilds struck a Map of the Empire whose size was that of the Empire, and which coincided point for point with it. The following Generations, who were not so fond of the Study of Cartography as their Forebears had been, saw that that vast Map was Useless, and not without some Pitilessness was it, that they delivered it up to the Inclemencies of Sun and Winters. In the Deserts of the West, still today, there are Tattered Ruins of that Map, inhabited by Animals and Beggars; in all the Land there is no other Relic of the Disciplines of Geography.[54]

The equally famous response to Borges' story is Baudrillard's opening in his *Simulacra and Simulation* in which the French critic credits Borges with writing "the most beautiful allegory of simulation," yet only to deplore the fact that the end of the twentieth century heralds not just simulation, but simulacra: what is being covered is not something tangible but the fact that there is nothing to be covered anymore. Baudrillard reverses the Borges story in that it is not the territory which comes before the map but the contrary: the map comes before in what he calls the "precession of simulacra." More, what is left in Baudrillard's deserts are not the vestiges of the map but those of the real itself.[55]

The Buddhist mandala provides an interesting example of the relationship between myth, mapping, and the existence of others planes of being. A mandala, in oriental art, is "a schematized representation of the cosmos, chiefly characterized by a concentric organization of geometric shapes, each of which contains an image of a deity or an attribute of a deity," the word being Sanskrit for "circle."[56] W. Y. Evans-Wentz, in his memorable 1927 translation of *The Tibetan Book of the Dead*, defined mandalas as "divine conclaves"[57] and "mystic groupings of deities"[58] and gave detailed descriptions of numerous mandalas, among them the "Great Mandala of the Peaceful Deities," painted in color on heavy cotton cloth, complete with innermost, subordinate, and top circles.[59]

Carl G. Jung, who contributed the "Psychological Commentary" to Evans-Wentz' edition, assigned psychological significance to the mandalas and added that "on a higher level of insight, the dead man knows that the real thought-forms all emanate from himself, and that the four light-paths of wisdom [corresponding to the four colours in the mandala] which appear before him are the radiations of his own psychic faculties." The mandala helps to destroy the *karmic* illusions so that "consciousness, weaned away from all form and from all attachment to objects, returns to the timeless, inchoate state of the *Dharma-Kāya*."[60] Further clarification is to be taken from Jung's *Psychology and Alchemy* where he says, in his chapter on the symbolism of the mandala, that the term denotes "the ritual or magic circle used in Lamaism and also in Tantric yoga as a *yantra* or aid to contemplation." Jung adds that no two mandalas are alike for the true mandala is "always an inner image, which is gradually built up through (active) imagination, at such times when psychic equilibrium is disturbed." Since Jung's book is primarily concerned with dreams and alchemical symbols, the meaning of the mandala is that as a symbol it "originated in dreams and visions…[and] not invented by some Mahayana church father."[61] The importance of the mandala to Jung—and here to me in this study—is the equation between the mandala and its mappable use as psychic center:

> It is not without importance for us to appreciate the high value set upon the mandala, for it accords very well with the paramount significance of individual mandala symbols…characterized by the same qualities of a—so to speak—"metaphysical" nature. Unless everything deceives us, they signify nothing less than a psychic centre of the personality not to be identified with the ego.[62]

Jung cautiously advanced the theory that if the mandala is an archetype, then it must be a collective phenomenon, and this despite the distinct variants he exposed throughout more than a hundred pages, and ended up by affirming that "the symbolism of the mandala is not just a unique curiosity; we can well say that it is a regular occurrence."[63] Jung is here, of course, hinting at his collective unconscious theory and trying to tentatively place the mandala as a universal symbol perceived throughout the ages:

> The archetype is, so to speak, an "eternal" presence, and the only question is whether it is perceived by the conscious mind or not. I think we are forming a more probable

> hypothesis, and one that better explains the observed facts, if we assume that the increase in the clarity and frequency of the mandala motif is due to a more accurate perception of an already existing "type," rather than it is generated in the course of the dream-series.[64]

Eliade, in the appropriately-titled *Myth and Reality*, defines the mandala as an "*imago mundi*," a "Cosmos in miniature," and its construction, by the initiates, as a "magical re-creation of the world."[65] What I suggest here is that the mandala, as mythical symbol, has re-surfaced not only in the dreams analyzed by Jung but, following Eliade, in the way it can serve as a framework to help us map cyberspace. This framework, like the mandala, is a fluid one, an inner image built by each cybernaut as they cross the continuously receding expanses of cyberspace.

Greg Bear, in *Queen of Angels*, has scientists enter, in what can be seen as a cyberspace-like manner, the "Country of the Mind" in order to fathom the secrets of the human psyche:

> Martin closed his eyes. On the edge of his vision fluttered a somber brightness limned by electric green. The electric green blossomed into an infinite regression of twirling fractals, inner-mind geometries familiar to all brain researchers; visual interference patterns from occipital lobe signal smear.[66]

The "twirling fractals" are quickly identified as mandalas which morph to mythical creatures symbolizing the innermost recesses of the mind's drives:

> Clouds. An endless cycle of clouds and rain again in a mandala, storms racing in a circle around a twisting wheel of lightning. The lightning threatened to turn into snakes. Martin exulted; they were on track, observing the layers of limbic signs, symbols exchanged between the brain's autonomic systems and higher personal systems. "Clouds and lightning, lightning trying to go back to the snakes layer again."[67]

Mandalas are also at the center of the futuristic training given to would-be mind scientists in Pat Cadigan's *Mindplayers*:

> I rolled over onto my back and stared at the meditation mandala on the ceiling. The colors reminded me of the colors from the relaxation exercise Segretti had hooked me into. The program had probably drawn on them, I realized, and for some reason, the idea was rather comforting.[68]

On a more mundane plane, the association between the new technologies and the mandala has also been observed. Dery quotes mythologist Joseph Campbell, co-author of *The Power of Myth*, as being "dazzled by the dizzy mandala of the computer's microcircuitry," and as exclaiming, upon opening up his own PC: "Have you ever looked inside one of those things?...You can't believe it. It's a whole hierarchy of angels—all on slats."[69]

Cyberspace-as-mandala belongs to myth in that it opens up, in a fulgurant manner, visions which have taken aeons to imagine, and in that it constructs, as Jung says above, a "psychic centre of the personality not to be identified with the ego." Here mysticism rejoins psychoanalysis in the building of an image not too far removed from the theories expounded by postmodernist thinkers about the idea of the self being not much more than a narrative construction, a fiction lacking a stable center where the ego—of the author, of the reader, of the critic—can find itself. Cyberspace re-constructs the mandala image and offers, at its center, not the stability of real life—the ego—but the play of possibilities.

Case, in Gibson's *Neuromancer*, goes through a kind of epiphany when, at the beginning of the novel, he is able to re-enter cyberspace. The mandala-like nature of the experience is described:

> He closed his eyes...
>
> And in the bloodlit dark behind his eyes, silver phosphenes boiling in from the edge of space, hypnagogic images jerking past like film compiled from random frames. Symbols, figures, faces, a blurred, fragmented mandala of visual information.[70]

Cyberspace as mandala serves, likewise, to open up the inner eye in the realization that the real world we have taken for granted may be but an illusion.

But as the tantric deities sometimes take on frightening shapes, so does cyberspace to the initiate and the non-initiate alike. Case experiences "the paneled room [folding] itself through a dozen impossible angles, tumbling away into cyberspace like an origami crane."[71] The vistas offered by cyberspace can be magical, but also disconcerting. To be put face to face with a space that defies the norms of our everyday life measurements is, to say the least, like going through a mystical experience where time and space cease to function as expected. Cyberspace is here available for anybody to enter, yet it remains an absence until it is actually used. Calvino presents, in *Invisible Cities*, the city of Fedora where in each room there is a small crystal globe with a different version of Fedora itself, each version being the form imagined as ideal by different travelers. Marco Polo tells the Khan about the meaning of this invisible city:

> On the map of your empire, O Great Khan, there must be room both for the big, stone Fedora and the little Fedoras in glass globes. Not because they are all equally real, but because all are only assumptions. The one contains what is accepted as necessary when it is not yet so; the others, what is imagined as possible and, a moment later, is possible no longer.[72]

Similarly, cyberspace offers itself like the little crystal globes: each cybernaut constructs cyberspace as the ideal to be reached, and while doing so, the stone Fedora, real life, is no longer the same anymore, changing a little bit with every dream, with every crystal globe being added. On the map of our big empire, an empire which must make room for the visible and the invisible, for the present and the absent, for the model and the simulation, for real life and cyberspace, there must be room for all Fedoras, for all modes of existence. As Marco Polo explains later to the Khan, "[t]he catalogue of forms is endless: until every shape has found its city, new cities will continue to be born."[73] Cyberspace's most important gift is that it has allowed us to tangibly experience infinity and not to be bound by a stone-like representation of reality. What has hitherto remained the jealously guarded possession of mystics and experimenters of mind-enhancing substances can now be made available for all.

Borges, in "The Book of Sand," feverishly describes a face-to-face encounter with infinity, in this case with a book the pages of which cannot be counted and can never be found again. Cyberspace puts us in front of a similar situation: the digital spaces we are faced with are of such a different substance and texture that they are only limited by the extent we use them, and anyone who has "surfed" the Internet for a substantial time would understand why its "pages" follow a route that can never be the same. The book, in Borges' story, is called the "Book of Books," and also the "Book of Sand," because "neither this book nor sand has a beginning or an end." The book comes to the narrator through a mysterious Bible seller who asks him, after telling him the origin of the book, to find the first page. The narrator tries but finds that such an easy action is impossible: pages keep coming out of the cover. Asked to find the last page, the narrator goes through the same ordeal in vain. The seller attempts an explanation:

> This is not possible, yet it *is*. The number of pages in this book is exactly infinite. Not one is the first, not one is the last. I do not know why they are paginated in such an arbitrary way. Maybe to mean that the components of an infinite series can only be paginated in an absolutely haphazard manner.[74]

He adds: "If space is infinite, we are in any point in space. If time is infinite, we are at any point in time."[75] Is cyberspace infinite space? Is cybertime infinite time? Probably, as long as we are *inside* it: actions can be undone as though nothing were final and second chances were always available; deletions, unlike our real-life terminations and deaths, can be reversed and the dead and sick brought back to life and pristine health; items can be copied so perfectly that the age-old concept of the original simply vanishes;[76] one item can be copied an infinite number of times in a manner reminiscent of mystical stories of bi-locality; items can be cut from one place and put anywhere else in a manner not very different from magical tele-transportation. Can there be any doubt that cyberspace, through apparently trivial commands, is offering the mythical equivalent of what humanity has been dreaming of since its beginning?

But a myth of these dimensions, as we have seen above, is, to many, a monstrosity, something that cannot be encompassed by our still-budding notions of time and space. The narrator in Borges' story realizes the extent of what the book of sand constitutes, not in its substance inasmuch as in its implications on reality:

> I understood that the book was monstrous. It meant nothing to realize that I myself was monstrous, I who was seeing it with my own eyes and was touching it with my own ten fingers and nails. I felt that it was an object of nightmare, an obscene thing which defamed and corrupted reality.[77]

What is more important than the narrator's understandable fright is the vague realization, somewhere deep inside, that he himself is similar to the book of sand, with no essential boundaries in time and space, with no beginning or end, himself a book the pages of which are infinite, constantly re-written, never the same. It is therefore obvious why the book of sand, the book of our own existence, when seen as an infinite entity, becomes an object of nightmare, obscene, a defamation and corruption of reality: it is simply because it allows us, like Blanchot's siren song, to glimpse into our own infinity, and the whole edifice of reality, patiently constructed through the millennia, crumbles to pieces before our very eyes. Cyberspace, like a monstrous mirror, reflects back the very infinity of reality, and the myth of cyberspace *is* the instant vision not only of a complex process, as McLuhan said, but of an *infinite* process. We live mythically in cyberspace as we glimpse infinite planes, and the vision is frightening because it allows us to look back at some original chaos which has been dormant all the time. Hakim Bey, in his famous *Temporary Autonomous Zone* writes, Nietzsche-like:

> CHAOS NEVER DIED. Primordial uncarved block, sole worshipful monster, inert & spontaneous, more ultraviolet than any mythology (like the shadows before Babylon), the original undifferentiated oneness-of-being still radiates serene as the black pennants of Assassins, random & perpetually intoxicated.[78]

Chaos, in early Greek cosmology, is the primeval emptiness of the universe, the original state of things, and Bey states that there is a Chaos still waiting to be acknowledged. Ovid, in the *Metamorphoses*, gives this picture of the beginning of times:

> Before there was any earth or sea, before the canopy of heaven stretched overhead, Nature presented the same aspect the world over, that to which men have given the name of Chaos. This was a shapeless uncoordinated mass, nothing but a weight of lifeless matter, whose ill-assorted elements were indiscriminately heaped together in one place...Nothing had any lasting shape, but everything got in the way of everything else; for, within that one body, cold warred with hot, moist with dry, soft with hard, and light with heavy.[79]

The attraction of cyberspace is the attraction of chaos, the seduction of places waiting to be transformed into spaces, the frontier myth again, since to the early colonizers the Indians—as "savages"—and the wilderness were symbols of evil, symbols of disorder waiting to be ordered by the civilizing hand of man.

Chaos as mandala is best represented as a labyrinth, and cyberspace as labyrinthine mandala possesses the one feature of all labyrinths: it can either lead to the center, to the secret, or it can lead to confusion and death. The most famous labyrinth and, appropriately, the most mythical, is Daedalus' labyrinth designed for King Minos of Crete. Ovid gives us this description:

> Daedalus, an architect famous for his skill, constructed the maze, confusing the usual marks of direction, and leading the eye of the beholder astray by devious paths winding in different directions...Daedalus constructed countless wandering paths and was himself scarcely able to find his way back to the entrance, so confusing was the maze.[80]

The labyrinth was to be the prison for the Minotaur who was the fruit of the union between Minos' wife Pasiphae and a bull sent forth initially by Poseidon to be sacrificed by the king—who didn't, such was the beauty of the bull. The Minotaur roamed the labyrinth, feasting on young men brought to him every nine years, and was eventually killed by Theseus with the help of Ariadne and her golden thread.

It is to Borges that we turn again for an interesting re-reading of the Minotaur's story based on Apollodorus' version of the myth. Asterion, the Minotaur, finds himself the unknowing prisoner of a peculiar labyrinth:

> It is true that I never leave my house, but it is also true that its doors (whose number is infinite) are open day and night to men and to animals as well...[anyone] will also find a house like no other on the face of the earth...Even my detractors admit there is not *one single piece of furniture* in the house.[81]

Asterion lives in a house the paths of which, like the monstrous book of sand above, are infinite, a house *which has no equivalent on earth*, a house with no furniture, i.e., with no physical moorings, or with no fixtures that can be used to accommodate humans from the outside world. Asterion is not a mere beast, on the contrary: Borges endows him with a high sensibility with which he tries to understand the place he has been locked in. Asterion has "meditated on the house":

> All the parts of the house are repeated many times, any place is another place. There is no one pool, courtyard, drinking trough, manger; the mangers, drinking troughs, courtyards, pools are fourteen (infinite) in number. The house is the same size as the world; or rather, it is the world...Everything is repeated many times, fourteen times, but two things in the world seem to be only once: above, the intricate sun; below, Asterion. Perhaps I have created the stars and the sun and this enormous house, but I no longer remember.[82]

Asterion's search for answers echoes our own quest(s) for the nature of reality. Gibson has one of his characters say, in *Count Zero*:

> 'Yeah, there's things out there. Ghosts, voices. Why not? Oceans had mermaids, all that shit, and we had a sea of silicon, see? Sure, it's just a tailored hallucination we all agreed to have, cyberspace, but anybody who jacks in knows, fucking *knows* it's a whole universe.'[83]

Compare the above with Case's description of the Villa Straylight—a construction half-physical, half-digital—in *Neuromancer*:

> 'The Villa Straylight...is a body grown in upon itself, a Gothic folly. Each space in Straylight is in some way secret, this endless series of chambers linked by passages, by stairwells vaulted like intestines, where the eye is trapped in narrow curves, carried past ornate screens, empty alcoves. . .'[84]

If Baudrillard uses the image of Narcissus bending over the spring, Borges has Asterion *inventing* a mirror image of himself: "But of all the games, I prefer the one about the other Asterion. I pretend that he comes to visit me and that I show him my house...Sometimes I make a mistake and the two of us laugh heartily."[85] Whether it is Narcissus or Asterion is not an issue to Baudrillard who says: "We dream of passing through ourselves and of finding ourselves in the beyond: the day when your holographic double will be there in space, eventually moving and talking, you will have realized this miracle." But Baudrillard hastens to add: "Of course, it will no longer be a dream, so its charm will be lost."[86] Likewise with Borges who, always ready to add a twist to his narrative, has Asterion's double come not in the shape of the self-created other, but in that of Theseus, not a denizen of Asterion's world and thus not a figment of the half-beast-half-man's imagination, but a man of flesh and blood, a man from *real life*. Not surprisingly, Asterion awaits Theseus and calls him his "redeemer." When the rather insensitive earthling kills the Minotaur, he is surprised by the ease of his deed:

> 'Would you believe it, Ariadne?' said Theseus. 'The Minotaur scarcely defended himself.'[87]

The tragic side of Asterion is mirrored by the uncouthness of Theseus; the tragedy of Asterion is that as a miscarried progeny, a freak crossbreed between a beast and a human being, ultimately a *simulation* because not essentially real, living in a closed world with entrances too many to be numbered, in a house where every part points to and is, at the same time, any other part; a simulation which has committed the unforgivable sin of *re-creating* himself, i.e., a simulation creating a simulation, the Platonic sin of a work thrice removed from reality. But Borges' story leaves, by the very characterization of its actors, a subtle hint or an interrogation which lingers after the narrative is told and the events acted out: could Asterion be right? Could he be the thinking consciousness which, by looking back at itself sees itself for the first time (for speculation and specular—mirror-like—share the same Latin root *speculor*, to observe[88])? Is Theseus then really the darker side of Asterion's nature who tragically puts an end to the Minotaur's inquisitive sensibilities? If cyberspace is the House of Asterion, who is this Theseus bent on ruthlessly killing the master of the domain?

Lévy also takes up the Minotaur-Theseus story and gives it another interesting twist, ascribing the myth to a re-writing, by the nascent Greek civilization, of what was originally a Cretan supremacy built on the love not of war, but of peace. Lévy reverses the original roles and Theseus, much like in Borges' story, is the rude barbarian incapable of meditating on the nature of reality:

> Who is then the Minotaur? Is it the frightening beast devouring the young Athenians?...This version of the Minotaur is that of the Greeks. But the polemic Greeks, sons of Mycenae and readers of the *Iliad*, could not understand Knossos, the enigma of an irenic civilization. The Minotaur, the man-bull hybrid, is nothing but the Minoan acrobat executing, on the sacred bull, perilous ritual jumps. The Minotaur, the man-bull hybrid, indeed appears in the center of the labyrinth, but it is really the central court of Knossos' palace. He appears in the open, light, gracious, in the sunny court of a large well of light...Theseus killing the Minotaur is the Mycenaeans occulting the Minoan civilization, an artistic, technical civilization with no weapons and no slavery.[89]

It is clear from the above that cyberspace, as is seen by many, is this "artistic, technical civilization with no weapons and no slavery," a realm which desperately wants to be above the destructive passions of the flesh or "meat," and which delights in its ritualistic acrobatic jumping and surfing along fluid hypertextual routes.

Still, Asterion as a figure cannot all by himself account for the creation of cyberspace, and the rich mythical lore patiently constructed by humanity over the millennia provides us with further building blocks with which to map cyberspace. The ubiquitous pair of one male and one female being the origin of the human species—the Adam and Eve of the Biblical creation story—has given cybertheorists food for thought. In cyberspace, creation is present in the form of the basic digital duality of 1 and 0, as explained in Stephenson's *Snow Crash*: "Computers rely on the one and the zero to represent all things. This distinction between something and nothing—this pivotal separation between being and nonbeing—is quite fundamental and underlies many Creation myths."[90]

Not only is this separation pivotal in creation myths, it is even more essential when one is dealing with cyberspace, where everything hinges around presence and absence: simulation, virtuality, decentering, and the absence of an ultimate signified. In fact, it is legitimate to say that the second half of the twentieth century bears the mark of this problematization of presence and absence. Jameson spoke of five fundamental depths that have been repudiated in contemporary theory: the hermeneutic model of inside and outside, the dialectical model of essence and appearance, the Freudian model of latent and manifest, the existential model of authenticity and inauthenticity, and the semiotic opposition between signifier and signified. To Jameson, depth in all five models has been replaced by surface.[91] We can also add to these five a spatial model, born with cyberspace, a model which, contrary to the other five, has not been repudiated, but has been on the contrary acknowledged as the supreme spatial model of presence and absence. Yet even a new model, to be palatable to human beings who, after all, have not physically evolved at the same speed as their own technologies, has to be clothed with myth, and the old *stories*, for lack of new ones, have to be adapted to fit the new models. This, in a few words, is what Stephenson admirably does, among other things, in *Snow Crash*. Eve, in cyberspace mode, is not the one who is tempted by Satan to eat the forbidden fruit of the tree of knowledge; instead, she is tempted to pluck out *data* from the common repository of binary knowledge and thus introduces a metavirus which is the cause of the creation of other viruses.[92] As a result, the whole of the avatars peopling cyberspace take their various shapes from the software design of the two main characters in the novel, Hiro and Juanita:

> She [Juanita] was the one who figured out a way to make avatars show something close to real emotion. That is a fact Hiro has never forgotten, because she did most of her work when they were together, and whenever an avatar looks surprised or angry or passionate in the Metaverse, he sees an echo of himself or Juanita—the Adam and Eve of the Metaverse. Makes it hard to forget.[93]

The above echoes Genesis' account of the creation of the world and God's making humanity after his image. Jeff Noon, in *Vurt*, uses similar imagery when describing trips to virtual realms accessed through "simulation feathers." "Vurt," the other side of reality—virtuality,—is equated with the garden of Eden, and the connection between knowledge, Paradise, and the Fall, is striking:

> Last time I saw my sister, for real, she was sitting opposite me, across an apple jam-smeared table, with a feather in her mouth, expecting to fly. It was me, the brother, holding the feather there, turning it all around inside of her mouth. And then moving it to my own mouth, and Desdemona's eyes were glazed already by the Vurt, as I twisted the feather deep, to follow her down. Wherever she was going, I was going too. I really believed that. We went down together, sister and brother, falling into Vurt, watching the credits roll; WELCOME TO ENGLISH VOODOO. EXPECT TO FEEL PLEASURE. KNOWLEDGE IS SEXY. EXPECT TO FEEL PAIN. KNOWLEDGE IS TORTURE. Last time I saw my sister, close up, intimate, in the Vurt world, she was falling through a hole in a garden, clutched at by yellow weeds, cut by thorns, screaming my name out loud."[94]

The descent to virtuality finds its best metaphor in the Fall of Adam and Eve. Gibson constructs a cyber-myth taken from the Bible but twisted to accommodate the new cyberspace model: Paradise is not the place on earth where God's newly created Adam and Eve bask in supreme innocence, it is cyberspace. Out of it is the Fall; back to *real* space is the casting out of Eden: "For Case, who'd lived for the bodiless exultation of cyberspace, it was the Fall."[95] The body, in a curious return to the religious paradigm, is the source of evil, but here its opposite is not the spirit, but *disembodied* existence in cyberspace, a return to the pure freedom of an a-physical world. Case and his cowboy buddies live in cyberspace like angels.

But cyberspace is a strange place indeed, and it must in a way contain real life in it, *prior* to it, if that is in any sense possible, and Case—as Ng in *Snow Crash* in the van episode cited previously—is capable of enjoying the "meat," flesh, but from the vantage point of cyberspace. It is as if the flesh or physicality were only pure in cyberspace, as if the body, in mystical parlance, could only be transcended by the grace of the holy cyber-spirit:

> There was a strength that ran in her [Linda]...Something he'd found and lost so many times. It belonged, he knew—he remembered—as she pulled him down, to the meat, the flesh the cowboys mocked. It was a vast thing, beyond knowing, a sea of information coded in spiral and pheromone, infinite intricacy that only the body, in its strong blind way, could ever read.[96]

And then the long-awaited union with Linda, the long search for her that spans, like a barely visible thread, the whole novel, is consummated, but only as Orpheus can consummate his love with Eurydice: in the realm of the dead. Yet both are, in some way, still alive:

> The zipper hung, caught, as he opened the French fatigues, the coils of toothed nylon clotted with salt. He broke it, some tiny metal part shooting off against the wall as salt-rotten cloth gave, and then he was in her, effecting the transmission of the old message. Here, even here, in a place he knew for what it was, a coded model of some stranger's memory, the drive held.[97]

Case is amazed to see that the "old message," that of the flesh, that of physical existence, is still valid and working in cyberspace, yet he doesn't know, at this stage, that even this "coded model" is a plane of existence that owes as much to virtuality as it does to real life.

As far as origins are concerned, then, myths in cyberspace are reversed and are seen as the mirror image version of their real life counterparts. Baudrillard, though with another agenda in mind, writes of such reversals: "Simulation…is the generation by models of a real without origin or reality: a hyperreal. The territory no longer precedes the map, nor does it survive it. It is nevertheless the map that precedes the territory…that engenders the territory."[98] The territory, real life, comes *after* and is *modeled after* the map, after cyberspace. When Case, at the end of the novel, "jacks in" and sees Linda and himself waving at him from the far reaches of cyberspace, he realizes that immortality, in whatever digital shape it may be, can survive real life and it is, in fact, his own life in the matrix which engenders the events of the novel. Case's experience is a satori-like sudden realization that phenomena are, in the digital complexity of cyberspace, undifferentiated. His enlightenment recalls that of Govinda in Herman Hesse's novel *Siddhartha* when, also at the end, Govinda sees in the smiling face of Siddhartha the kaleidoscopic vision of different planes of being:

> He no longer saw the face of his friend Siddhartha. Instead he saw other faces, many faces, a long series, a continuous stream of faces—hundreds, thousands, which all came and disappeared and yet all seemed to be there at the same time, which all continually changed and renewed themselves and which were yet all Siddhartha.[99]

Govinda's search mirrors our own: trying to resolve the conflict between Nirvana and Samsara, between the un-nameable, the end of the existence of the ego, and the world of illusions, the world we live in. When faced with the riddle of cyberspace, when cyberspace becomes a Zen *koan*, we strive to resolve the conflict as well. Which is which? Is cyberspace a world of illusion, Mara the seducer,[100] or is it the answer to our questions and the end of our quest?

Slavoj Žižek is skeptical about the enthusiasm projected by cyberspace and problematizes the issue of self and identity, asking whether we are "nobody and nothing," only an illusion of self-awareness similar to what is experienced by hallucinogenic drug-takers:

> No wonder, then, that the old heroes of the LSD scene like Timothy Leary were so eager to embrace virtual reality: does the prospect of VR not offer the drug journey into the ethereal space of new perceptions and experiences WITHOUT direct chemical intervention in the brain, i.e. by providing from the outside, through the computer generation, the scenes that our brain itself had to create when enhanced by the drug substance?[101]

Žižek is mainly afraid that we, as human beings, will be, after the genome project completion, defined as a mere code "that can be compressed onto a single CD"[102] and that our cherished individuality will disappear and melt in a giant "brain-in-the-vat" scenario. The prospect of downloading "the entire human brain (once it is possible to scan it completely) onto an electronic machine more efficient than our awkward brains"[103] seems very real to him. However, Žižek's fears, like those of others, stem from a hasty reduction of possibilities into a dark apocalyptic scenario. Stahl Stenslie clarifies the "brain-in-the-vat" controversy:

> Future communication will go beyond the interface as we know it. Not into an absurd "uploading of the body" or the disappearance of the body in information, but rather in the re-emerging of the body as interface; an unpredictable, unreliable, unstable, and emotional interface, susceptible to hormonal flux and biological decay, but with a "fuzzy" logic guaranteeing information digestion/exchanges in bit rates higher than any contemporary, "logic" interface.[104]

But Žižek is in fact unable, in a chapter appropriately called "Against the Digital Heresy," to escape the lure of linking cyberspace with myth, for he writes:

> In this sense, the claim that cyberspace contains a Gnostic dimension is fully justified: the most concise definition of Gnosticism is precisely that it is a kind of *spiritualized materialism*: its topic is not directly the higher, purely notional, reality, but a "higher" BODILY reality, a proto-reality of shadowy ghosts and undead entities.[105]

Erik Davis goes to the extent of saying that Gnosticism in fact "anticipates cyberculture" with "its obsession with simulacra and encoded messages, as well as its almost libertarian hatred of traditional authority and a corresponding emphasis on spiritual autonomy."[106] Lévy, in turn, situates the issue of this higher reality in the context of his overall theory of collective intelligence, defining it as "an intelligence distributed everywhere, constantly valorized, coordinated in real time, leading to an effective mobilization of competences," with the aim of "mutually recognizing and enriching people."[107] Lévy adds: "Far from fusing together individual intelligences in a kind of indistinct magma, collective intelligence is a process of growing up, of differentiation and of mutual re-energizing of singularities."[108] Gibson, in a passage cited previously, could not have said this better when Case, only in cyberspace, recovers a long-lost relationship with the flesh and discovers that his cyberspace body is in a way *more real* than the one he carries in real life. Žižek is aware of the consequences of such meditations: "However, the ultimate lesson of cyberspace is an even more radical one: not only do we lose our immediate material body, but we learn that there *never was* such a body—our bodily self-experience was always-already that of an imaginary constituted entity."[109]

Apocalyptic brain-in-the-vat visions are not, however, conducive to a dispassionate appraisal of what cyberspace can offer. If we follow the mythical path, we will see that cyberspace is home to a full-fledged cosmogony which can be seen as threatening or as benign as its counterpart in real life. The Babel story is certainly a recurring motif in the literature of cyberspace. From the Bible we read the following narrative:

> And the whole earth was of one language, and of one speech… And the LORD said, Behold, the people *is* one, and they have all one language; and this they begin to do: and now nothing will be restrained from them, which they have imagined to do. Go to, let us go down, and there confound their language, that they may not understand one another's speech. So the LORD scattered them abroad from thence upon the face of all the earth: and they left off to build the city. Therefore is the name of it called Babel; because the LORD did there confound the language of all the earth.[110]

Babel/Babylon, the confusion of languages, is seen by Gibson as cyberspace, and he has the Zionites, in *Neuromancer*, go with Case on his journey. They provide a counterpart to his cowboy-in-the-matrix identity by having turned their back to the main system and founded the Zion colony. Case has Aerol, one of the Zionites, have a try at cyberspace:

> 'Try it,' Case said.
>
> He took the band, put it on, and Case adjusted the trodes. He closed his eyes. Case hit the power stud. Aerol shuddered. Case jacked him back out. 'What did you see, man?'
>
> 'Babylon,' Aerol said, sadly, handing him the trodes and kicking off down the corridor.[111]

Shortly after, Case meets the two surviving founders of Zion who speak a peculiar language, a mixture of prophecy and technological awareness: "'Soon come, the Final Days . . . Voices. Voices cryin' inna wilderness, prophesyin' ruin unto Babylon…We monitor many frequencies. We listen always. Came a voice, out of the babel of tongues, speaking to us. It played us a mighty dub'." [112] The Zionites are Neo-Luddites who are forced to accompany Case on his quest which will, paradoxically, end with the unification of the two great AIs, (Artificial Intelligence), Wintermute and Neuromancer, into the matrix. It is as if Wintermute and Neuromancer were attempting to reverse the Babel of tongues, to re-instate one unified language. But Gibson remains skeptical as to whether the end justified the enormous means in the final dialogue between Case and the newly-formed AI:

> 'But you're the whole thing. Talk to yourself?'
>
> 'There's others. I found one already. Series of transmissions recorded over a period of eight years, in the nineteen-seventies. 'Til there was me, natch, there was nobody to know, nobody to answer.'[113]

The reversal of Babel, the re-unification of languages, the tremendous effort at becoming a unity again has not had the expected results, for the new AI, the matrix, has alienated itself from both the outside world and cyberspace, resorting to communication attempts with different solar systems. Yet, as seen earlier, parallel lives and unwritten existences still continue their life in cyberspace, as if unaware of the battle that has been fought. Could this mean that, as the new technologies rise and fall, as schemes of power, enslavement, and illusion thrive, there remains the fact that cyberspace is a viable alternative to real life? Neither the Zionites, who helped Case with their music tear the fabric of the illusion played on him, nor Wintermute-Neuromancer possess the key to immortal omnipotent life. It is on the individual level, that of Case and Linda, that cyberspace offers solutions of continuity and hope. As I will show later, it is indeed on the personal level, as *guerrilla warfare*, that cyberspace can be mapped and occupied.

The Tower of Babel as myth has also intrigued writers of the city who, like Paul Auster, are ready to re-shuffle the notions of space and time. The protagonist of *City of Glass*, Quinn, takes up an investigation which turns out to be everything but a normal case. As he follows Peter Stillman, the prime suspect, he discovers, to his utter horror, that the man, through his apparent wanderings in the city, is in fact tracing a very precise itinerary and actually constructing a sentence *onto* the streets out of his daily wanderings. Quinn draws up a map of Stillman's daily walks which produce the phrase "THE TOWER OF BABEL." What horrifies Quinn—and infinitely seduces Auster and his readers—is, in a way reminiscent of the individuality or uniqueness of Jung's mandala, that Stillman was mapping, in a de-Certeau-like manner, his own myth-city through his own individual movements:

> For Stillman had not left his message anywhere. True, he had created the letters by the movement of his steps, but they had not been written down. It was like drawing a picture in the air with your finger. The image vanishes as you are making it. There is no result, no trace to mark what you have done.[114]

We do not, so to speak, leave our messages anywhere when we communicate in cyberspace, except on hard disks if we choose to, or if they are kept for us on purpose.[115] Yet where are they *at the moment of production*? If on the screen, they are a combination of 1s and 0s, digitized pixels hitting the screen to be replaced by others in quick succession, and stored temporarily in memory. The digital message, even when stored on disks, is problematic, for where is it when the computer is turned off? Under what language is it stored? What we see on the screen is a translation from the essential machine language—what is called low-level language—which computers use to communicate with each other before end-users are allowed to look. We, like Stillman, create the letters by the movements of our fingers on a keyboard, but they are not written down. Until—and if—they are printed out, they remain electrical signals, a bewildering combination of "on" and "off" switches making up bytes. Is this similar to drawing a picture in the air with our finger? Is our mapping done through writing, as Stillman is doing? The Babel myth is the best metaphor for this movement in cyberspace: the digital world, cyberspace, the world before the Fall, is the perfect space for the perfect movement which can take any form and which can even disappear without leaving a trace. It is only in real life, in the real world, that movement acquires, because of the Fall, this heavy quality alongside with the confusion of languages and their consequent inability to re-map a lost original ideal, what Stephenson, in *Snow Crash*, calls an "informational disaster," the "Infocalypse" following the stopping of the Tower of Babel project and the confusion of languages.[116]

With Paradise followed by the Fall and then by the confusion of tongues comes a double identity, one that partakes of the divine, or of the original state, and one that is bound to the flesh. It will be no surprise, then, to see that the myths constructing cyberspace are also very much indebted not only to a paradise, a fall, and a confusion of tongues, but also to the idea of a double identity. In fact, the denizens peopling Active World, as well as those in Stephenson's *Snow Crash*, are called "avatars," a term taken from Hindu mythology. *Webster's Dictionary*'s definition of avatar is interesting:

> 1. *Hindu Myth.* the descent of a deity to the earth in an incarnate form or some manifest shape; the incarnation of a god.
>
> 2. an embodiment or concrete manifestation, as of a principle, attitude, view of life, or

> the like. [<Skt *avatara* a passing down…][117]

The Hindu avatar *descends* to the earth and embodies a concrete manifestation or principle. In *Snow Crash* and in Active Worlds, the movement is in the opposite direction: the real-life user *connects* to the Metaverse and to the online community and embodies a concrete manifestation or principle of reality. As Stephenson himself shows with Ng, it is possible to control real life *from* cyberspace; it is possible to forsake the physical body, to keep it barely functioning and, acquiring a brand new virtual body, a brand new virtual life, and brand new virtual conditions, to control, if needed, the physical body for menial chores, as if in contempt. The creation of this perfect virtual world is the mythical—and deeply tragic—attempt to go back to an Edenic past, and Ng spares no effort designing it:

> He has a large office with French doors and a balcony looking out over endless rice paddies where little Vietnamese people work. Clearly, this guy is a fairly hardcore techie, because Y.T. counts hundreds of people out in his rice paddies, plus dozens more running around the village, all of them fairly well rendered and all of them doing different things. She's not a bithead, but she knows that this guy is throwing a lot of computer time into the task of creating a realistic view out of his office window.[118]

Yet Stephenson quickly adds that, unlike in the real world where people physically feel each other, avatars in the Metaverse can't and, therefore, bow but do not shake hands because this would painfully remind them of their virtuality.

But hasn't the flesh been the principal enemy of the Judeo-Christian tradition for centuries? Obviously, a departure from the physical into a realm of pure thought and pure rationality could not be too alien to the western mind. As the movie *The Thirteenth Floor* brilliantly suggests, we could ourselves be the avatar(s) of a super-user, a "deity" descended to our real life. The mere fascination and the stupendous *facility* and *adaptability* of such myths to the medium of cyberspace is worthy of notice. As a new mode of existence, cyberspace embodies both our wildest and most spiritual fantasies quickly, effortlessly, and with a high degree of versatility. An example is the ease with which Voodoo myth has been adapted by Noon as shown previously and specially by Gibson where Oungans, Mambos, Loas, Pappa Legba, Ezili Freda, Baron Samedi, Similor, Madame Travaux, Grande Brigitte and others rub elbows with advanced technology. In a passage from *Count Zero*, humans are "decks," Danbala is the "program," and the world is cyberspace:

> When Beauvoir or I talk to you about the loa and their horses, as we call those few the loa choose to ride, you should pretend that we are talking two languages at once. One of them, you already understand. That's the language of street tech, as you call it. We

> may be using different words, but we're talking tech. Maybe we call something Ougou Feray that you might call an icebreaker, you understand? But at the same time, with the same words, we are talking about other things, and *that* you don't understand...'Okay,' Bobby said, getting the hang of it, 'then what's the matrix? If she's [Jackie] a deck, and Danbala's a program, what's cyberspace?' 'The world,' Lucas said.[119]

Indeed, Dery notices that in Gibson's novels "cyberspace is inhabited by artificial intelligence (AI) programs that have evolved into something rich and strange: a pantheon of voodoo deities known as the *loa*," and points out that the proliferation of programs in cyberspace "has given rise to artificial entities that assume the appearances and attributes of voodoo gods."[120]

Avatars, as embodiment of the pre-Fall creatures, are therefore embodiment of Chaos, the original undifferentiated unity, sometimes also represented as Dionysus. Bey judiciously puts the three together: "Avatars of chaos act as spies, saboteurs, criminals of amour fou, neither selfless nor selfish, accessible as children, mannered as barbarians, chafed with obsessions, unemployed, sensually deranged, wolfangels, mirrors for contemplation, eyes like flowers, pirates of all signs & meanings."[121]

In the context of mirrors, it is interesting to note that the Narcissus myth, briefly mentioned previously, has also played an important role in the construction of cyberspace. The master of myth, Ovid, tells us the wonderful story of Narcissus discovering his reflection in the clear pool:

> While he sought to quench his thirst, another thirst grew in him, and as he drank, he was enchanted by the beautiful reflection that he saw. He fell in love with an insubstantial hope, mistaking a mere shadow for a real body. Spellbound by his own self, he remained there motionless, with fixed gaze, like a statue carved from Parian marble...Unwittingly, he desired himself, and was himself the object of his own approval, at once seeking and sought, himself kindling the flame with which he burned...But he could not lay hold upon himself.[122]

Are we spellbound by our own reflection in cyberspace? Are we deluded, like Narcissus by a reflection of ourselves which we have not been able to see before? Have we tricked ourselves and are we now trapped in a deadly mirror image? Ovid issues a strong warning to Narcissus:

> Poor foolish boy, why vainly grasp at the fleeting image that eludes you? The thing you are seeing does not exist: only turn aside and you will lose what you love. What you see is but the shadow cast by your reflection; in itself it is nothing. It comes with you, and lasts while you are there; it will go when you go, if go you can.[123]

This would be simple and settled yet Ovid takes the problem to its ontological extreme and Narcissus appears to us not as a foolish teenager tricked by his own arrogance but as a tragic representation of human nature as it battles to understand itself and to find perfection. Narcissus, addressing his surroundings, utters these words: "Alas! I am myself the boy I see. I know it: my own reflection does not deceive me. I am on fire with love for my own self. It is I who kindle the flames which I must endure...How I wish I could separate myself from my body!"[124] The initial separation, be it that following the Greek Chaos or that of the Judeo-Christian Fall, is to be mended by another separation, this time between the body and the soul. Our fall from a state of happiness, whatever it may be, is to be met by an amputation that will, paradoxically, make us whole again. Our construction of cyberspace has amputated us from our physical body and what we have lost is given back to us in different ways. McLuhan, in "The Gadget Lover: Narcissus as Narcosis," says the point of the Narcissus myth, transposed to our relationship with the new technologies, is "the fact that men at once become fascinated by any extension of themselves in any material other than themselves."[125] He goes on to explain that any invention, especially in this age, is an extension or a self-amputation of our physical bodies, and humanity becomes the "sex organs of the machine world," serving it and being served by it, in a mutually beneficial relationship.[126]

This process, which Baudrillard finds, through the invention of the hologram, fascinating, is represented in cyberspace by our avatar, our mirror image. Benjamin writes: "Let two mirrors reflect each other; then Satan plays his favorite trick and opens here in his way...the perspective on infinity,"[127] and Sterling, in an interview conducted by Rosie Cross, admits that it is "very difficult to get your bearings in the world of cyberspace; it really is a place of fun house mirrors."[128] Cyberspace and real life are two mirrors, quickly becoming with every passing day more and more polished, reflecting each other better and better until the time when one would not know which was originally which. Fascination or ultimate temptation? What to do with such a dilemma? Myth is able to give an answer, as it has done for millennia, and its lore provides us with yet other ways to deal with cyberspace.

Daoism is one of the earliest mystical systems to have provided a clue to the relationship between two states of being, the original undifferentiated First Principle, and the state brought about by everyday confusion and turmoil. The Dao, or "Way," is the path to re-implanting in oneself the features of that original principle. Speaking of the Dao[129], Lao Zi, in his famous *Dao De Jing*, says:

> Tao is a hollow vessel,
>
> And its use is inexhaustible!

> Fathomless!
>
> Like the fountain head of all things.
>
> Its sharp edges rounded off,
>
> Its tangles untied,
>
> Its light tempered,
>
> Its turmoil submerged,
>
> Yet dark like deep water it seems to remain.[130]

Cyberspace obviously evokes in the minds of many users a vast, inexhaustible, and dark realm which can scarcely be fathomed as it is continuously expanding and changing its own boundaries. The similarity with the American wilderness, mentioned previously, is also striking. Lao Zi, when saying

> Great space has no corners[131]

would offer the would-be cybernaut cartographer with a situation similar to that faced by the early explorers and to the space/place pair mentioned by De Certeau. Is our new "Great space" really without corners, or are we still in the infancy of a new method of mapping the New World of cyberspace? Yet, for the first time, the idea of dealing with a space which is *inherently* unbounded seems fascinating, especially since it also implies the attractive possibility that if a space is infinite, then its center can be anywhere, and if its center is anywhere, then taking up any position in this space would be equivalent to standing on one of its infinite centers. Then one would be able to dream, with Lao Zi, of accomplishing the marvelous miracle of knowing all that happens everywhere else:

> Without stepping outside one's doors,
>
> One can know what is happening in the world,
>
> Without looking out of one's windows,
>
> One can see the Tao of Heaven.[132]

And is this not the main fascination of cyberspace—now in its Internet-like manifestation—to be able to sit in one place, in front of a computer screen, and access the whole digitized world and communicate with it? Sterling marvels at this new capability, saying: "But it's this sense that there—sitting there in my study is access to the information of the world."[133] The old dream of omnipresence and omniscience is becoming, everyday, more and more a reality.

But alongside the myth of rebirth comes that of sacrifice. Indeed, the two worlds, that of reality and cyberspace, are connected by—and share—a myth of sacrifice and celebration performed by officiants. Georges Bataille gives an interesting interpretation of sacrifice:

> [T]he destruction operated by sacrifice is not annihilation. It is the thing—only the thing—which sacrifice wants to destroy in the victim. Sacrifice destroys the links of real subordination of an object, it tears the victim away from the world of utility and brings it back to the world of unintelligible fancy.[134]

Transposed to cyberspace, this means that if the matrix is seen by many as a danger to real life, a destroyer of physicality, then the sacrifice of the old (real life) is in fact the realization that the sheer physicality of our world has to be purged by the fires of the digital in order to free it from its bonds. Cyberspace comes as a sacrificer to sever the age-old subordination of the sacred to the profane, yanking our old self from utility to the pure realm of imagination. In this sense, the sacrifice of the real to the virtual is a necessity when the physical, the object as "thing," has become too ponderously predominant: "When the offered animal enters in the circle where the priest will immolate it, it moves from the world of things…to that which is immanent to it, *intimate*."[135] Cyberspace comes back, like an avenging angel, to *purify* the physical world and at the same time to *redress* the wrong committed against this world by the object and then, to Bataille, "the putting to death appears like a way to repair the offense made to the animal, miserably reduced to the state of thing."[136] And the sacred, in Bataillian terms, is a prodigal boiling which, in order to effect the required changes, has to violently assert itself in an unboundedness not unlike madness and the full expenditure of accumulated energy. Cyberspace is violently knocking at the door(s) of real life and the voice heard outside terrifyingly fills us, the denizens of real life, with awe and wonder. Bataille says: "The divine world is contagious and its contagion is dangerous."[137]

The officiants to this mystery are more akin to shamans than to priests, for if priests are needed for Apollonian rituals, shamans are the only possible officiants for the Dionysian cults. Real life is an ordered paean to Apollo, "any song of praise, joy, or triumph" and cyberspace is a dithyramb to Dionysus, a "choral song or chant of vehement or wild character and of usually irregular form."[138] Henri Jeanmaire, the authority on the cult of Dionysus, says that as Apollo gave birth to the soothing and solacing institution of religion, Dionysus retained the mysterious, dark, and frantic aspects of early cults.[139] The followers of Dionysus, the "mad" female Maenads, were known, during feasts in honor of the god, to collectively and brutally seize a fawn, tear it to pieces with their bare hands, and eat it raw, an enactment of their god's passion, death, and rebirth.[140] Here again, the divine is contagious and is certainly dangerous for, as Walter F. Otto writes:

> [T]he magnificence of the god [Dionysus] to whom all the treasures of the world are made available is suddenly darkened by deep tenebrae. Behind the enchanted truth rises another truth, a truth which makes the female dancers tremble and which takes them to a madness not amiable but sinister.[141]

Otto explains that Dionysus is not only the "Happy" but also the "Terrible," and that he would offer himself in sacrifice to himself: "The obscure truth which brings madness shows its horrible face less in the actions of the god than in what he himself goes through."[142] Our divided stances toward cyberspace show how this dual nature is at work, not only on a personal and limited level, but on a worldwide scale on the verge of covering any and all facets of our existence. Dibbell, talking about D&Ds, compares Dungeon Masters to shamans who have to "mentally picture" the map of their dungeons, uncannily creating, with the mere power of the imagination, a full-fledged realm where characters will wander, battle, and die; and Bey advocates the return to shamanistic practices in order to deal with the emerging world(s):

> To shed all the illusory rights & hesitations of history demands the economy of some legendary Stone Age—shamans not priests, bards not lords, hunters not police, gatherers of paleolithic laziness, gentle as blood, going naked for a sign or painted as birds, poised on the wave of explicit presence, the clockless nowever.[143]

Bey equates chaos with the Dionysian frenzy when he says:

> Agents of chaos cast burning glances at anything or anyone capable of bearing witness to their condition, their fever of *lux et voluptas*. I am awake only in what I love & desire to the point of terror—everything else is just shrouded furniture, quotidian anaesthesia, shit-for-brains, sub-reptilian ennui of totalitarian regimes, banal censorship & useless pain.[144]

Bey, in terms reminiscent of de Certeau, sees cyberspace as the last yet formidable haven for freethinkers in their building of "Temporary Autonomous Zones" where their survival is conditioned by how much "sorcery" they can yield in a place/space dichotomy: "Sorcery works at creating around itself a psychic/physical space or openings into a space of untrammeled expression—the metamorphosis of quotidian place into angelic sphere...Imaginal Yoga."[145] Caillois ascribed a double function to the inner workings of the mind: one is magical, and evinces attitudes of conquest, intelligence, and power, an attempt to extend the field of consciousness to integrate in it the super-sensible world; the other is mystical, and shows qualities of effusion and passivity.[146] Magic, shamanism, and sorcery perfectly describe the nascent cyberspace as a place to be conquered, colonized, and transformed, through mythical metaphors and practices, into a new space.

After this brief foray into the myth of cyberspace, it is time to answer Eliade who asks, quite justifiably, what has become of myth in modern societies. He bemoans the fact that "certain 'participations' to myths and to collective symbols still survive in the modern world, but they are far from filling the central role played by myth in traditional societies: in comparison, the modern world appears devoid of myths."[147] Eliade tries to search for modern ideologies that have taken the place of myth and cites Marxist communism and national socialism as having, for a time, fulfilled the role, but ends by saying that "outside of these two political myths, modern societies do not seem to have known others of a comparable amplitude."[148] But Eliade does not quite give up and thinks that myth has found refuge back in a realm long thought to be its own, that of writing, and reminds his readers that mythical archetypes survive in one way or another in the big modern novels. In particular, poetry takes up the missing place of myth in modern societies for the very fact that poetry can, almost magically, "re-create" language, and can "abolish common language, that of everyday life, and invent a new one, personal and private, ultimately *secret.*"[149] The great myths of creation, transformation, and death are being played everyday whenever one is writing, especially poetry, for it is in poetry that the greatest license is permitted. Likewise, I see cybernauts, with the help of software programmers, creating worlds, interacting with and *in* them, and being able to destroy them with a simple command. The creation of digital folders, files, and documents; the amazing flexibilities offered for editing almost anything from a simple image to a long document; the magical facility with which anybody can copy, almost ad infinitum, any file and delete it as easily; all these actions partake of myth. If one is not a programmer, mythical actions are still as conspicuous, as Eliade says about the modern act of reading:

> Reading not only replaces oral literature…but also the telling of myths in archaic societies. Reading, indeed, maybe more than spectacle, produces a rupture of duration and therefore a "slipping out of time" phenomenon. Whether we "kill" time with a detective novel, or we enter into a foreign temporal universe, that represented by any novel, reading projects the modern out of his duration and integrates him to other rhythms, makes him live other stories…[and] gives him the illusion of a *mastery of time* in which we can suspect a secret desire to spirit himself away from the implacability which leads to death.[150]

Cybernauts of all kinds are daily constructing a writerly text with the trustworthy tools offered by myth in a tragic attempt to escape the limitations of time and the fatality of death. Never before have twenty-first-century human beings been given such an opportunity to *mythically re-write* their fate, and this in the seemingly innocuous act of accessing the Internet, "surfing" the web, sending emails across the planet, and constructing simulations. The human species' frenzied virtual activity, where millions are simultaneously online, is unprecedented. Luddite scenarios about the end of the human race and other apocalyptic visions misread the obvious: in the absence of myth, in the absence of God, cybernauts have built, only as *bricoleurs* can, a new space teeming with the re-constructed myths that have shaped the collective human race for millennia. The mythopoeic dimension of cyberspace is being mapped everyday by the daring colonizers of virtuality, a map as rich in imaginative meaning as that of the first explorers sailing across the voids of the great oceans.

Let us now turn now to the characteristics of this writing of myth and see how it is also a mythical writing, an *écriture*, a "semiophany,"—as Barthes called it in not a very different context[151]—which has so dramatically changed our view of the universe and which, to take up again Lévi-Strauss' term, has allowed almost anybody to share in the construction of a "science of the concrete," and to become a bricoleur in the continuously expanding new realm of cyberspace. Cyberspace as the re-construction—and probably last haven—of myth is to be informed by cyberspace as *écriture*.

NOTES

1 J. Hillis Miller, *Ariadne's Thread: Story Lines* (New Haven: Yale University Press, 1992), 10.

2 Starrs, "Sacred," 193.

3 Greg Bear, *Queen of Angels* (London: Millennium, 2000), 468.

4 Starrs, "Sacred," 196. Bishop Gaillot's page is, almost ten years later, very much alive at http://www.partenia.org [Last accessed Oct. 12, 2006]. In the section on the history of Partenia, Gaillot writes: "Since Partenia does not exist anymore, it has become the symbol of all those who, in society as well as in the Church, have the feeling of not existing anymore. It is an immense diocese without frontiers where the sun never sets" (http://www.partenia.org/histoire_f.htm).

5 Qtd in Starrs, "Sacred," 197.

6 Ibid., 197.

7 Margaret Wertheim, "The Medieval Return of Cyberspace," in Beckmann, *Virtual Dimension*, 47–60, 47–48.

8 Ibid., 53.

9 Ibid., 57.

10 Benedikt, "Cyberspace: First Steps," 32.

11 Ibid., 32–33.

12 Ibid., 33.

13 Dery, *Escape*, 15. Dery defines technopaganism as "the convergence of neopaganism (the umbrella term for a host of contemporary polytheistic nature religions) and the New Age with digital technology and fringe computer culture." Quoting Erik Davis, a critic of cyberculture and "long-time participant-observer in the Pagan community," he further defines technopagans as "a small but vital subculture of digital savants who keep one foot in the merging technosphere and one foot in the wild and woolly world of Paganism." Davis puts their number between one hundred and three hundred thousand in the United States (Dery, *Escape*, 50).

14 Ibid., 50–51.

15 Ibid., 66.

16 J. Hillis Miller, *On Literature* (London: Routledge, 2002), 21–22.

17 *Webster's*, 946.

18 Mircea Eliade, *Mythes, rêves et mystères* (Paris: Gallimard, 1972), 21–22.

19 Mircea Eliade, *Myth and Reality* (New York: Harper & Row, 1975), 5–6.

20 Calvino, *Invisible*, 110.

21 Ibid., 110.

22 McLuhan, *Understanding Media*, 25.

23 Paul Virilio, *Desert Screen: War at the Speed of Light* (London: Continuum, 2002), 42.

24 Lévy, *Technologies*, 10.

25 John Perry Barlow, "A Declaration of the Independence of Cyberspace," *The Humanist* 56.3 (May–Jun. 1996), 18–19.

26 Dyson, "Space," 35–36.

27 Timothy Leary, "The Cyberpunk: The Individual as Reality Pilot," in Bell and Kennedy, *Cybercultures*, 529–39, 529.

28 Ibid., 530.

29 Ibid., 530.

30 Ibid., 531–32.

31 Ibid., 534.

32 John Perry Barlow, "Crime and Puzzlement: In Advance of the Law on the Electronic Frontier," *Whole Earth Review* (Fall 1990), 44–57, 45.

33 Barlow's web page can be found at http://homes.eff.org/~barlow [Last accessed Oct. 12, 2006].

34 Kroker and Weinstein, *Data Trash*, 15.

35 Florian Röetzer, "Outer Space or Virtual Space? Utopias of the Digital Age," in Beckmann, *Virtual Dimension*, 121–43, 131.

36 Given originally as an address to the American Historical Association in 1893 and published later, in 1920, in *The Frontier in American History*.

37 The abuses of the Internet are, of course, obvious. But take, for example, Phil Zimmerman's PGP cryptographic software. A free product, it has helped many institutions and bodies in the world communicate vital life-saving information in secure, untampered-with, channels.

38 Adams, "Cyberspace and Virtual Places," 161.

39 Arthur and Marilouise Kroker, *Hacking the Future: Stories for the Flesh-Eating 90s* (Montreal: New World Perspectives, 2001), 12.

40 Ziauddin Sardar, "Alt.Civilizations.Faq: Cyberspace as the Darker Side of the West," in Bell and Kennedy, *Cybercultures*, 732–52, 734.

41 Ibid., 735.

42 Stefan Zweig, *Amerigo: Récit d'une erreur historique* (Paris: Pierre Belfond, 1994), 23–24.

43 *Webster's*, 515.

44 François de Closets et Bruno Lussato, *L'Imposture informatique* (Paris: Fayard, 2000), 80.

45 Lévy, *Technologies*, 64.

46 Ibid., 93.

47 Roger Caillois, *Le Mythe et l'homme* (Paris: Gallimard, 1972), 151.

48 Andrew Richard Albanese, "Cyberspace: The Community Frontier - LJ Talks with Electronic Frontier Foundation Cofounder John Perry Barlow," *Library Journal* 127.19 (Nov. 15, 2002), 42–44.

49 Dibbell, *My Tiny Life: Crime and Passion in a Virtual World*, ch. 1.

50 Claude Lévi-Strauss, *The Savage Mind* (Chicago: The University of Chicago Press, 1966), 16. For a more complex study of myth, see Lévi-Strauss' "The Structural Study of Myth," *Journal of American Folklore* 78.270, (Oct.–Dec. 1955), 428–44. The article has been translated back into French as "La Structure des mythes" in Lévi-Strauss' *Anthropologie Structurale* (Paris: Plon, 1974).

51 Ibid., 16–17.

52 Ibid., 19.

53 Ibid., 10–11.

54 Jorge Luis Borges, "On Exactitude in Science," in *Collected Fictions* (New York: Viking Penguin, 1998), 325.

55 Baudrillard, *Simulacra*, 1.

56 *Webster's*, 870.

57 W. Y. Evans-Wentz, ed., *The Tibetan Book of the Dead* (Oxford: Oxford UP, 1985), xxvii.

58 Ibid., 217.

59 Ibid., xxviii–xxix.

60 Ibid., xlviii–xlix.

61 Carl G. Jung, *Psychology and Alchemy* (Princeton: Princeton UP., 1993), 95–96.

62 Ibid., 98–99.

63 Ibid., 222.

64 Ibid., 221–22. See also Jung's *Das Geheimnis der Goldenen Blüte* (*The Mystery of the Golden Flower*) translated to French as *Commentaire sur le mystère de la fleur d'or* (Paris: Albin Michel, 1979), for examples of European mandalas drawn by patients in the book's index (87–107). Jung is careful to say that all the drawings (the earliest dating from 1916) "have been realized independently of any oriental influence" and "clearly illustrate the parallelism between oriental philosophy and the unconscious mental processes in the Occident" (87).

65 Mircea Eliade, *Myth and Reality*, 25.

66 Bear, *Queen of Angels*, 318.

67 Ibid., 319.

68 Pat Cadigan, *Mindplayers* (London: Victor Gollancz, 2000), 35.

69 Dery, *Escape*, 72.

70 Gibson, *Neuromancer*, 68.

71 Ibid., 208.

72 Calvino, *Invisible*, 32–33.

73 Ibid., 139.

74 Jorge Luis Borges, *El Libro de arena* (Madrid: El Libro de Bolsillo, 2000), 133. My translation.

75 Ibid., 133–134.

76 See Walter Benjamin's famous essay "L'Oeuvre d'art à l'époque de sa reproduction mécanisée," in *Écrits français* (Paris: Gallimard, 2003), 177–220.

77 Borges, *Libro*, 136.

78 Hakim Bey, *T.A.Z.: The Temporary Autonomous Zone, Ontological Anarchy, Poetic Terrorism* (NY: Autonomedia, 2003), 3.

79 Ovid, *Metamorphoses* (Harmondsworth: Penguin, 1980), 29.

80 Ibid., 183.

81 Jorge Luis Borges, *Labyrinths* (London: Penguin, 2000), 170.

82 Ibid., 171–72.

83 Gibson, *Count Zero*, 170.

84 Gibson, *Neuromancer*, 206.

85 Borges, *Labyrinths*, 171.

86 Baudrillard, *Simulacra*, 105.

87 Borges, *Labyrinths*, 172.

88 Auzanneau and Avril, *Dictionnaire latin*, 580.

89 Lévy, *Intelligence*, 239.

90 Stephenson, *Snow Crash*, 195.

91 Jameson, *Postmodernism*, 12.

92 Stephenson, *Snow Crash*, 216–17.

93 Ibid., 59.

94 Jeff Noon, *Vurt* (New York: St. Martin's Griffin, 1993), 82.

95 Gibson, *Neuromancer*, 12.

96 Ibid., 284–85.

97 Ibid., 285.

98 Baudrillard, *Simulacra*, 1.

99 Herman Hesse, *Siddhartha* (New York: Bantam, 1976), 150.

100 "Lit. 'murder, destruction', the Devil of the Sixth Heaven…Although the embodiment of death, Mara symbolizes in Buddhism the passions that overwhelm human beings as well as everything that hinders the development of wholesome roots and progress on the path of enlightenment," *The Seeker's Glossary of Buddhism* (New York: Sutra Translation Committee of the United States and Canada, 1998), 360.

101 Slavoj Žižek, *On Belief* (London: Routledge, 2003), 53–54. See also the controversial works of Carlos Castaneda depicting his initiation to peyote.

102 Ibid., 48.

103 Ibid., 51.

104 Stahl Stenslie, "Flesh Space," in Beckmann, *Virtual Dimension*, 19–23, 19.

105 Žižek, *On Belief*, 54–55.

106 Erik Davis, "Techgnosis: Magic, Memory, and the Angels of Information," in Spiller, *Cyber_Reader*, 192–94, 192.

107 Lévy, *Intelligence*, 29.

108 Ibid., 33.

109 Žižek, *On Belief*, 55.

110 *The Bible*, King James' Version, Genesis 11:1–9.

111 Gibson, *Neuromancer*, 131.

112 Ibid., 135. See also Benjamin Fair, "Stepping Razor in Orbit: Postmodern Identity and Political Alternatives in William Gibson's *Neuromancer*," *Critique* 46.2 (Winter 2005), 92–103, for a discussion of Zionite political allusions in the novel.

113 Ibid., 316.

114 Paul Auster, *The New York Trilogy* (New York: Penguin, 1990), 85–86.

115 I am aware of the tremendously advanced ways various governments are using the new technologies to spy on their own citizens and on citizens of other nations. The European Parliament's commissioning of an investigation into the suspected existence of a covert data-gathering system nicknamed "Echelon" is one of many proofs about the insecurity of data in cyberspace (the EP's report is available, in full, in various places on the Internet as a PDF document). However, these issues fall beyond the scope of this study as they are amply addressed by other writers.

116 Stephenson, *Snow Crash*, 101, 203.

117 *Webster's*, 102.

118 Stephenson, *Snow Crash*, 206.

119 Gibson, *Count Zero*, 163.

120 Dery, *Escape*, 55.

121 Hakim Bey, *T.A.Z.*, 4.

122 Ovid, *Metamorphoses*, 85.

123 Ibid., 85.

124 Ibid., 86.

125 McLuhan, *Understanding Media*, 41.

126 Ibid., 46.

127 Walter Benjamin, *The Arcades Project* (Cambridge, MA: The Belknap Press of Harvard UP, 1999), 538.

128 Rosie Cross, "Surfing the Internet" aired Apr. 3, 1994, *Radio Eye, Sunday Night on Radio National.*

129 I will be using the official pinyin transliteration system whenever mentioning Chinese terms. The old Wade system, though still found in some places, is misleading for pronunciation.

130 Lin Yutang, *The Wisdom of Laotse* (New York: The Modern Library, 1948), 63. Lin Yutang calls Lao Zi's famous book "The Book of Tao" but many other renderings exist for the original Chinese "Dao De Jing."

131 Ibid., 211.

132 Ibid., 227.

133 Rosie Cross, "Surfing the Internet."

134 Georges Bataille, *Théorie de la religion* (Paris: Gallimard, 1999), 58–59.

135 Ibid., 59.

136 Ibid., 61.

137 Ibid., 72.

138 *Webster's*, 1036 and 418.

139 Henri Jeanmaire, *Dionysos: Histoire du culte de Bacchus* (Paris: Payot, 1978), 194.

140 Ibid., 175.

141 Walter F. Otto, *Dionysos: Le Mythe et le culte* (Paris: Mercure de France, 1992), 110.

142 Ibid., 112.

143 Hakim Bey, *T.A.Z.*, 4.

144 Ibid., 4.

145 Ibid., 22.

146 Caillois, *Mythe*, 9.

147 Eliade, *Mythes, rêves*, 23.

148 Ibid., 26.

149 Ibid., 36.

150 Ibid., 36–37.

151 Roland Barthes, *Sade, Fourier, Loyola* (Paris: Seuil, 1980), 55. Barthes describes Loyola's "Spiritual Exercises" as a new language, a "semiophany."

Chapter Five

Cyberspace as *Écriture*: The Metaverse

> Go ye wa no: *I am about to make words*. Melanesian expression.
>
> Maurice Leenhardt, *Do Kamo*[1]

> What is a myth today? I will immediately give a very simple first answer perfectly in line with etymology: *myth is a discourse*.
>
> Roland Barthes, *Mythologies*[2]

The different myths re-interpreted in the preceding chapter to fit the context of a mapping of cyberspace can only be situated within the framework of language and of a *magical* use of discourse. Speaking of myths and mythemes, Lévi-Strauss said: "If we want to account for the specific characters of mythical thought, we must therefore establish the fact that myth is simultaneously inside language and beyond it."[3] Can we, likewise, attempt to map cyberspace in conjunction with myth and writing? In this chapter I will try to show how cyberspace is indeed an *écriture* which constructs and maps out a space for cybernauts.

Borges, in *Atlas*, played the following game with the notion of the labyrinth where discourse becomes itself an unending maze:

> This is the labyrinth of Crete. This is the labyrinth of Crete whose center was the Minotaur. This is the labyrinth of Crete whose center was the Minotaur that Dante imagined as a bull with a man's head in whose stone net so many generations were as lost as María Kodama and I were lost. This is the labyrinth of Crete whose center was the Minotaur that Dante imagined as a bull with a man's head in whose stone net so many generations were as lost as María Kodama and I were lost that morning, and remain lost in time, that other labyrinth.[4]

The starting point is a *place*, the labyrinth of Crete, and Borges uses language to construct a narrative, beginning with "whose center was the Minotaur," and building over it until that place becomes a *space* filled with history's events, memories, actors, and expectations. From the heart of the labyrinth language has magically built upon itself to create a vibrant life-like realm. The labyrinth remains a monological place, closed upon itself, self-reflecting and ultimately sterile until a narrative discourse, dialogic and reflecting the voices of the world, reaches out to map out its bearings.

Lévy, in the context of knowledge versus power as the coming order of cyberspace, also equates the labyrinthine qualities of the new technologies with writing:

> Instead of thickening the bastions of power, let us refine the architecture of *cyberspace*, the ultimate labyrinth. On every integrated circuit, on every electronic chip, we see but cannot read the secret number, the complex emblem of collective intelligence, scattered irenic message.[5]

To Lévy, cyberspace has allowed us to genuinely treat the text as it was meant to be treated, as *tissue*:

> As we tear the text by reading or listening, we *ruffle* it. We fold it upon itself. We link the passages which correspond to each other. We sew together the limbs scattered and dispersed over the surface of the pages or in the linearity of discourse: to read a text is to recover the textile gestures which gave it its name.[6]

He adds that cyberspace has also brought writing back, thanks to it basic programming language, to its original simplicity:

> Informatization accelerates the movement begun by writing by reducing any message to combinations of two elementary symbols, zero and one. These characters are the least significant possible, identical on all the supports of memory...Information technology is the most virtualizing of techniques because it is also the most grammaticalizing.[7]

Taken back to its bare binary pair of 1 and 0, information technology uses the two basic building blocks of creation, the mythical Adam and Eve, the mythical yin and yang of all differentiated beginnings. Any original language, whether "primitive" or "basic" such as that of IT, is thought to be imbued with power. Maurice Leenhardt, in 1947, wrote his phenomenal study on the person and the myth in the Melanesian world. A friend of Lucien Lévy-Bruhl and Marcel Mauss, he wrote the following lines in *Do Kamo*:

> When a great endeavor succeeds, like the bringing down of a log from the mountain to the sea to make a boat, they [the inhabitants] immediately explain the success of the event without mishaps, without broken leg or other damage, by properly saying: the words (*no*, action) have been good because we have followed the words (*no*, action

revelation) of someone, and they name a god…they have remained in the mythical.[8]

From Leenhardt to J. L. Austin's 1962 *How to do Things with Words*, the performative uses of discourse have fascinated human beings. One of the earliest recorded acts of mythical—and almost magical—creation through words is, in the Judeo-Christian tradition, the fiat of God in Genesis 1:3: "And God said, Let there be light: and there was light." Are we still, millennia later, working our way through technology and thinking, like Leenhardt's Melanesians, that we are in fact giving our words a magically performative quality? Let us remember first de Certeau's practices which allow everyday people to construct stories in order to thwart modes of delimitation and control: story-making transforms places into spaces. If we also remember that one of the main definitions of myth is that of a "traditional or legendary story," and Eliade's pronouncement that myth is a true story, the connection between space, mapping, myth and narrative becomes clear.

How myth becomes a narrative and, specifically, literature, is explained by Caillois who writes that "it is precisely when myth loses its moral restricting power that it becomes literature and object of esthetic pleasure," and adds, interestingly: "It is the moment when Ovid writes the *Metamorphoses*."[9] In one sweeping gesture, Caillois helps us put together the diverse elements which make up the cyberspace jigsaw puzzle: when myth loses ground in front of its one formidable enemy, science, mythical construction goes underground, wages guerrilla warfare and wins on different fronts. Through language, writing, and literature, myth is alive again, and cyberspace becomes the *metamorphosis* of myth from the physical to the virtual. Isn't one of the definitions of matrix the mold used in printing for casting typefaces? If the matrix is the mold, the original, is not the real world, maybe, also the *writing* done by cyberspace? Are we Eusapians dictating—the verb "to dictate" comes from the Latin *dīcere*, to say, speak[10]—fashion to the other world, that of simulation and virtuality, or is the opposite also true? The mirror and the double are the locus of a duplicity, two edges rubbing each other and forcing beholders to acknowledge/discover their own nature in the process. To repeat Barthes' theory, the writerly nature of modern texts comes from their allowing us as readers to experience the duplicity inherent wherever the *fissure* between two edges is present.

Cyberspace is such a text, probably the first fully writerly text in the history of human thought. Cyberspace is a gigantic and, yes, probably a monstrous book; an obscene book which defies and defames our age-old respect for the orderly, the delimited, and the clearly mapped out; a mandala dictated to us and, at the same time, drawn with our very hands; a polymorphous and, at the same time, amorphous rhizome where the only rules are those of a

Dionysian frenzy which turns us into Maenads not knowing anymore which is first and which is last. Our writing in cyberspace is that of a book connected to all other books, a book-plateau, as Deleuze and Guattari say:

> We call "plateau" any multiplicity connectable to others through superficial subterranean stems, in order to form and extend a rhizome. We are writing this book as a rhizome. We have made it of plateaux. We have given it a circular form, but it was a way of joking. Every morning we would wake up, and each one of us would ask himself what plateaux he would take, writing five lines here and ten lines there.[11]

Like the founders of French surrealism, André Breton and Philippe Soupault, Deleuze and Guattari were in their own way attempting to get to the source of the original language, the language before the Fall. Interestingly, the machine language of cyberspace is, as Stephenson points out in *Snow Crash*, long strings of 1s and 0s which bring up myriads of words, colors, and sounds. Almost all the human sensoria, in cyberspace, can be brought back to this fundamental language, a process so dazzling in both its simplicity and complexity that it approaches the realm of myth.

Eliade's assertion that poetry is a prolongation of myth and is a private, personal, and secret realm where reality is metamorphosed is, in many ways, verifiable in cyberspace. If we go back again to *Webster's Dictionary*, we read that the definition of "universe" is:

> 1. the totality of known or supposed objects and phenomena; all existing things, including the earth and its creatures, the heavenly bodies, and all else throughout space; the cosmos; macrocosm.
>
> 2. a world or sphere in which something exists or prevails.[12]

"Universe" comes from the Latin "universus," a word made up of *unus* and *verto*, "one" and "to turn." Now, the word for "verse," meaning a poem or piece of poetry comes from the Latin *versus*, "a line of writing," which *also* comes from the same Latin root *verto*, to turn, for writing is a turning of words, images, and figures together. *Verto* also means to turn back, to switch and to flip.[13] Two modes, two sides of one coin, are therefore present both in "universe" as a physical world and in "verse" as a mode of writing, as *écriture*.

Let us recapitulate: if myth is an attempt to explain the phenomena of the world in a narrative; if myth perpetuates itself in language; if our word for the known or supposed world is "universe" and our word for poetry is "verse," and both share the same root, then myth, language, and the known and unknown worlds are uncannily, yet unmistakably, related. But is our "one turn" universe enough to accommodate the new modes of being created by the new technologies? Language's "turning" of words to create, like a potter working on a wheel or a glassmaker blowing and turning new forms, myth anew is able to give the universe *yet another turn* which will flip it upside down, and create, as we have seen earlier, a mirror image where gazer and gazed at are irremediably and forever confused.[14]

The three elements of myth, narrative, and universe are masterfully joined in Stephenson's "Metaverse" mentioned earlier. That this Metaverse is, if we follow the Greek and Latin etymologies, an "after, behind, and/or beyond the turn/return," provides us with exciting mirror-like complexities. The relationship between the Metaverse and metaphorical language is clear in *Snow Crash* when a sword-fight occurs between Hiro and a Japanese businessman, a fight, in fact, between their two avatars:

> The Nipponese businessman lies cut in segments on The Black Sun's floor. Surprisingly (he looks so real when he's in one piece), no flesh, blood, or organs are visible through the new cross-sections that Hiro's sword made through his body...But the air does not rush out of him, he fails to collapse, and you can look into the aperture of a sword cut and see, instead of bones and meat, the back of the skin on the other side. It *breaks the metaphor.*[15]

Bodies in cyberspace are the *poetical oeuvre* of computer programmers and hackers. In fact, *all* of cyberspace is a big text written in its entirety with a language not too different, in its essence, from the language of literature. It is a specialized jargon which can be understood by most but appreciated by few. Its authors form a close-knit society with its craft, lore, and traditions. In the context of intertextuality and hypertextuality, Michael Riffaterre wrote:

> The institutions of interpretation have remained largely unchanged since Aristotle, with one exception. Born almost unnoticed initially in the backyard of the humanities, first mistakenly seen as a mere improvement in the techniques of inquiry available to literary scholars, computer programming evolved almost overnight from a system of information retrieval to one of real analysis, to one capable of producing first critical discourse and later creative writing. This last *avatar* is the significant one, the first break with traditional humanism.[16]

But programmers and hackers enjoy the added benefit of seeing their work taking *actual* shape and performing *actual* actions that are slowly becoming more far-reaching as the writing technologies advance. For it is indeed a writing which is involved, the writing of a code which translates, in a fulgurant manner, into immediate and measurable results. Like their pen-and-paper or typewriter forefathers, the "poetry" of code-writers is highly metaphorical; in fact, it can *only* be metaphorical since whatever it constructs lives in the realm of simulation and virtuality. Yet, how potent such metaphorical language is can be taken as the confirmation that what takes place in real life is not less bound to the dicta of language. Gibson shows the relation between cyberspace and narrative in the following passage from *Count Zero*:

> It came on, again, gradually, a flickering, non-linear flood of fact and sensory data, a kind of narrative conveyed in surreal jumpcuts and juxtapositions. It was vaguely like riding a rollercoaster that phased in and out of existence at random, impossibly rapid intervals, changing altitude, attack, and direction with each pulse of nothingness, except that the shifts had nothing to do with any physical orientation, but rather with lightning alternations in paradigm and symbol-system.[17]

The fascination of language-as-virtuality is told by Miller: "I have used, and will go on using, the word 'magic' to name the power that words on the page have to open up a virtual reality when they are read as literature."[18]

If narrative is a story being told in language, and cyberspace is a narrative construction and re-creation of myth, then it is important to see how the relationship between narrative and the new technologies that have allowed the translation to cyberspace is perceived. Worthington sees the problem clearly when she writes: "Narrative…is more essential than ever as a tool for understanding the myriad conjunctions between postmodernism and technology and for devising a possible place for ourselves as active subjects within those conjunctions."[19] In fact, it is George P. Landow who first put together the theories of the postmodern age and the new discoveries of technology. In his *Hypertext 2.0: The Convergence of Contemporary Critical Theory and Technology*, he writes that we are witnessing the clear coming together of literary theory and hypertext, i.e., literary theories finding their practical confirmation in the narratives of cyberspace:

> The parallels between computer hypertext and critical theory are of interest at many points, the most important of which, perhaps, is that critical theory promises to theorize hypertext and hypertext promises to embody and thereby test aspects of theory, particularly those concerning textuality, narrative, and the roles or functions of reader and writer. Using hypertext, critical theorists will have, or now already have, a laboratory in which to test their ideas.[20]

Cyberspace is seen, as shown previously, as a lab in which the theories of the last half of the twentieth century are being—very successfully, one may say—tested. Landow builds his thesis not around figures who have shaped the new technologies inasmuch as around the very same critics/writers I have introduced like Barthes, Baudrillard, Benjamin, Borges, Jameson, Calvino, de Certeau, Derrida, Gibson, Lévi-Strauss, Miller, and others. Talking about the Deleuze and Guattari concept of the rhizome, he writes:

> Anyone considering the subject of this book [*A Thousand Plateaus*] has to look closely at their discussion of rhizomes, plateaus, and nomadic thought for several obvious reasons, only the most obvious of which is that they present *A Thousand*

> *Plateaus* as a print proto-hypertext...Certainly, many of the qualities Deleuze and Guattari attribute to the rhizome require hypertext to find their first approximation if not their complete answer or fulfillment...Like Derrida and like the inventors of hypertext, they propose a newer form of the book that might provide a truer, more efficient information technology.[21]

What Jean-François Lyotard describes as the "return of the narrative in the non-narrative"[22] is the converging moment between technology and writing when contemporary critical theory, after having almost exhausted its interpretive methods in the physical world,[23] is now ready to effectively measure, on a scale never expected before, the truth or untruth of its assertions. Miller masterfully shows the extent to which the new technologies are replacing more traditional modes of reading and writing, and compares two users of the language, one he calls Horace, the "book or paper person," the other he calls Jimjim, a "cyberperson" spending the many hours of the night on his computer chatting with friends online and using the many possibilities offered by the Internet:

> It does not go without saying that Jimjim is necessarily inferior to Horace. Jimjim's involvement with his media is active, interventionist. Jimjim writes a lot, with fluency and power, while Horace is in danger of being passively determined by other people's words. Reading books does not necessarily make one a good writer, whereas instant messaging is superb training in succinctness and economy, even elegance, of style.[24]

The fear of losing traditional modes of reading and writing is not grounded in valid reasons. In fact, what we take as a battle for narrative between the real and the virtual ignores the fact that the book, writing, and the text have always been virtual objects and activities. Ryan writes:

> As a generator of potential worlds, interpretations, uses, and experiences, the text is thus always already a virtual object. What the marriage of postmodernism and electronic technology has produced is not the virtual text itself, but the elevation of its built-in virtuality to a higher power. In no form is this exponentiation more obvious then [sic] in hypertext.[25]

Lévy concurs when he says that writing, because of its virtualizing quality, "desynchronizes and delocalizes," and helps bring forth "a mechanism of communication in which messages are often separated in time and space from their emitting source, and thus received out of context."[26] The new writing heralded by cyberspace takes our already-virtualized communicative abilities to their ultimate development and brings about a revolutionary change:

> Compared to old techniques of reading as network, digitalization introduces a small Copernican revolution: it is not the navigator who follows the reading instructions and physically moves in hypertext, turning pages, moving weighty volumes,

> wandering in libraries, but it is now a mobile and kaleidoscopic text which presents its facets, turns, folds and unfolds itself at will in front of the reader.[27]

It is not only us, humans, who have become, to anxious Neo-Luddites, deterritorialized, but it is also the text which, freed from its fetters, is fully spreading its wings and showing itself in its true colors: fully metaphorical, fully flexible, ungraspable because forever mutating. Lévy explains:

> Hypertextual mechanisms present in digital networks have *deterritorialized* the text. They have brought forth a text without clear borders, without definable interiority. Now there is *some text*, as one says some water or some sand. The text is put in motion, caught in a flux, vectorized, metamorphic. It is thus closer to the movement of thought itself.[28]

Virtualization, to Lévy, "brings about the becoming of the text," and begins the real "adventure of the text." Humanity has, finally, "invented writing."[29]

Cyberspace is indeed a textual space *par excellence*. One of the current manifestations of this textual space is hypertext, defined by Landow in the context of theorists of textuality as follows:

> Like almost all structuralists and poststructuralists, Barthes and Foucault describe text, the world of letters, and the power and status relations they involve in terms shared by the field of computer hypertext...*Hypertext*, as the term is used in this work, denotes text composed of blocks of text—what Barthes terms a lexia—and the electronic links that join them...*Hypertext* denotes an information medium that links verbal and nonverbal information.[30]

Landow is referring to Barthes' *S/Z*, the masterfully minute re-reading of Balzac's novel *Sarrasine*. In it, Barthes writes about an ideal writerly text where "systems of meaning can take over this absolutely plural text, but their number is never closed, based as it is on the infinity of language."[31] Is it necessary to point out that cyberspace is precisely this "ideal text"? What were hitherto scholarly theses, experimentations, and viewpoints almost exclusively aimed at the academic elite can now be practically experienced by any cybernaut. Lévy, who defines hypertext as a "universe of meaning" and "worlds of signification," also sees it as a *metaphor* valid for all spheres of reality where "significations" are involved.[32] He characterizes hypertext as following the principles of metamorphosis, heterogeneity, multiplicity and embedding of scales, exteriority, topology, and mobility of centers. What he says about topology is interesting to our mapping concerns:

> In hypertexts, everything works according to proximity and neighborhood. The course of events is a question of topology, of paths. There is no homogeneous universal space where forces of linking and unlinking, where messages could freely circulate. Everything which moves must do so on the hypertextual web as it is, or has

> to modify it. The web is not in space, it *is* space.[33]

The peculiar topology of texts seen in a post-structuralist context is best exemplified by Barthes' statement that the "text, in its mass, is comparable to a sky, at once flat and smooth, deep, without edges and without landmarks; like the soothsayer drawing on it with the tip of his staff an imaginary rectangle wherein to consult, according to certain principles, the flight of birds." [34] As the text is, to follow Barthes' famous expression, "*étoilé*"—"starred,"—so is cyberspace: a deep mass without edges and without landmarks, wherein cybernauts as travelers, be it for a minute or for days, are marking their private, personal, and secret path, secret not because it is confidential but because it remains the representation of what lies at the deepest core of each traveler. A mapping of cyberspace taking the text as its progenitor would use mobile, starred landmarks which can be likened to the *lexias* used by Barthes for the first time in his starring of Balzac's *Sarrasine*. These lexias are

> brief, contiguous fragments…[and] will include sometimes a few words, sometimes several sentences; it will be a matter of convenience: it will suffice that the lexia be the best possible space in which we can observe meanings; its dimension, empirically determined, estimated, will depend on the density of connotations, variable according to the moments of the text.[35]

In other words, cyberspace as textual space is a construct which, as Lévy said above, works according to proximity or, as Barthes would say, is made of contiguous fragments in continuous movement and change displaying the metamorphosis quality of hypertexts. Cyberspace mapping will consist of what I call *cyberlexias*, or the brief units of information generated by our journeys in virtuality. Such journeys might consist of shorter or longer bursts of information exchanges. The dimension of such cyberlexias would, as in a text, depend on the density of information given or taken. As technologies progress, a convergence will most probably occur where our movements in hypertext will be essentially similar to those in cyberspace. Silvio Gaggi writes in this context:

> When, in the near future, hypertextual systems…become our dominant textual vehicle, both the way we read and what we understand literature to be will be altered…The distinction between text and context will dissolve and intertextuality will cease to be regarded as such because there will be, in fact, only one text, one intertext, one hypertext…In hypertext there is no primary axis, no clear road in or out, no coordinates that have priority over any other coordinates—except as the reader determines.[36]

In a way reminiscent of Kurzweil's troubling predictions, Gaggi is envisioning a future where hypertext becomes the *only* mode of reading and writing. What we can equally infer is that *all* modes of communication and thus of being might be incorporated in cyberspace. Every unique, non-duplicatable path each and every reader/cybernaut draws in the flat and smooth sky of cyberspace will determine, and therefore map up, the lexias making up each *cybertext*. As in Borges' "The Book of Sand," the awesome monstrosity or *obscenity* of cybertextuality resides in the fact that never will anyone be able to find the first or the last page, and never will anyone be able to find the same page again, that is, to *read* and *write* the same cybertext. Sven Birkerts writes:

> Stripping the work of its proud material trappings, its solid three-dimentionality, [screen technologies] further subject it to fragmentation...We can enter cleanly and strategically at any number of points; we can elide passages or chapters with an elastic ease that allows us to *forget the surrounding textual tissue*.[37]

Derrida foresaw the end of reading and writing as we have known it and writes in *Of Grammatology* of a new age where technological developments have forced us to re-evaluate our reading and writing habits:

> The end of linear writing is indeed the end of the book, even if, even today, it is within the form of a book that new writings—literary or theoretical—allow themselves to be, for better or for worse, encased. It is less a question of confiding new writings to the envelope of a book than of finally reading what wrote itself between the lines in the volumes. That is why, beginning to write without the line, one begins also to reread past writing according to a different organization of space...Because we are beginning to write, to write differently, we must reread differently.[38]

The *cyberspace* of reading and writing is both the locus of a Derridean arch-writing—a writing working as a mold for all reading, writing, and speaking—activity and a site where readers—who have also become aware that they have also always been writers—are positioned. Miller clarifies this new discursive space:

> The Internet is not a "space," if one means by that a Euclidean manifold in which each thing is in one place and has identifiable relations by coordinates to all other things and to the borders that define regions within the volume. In the nonspaced space or spaced-out space of the Internet, everything is in a sense everywhere at all times, and everything is juxtaposed to everything else, in a pell-mell confusion.[39]

Faced with the inherent difficulty of mapping a space which defies the common acceptance of the term, Lévy links that space with language and coins the term "cosmopedia" as a replacement for "encyclopedia":

> Rather than having to deal with a text with *only one* dimension, or even with a hypertexual *network*, we are faced with a *multidimensional space* of dynamic and

> interactive representations. To the face-to-face of the fixed image and the text, characteristics of the encyclopedia, cosmopedia opposes a very large number of forms of expression: fixed image, animated image, sound, interactive simulations, interactive maps, expert systems, dynamic ideographies, virtual realities, artificial lives, etc."[40]

Cyberspace is so intimately reliant on language that words, as Shawn P. Wilbur writes, have come back with a vengeance: "We use words as tools, as individuals and as scholars. On the Internet we use little else. Whatever else Internet culture might be, it is still largely a text-based affair."[41] Heim says that the new technologies have driven "our verbal life faster and faster," and that word processors are "computerizing our language."[42]

What can be seen as a monstrosity is paralleled by the proliferation, during the last thirty years or so, of programming languages. As if the initial strings of 1s and 0s were not enough, programmers have vied to create more and more powerful and versatile languages. Kittler calls the implosion of programming languages a "postmodern tower of Babel."[43] Indeed, the Babel myth again serves a useful metaphor for this excess of languages, an excess which can take the form, in the new technologies, of viruses, which are nothing else than a malicious written code. In Stephenson's *Snow Crash*, one of the characters, a hacker guru, is infected by a very special virus and says:

> "What did the Brandy whisper in your ear?"
>
> "Some language I didn't recognize," Da5id says. "Just a bunch of babble."
>
> *Babble. Babel.*
>
> "Afterward, you looked sort of stunned."[44]

Writing is a Babel-like activity where languages, codes, and modes are shuffled, modified, and transformed in a dizzying whirlwind. After God "descended" to see what mankind was doing and confounded their language, humanity was stunned. Attempts to go back to the original pre-Babel tongue are as numerous as they are simplistic and/or extremist. The earliest recorded endeavor of this kind is reported by Herodotus in his *Histories* when the Pharaoh Psammetichus wanted to ascertain through language who the most antique people was and, taking two children and isolating them, came to the conclusion that since the first word they said was "becos," the Phrygian word for bread, the oldest language was therefore Phrygian and not, as he formerly thought, Egyptian.[45]

Paul Auster, in *City of Glass*, takes up the Herodotus story and mentions two other instances, one during the Middle Ages and another in the early sixteenth century. But Auster's own narrative turns around the fictional Peter

Stillman who, obsessed by the same search for the original pre-Babel language, locked up his son, also named Peter, in a dark room for nine years. After recognizing the failure of his project, Peter Stillman the father burned his records, accidentally setting fire to the whole house and unwillingly saving his son from his confinement. The father is tried and found insane, and the son is sent to a hospital to recover. His speech, however, is forever tainted with the Babel curse: Peter Stillman the son can only *babble*:

> "Wimble click crumblechaw beloo. Clack clack bedrack. Numb noise, flacklemuch, chewmanna. Ya, ya, ya. Excuse me. I am the only one who understands these words...Wimble click crumblechaw beloo. It is beautiful, is it not? I make up words like this all the time. That can't be helped. They just come out of my mouth by themselves. They cannot be translated...I am mostly now a poet. Every day I sit in my room and write another poem. I make up all the words myself, just like when I lived in the dark.[46]

The link between poetry and myth, noted above, is striking. When myth forsakes its guiding role in societies, it is incorporated—or recuperated—by literature, by writing. Peter Stillman the son and Peter Stillman the father are one and the same person representing the search for the pre-Babel language, its loss, and its re-tracing. As the elderly Stillman leads Quinn the detective in his walks in New York and spells out the phrase "The Tower of Babel" on the actual map of the city, cyberspace is constructed by users who write their own journeys. To Lévy, cyberspace is the computer of Babel:

> One could say that there is only one computer, only one support for text, but it has become impossible to trace its limits, to fix its outline. It is a computer the center of which is everywhere and the circumference nowhere; a hypertextual computer, dispersed, alive, pullulating, unfinished, virtual, a computer of Babel: cyberspace itself.[47]

The writing of cyberspace takes this anxiety a notch further. In the world of the matrix, the dichotomy between the basically simple 1s and 0s strings and the dazzling graphics, sounds, and—soon?—feelings such strings can produce, is tantamount to pure myth. Stephenson has his protagonist wonder over a picture of Hammurabi as the latter is given by Marduk, the chief Babylonian god, some sort of scepter in the shape of a one and a zero; these are explained as emblems of royal power, the origin of which is "obscure."[48] Power belongs to the one who can go back to the mythical pre-Babel tongue. If myth, as noted earlier, is the attempt to put in one fulgurant vision the essence of a concept which has taken millennia to develop, then cyberspace offers an infinitely varied virtual world through a mere binary code. Hardly a new concept, true, for most myths speak of an original pair of beings who are either created or re-created after some divinely-imposed catastrophe. But that a myth has actually taken form is what can be seen as the miracle of cyberspace.

From myth (Herodotus) to fiction (Auster) the progression takes us to cyberspace. Stephenson's Babel, in *Snow Crash*, is aptly called "Infocalypse": the building of the tower had to be stopped because of an "informational disaster,"[49] and it is indeed a proliferation of information that constitutes one of the main results of cyberspace. The divine name is, in terms of new technologies, the machine language of the world:

> At the lowest level, all computers are programmed with strings of ones and zeroes. When you program in machine language, you are controlling the computer at its brainstem, the root of its existence. It's the tongue of Eden. But it's very difficult to work in machine language because you go crazy after a while, working at such a minute level.[50]

Peter Stillman the father was trying to "work in machine language" but went crazy; likewise, human beings need a language-buffer, as it were, which will only imperfectly point to the original parent language, if indeed it does exist. The proliferation of languages is paralleled, in cyberspace, by a proliferation of programming languages.[51]

But at the same time, paradoxically, the proliferation of languages as a confusion visited by God is also pictured as the gift of speaking in tongues. Here again the connection between language and myth is striking: glossolalia—"speaking in tongues"—is, according to *Webster's Dictionary*, "a prayer characterized chiefly by incomprehensible speech," from the Greek *glossa*, meaning tongue, and *-lalia*, originally meaning a speech defect specified by the preceding element, in this case *glôssa.*[52] It is also revealing to find that the old name for linguistics was "glossology." One of the most important events to be recorded in the New Testament was the apostles' speaking in tongues during the feast of the Pentecost:

> And suddenly there came a sound from heaven as of a rushing mighty wind, and it filled all the house where they were sitting. And there appeared unto them cloven tongues like as of fire, and it sat upon each of them. And they were all filled with the Holy Ghost, and began to speak with other tongues, as the Spirit gave them utterance.[53]

The antique punishment recorded in the Old Testament is here repeated but in a different direction and different motives: glossolalia as defect and as means of confusion becomes the speaking in tongues as divine gift and as a means of re-unification and universal understanding through the gospels. The confusion of the bystanders is also the mirror image, reversed of course, of the confusion in the Babel story:

> Now when this was noised abroad, the multitude came together, and were confounded, because that every man heard them speak in his own language. And they were all amazed, and marvelled, saying one to another, Behold, are not all these which speak Galilaeans? And how hear we every man in our own tongue, wherein we were born?[54]

What is the role of the proliferation of tongues in cyberspace? Is it a glossolalia of confusion or a return to unification through multiplicity? Hypertext is one form of glossolalia for, as Lévy says in this context: "Each one according to their means, the communication actors or the elements of a message construct and remodel universes of meaning."[55] Stephenson devotes three full pages in *Snow Crash* to a discussion between Hiro and the virtual librarian on the meaning and cyberspace implications of glossolalia. The librarian tells Hiro that "[m]any Pentecostal Christians believe that the gift of tongues was given to them so that they could spread their religion to other peoples without having to actually learn their language. The word for that is 'xenoglossy'."[56] And isn't the widely-advertised concept of "global village" precisely built around a missionary-like movement to hook the whole planet online and achieve cyberspace xenoglossy?

Glossolalia, to others, represents the ultimate chance for human beings to fully construct a Babel language which is neither one of confusion nor one of unity. Instead, it is language of pleasure, and it is again to Barthes that I turn to borrow these lines from his study of relations in Sade:

> The meaning of the chain is to posit the infinite of erotic language (isn't the sentence itself a chain?), to break the mirror of enunciation, to make sure that pleasure does not go back to where it came from, to waste the exchange by dissociating the partners, not to return back to those who have given to you, to give to those who will not return back, to deport the cause, the origin, *away*, to make one finish the gesture begun by another: every chain being open, saturation is only momentary: nothing internal happens there, nothing *interior*.[57]

Cyberspace, then, is not only a simple mirror or a hologram which puts two worlds in specular reflection. The problem of the proliferation of languages, tongues, and voices in virtuality is elegantly solved with the help of the post-structuralist theory of the multiplicity of narratives in a chain which does not end, and which is made of links written by each and every reader. The pleasure of cyberspace textuality is not only the uncertainty of who will read what, and in which order, but also who will *re-write* the offered text. Barthes is also touching upon the Bakhtinian notion of dialogism and the centrifugal power of narrative *away* from a pure reflexivity that can only lead to closure. Bakhtin, unlike Eliade, ascribes to poetry a centripetal power which, instead of reaching out, confines poets inside their own unique mythical bubbles.[58] His concept of the prose writer, on the other hand, differs markedly from that of the poet. He writes:

> The prose writer does not purify his discourses from their intentions and from the tonalities of other people, he does not kill in them the embryos of social plurilinguism, he does not put aside these linguistic figures, these ways of speaking, these *virtual* story-telling-personas who appear, in transparence, behind the words and the forms of his language; but he disposes all these discourses, all these forms, at different distances from the ultimate semantic core of his work, from the center of his personal intentions.[59]

The above can be read by cybernauts as one of the features which have made cyberspace the point of convergence of different and differing voices from all over the planet. It is only through a dialogic writing that the global village can be made possible. Bakhtin says that polylinguism as introduced in the novel

> is *the discourse of the other in the language of the other*, serving to refract the expression of the author's intentions. This discourse presents the singularity of being *bivocal*. It simultaneously serves two locutors and expresses two different intentions...Such discourse contains two voices, two meanings ["sens"], two expressions...In all of these [bivocal discourses] is found the seed of a potential dialogue, un-deployed, concentrated on itself, a dialogue of two voices, two conceptions of the world, two languages.[60]

The "two conceptions of the world" is an interesting point in the context of cyberspace. As seen above, the current debate is precisely about the existence of this *other* world or virtuality, whether it is a mirror image, a double, a hologram, or a post-structuralist chain of unending signifiers. Bakhtin's dialogical discourse is useful in that *all* narrative discourse contains, in its essence, the seeds of an *other*, and dialogue makes this other's universe not only an intelligible world but also a shareable one.

The sharing of voice(s) in polylinguism and bivocality can also be usefully related to the notions of gift, prodigality, and excess. Mauss, in his famous "Essai sur le don," defines the specific kind of gift known as *potlatch* as an institution characterized by "total prestations of agonistic type." A potlatch, in various North-American Indian tribes, is the obligation of giving, receiving, and returning gifts in an increasingly excessive display of generosity. Mauss says about this remarkable excess or rivalry and antagonism: "One reaches the level of battles until the putting to death of the chiefs and nobles affronting each other. One also reaches the purely sumptuary destruction of accumulated wealth to overshadow the rival—and at the same time associate—chief."[61] Cyberspace is a giant arena where, through the expansion, at an exponential rate, of technologies undreamt of before, cybernauts are engaged in private and public displays of potlatch-like giving, receiving, and returning gifts.

However, the economy of excess in cyberspace is not, contrary to that of the physical world, one of matter: what is being given, received, and returned is information, the twenty-first-century commodity *par excellence*, a commodity at the same time intangible and supremely potent. Mauss was aware of the non-physicality of the potlatch:

> And all these institutions uniquely express only one fact, one social regime, one defined mentality: everything, food, women, children, goods, talismans, soil, labor, services, sacerdotal offices and ranks, is matter for transmission…Everything comes and goes as if there existed a constant exchange of a spiritual matter comprising things and men between the clans and the individuals, spread over the ranks, the sexes, and the generations.[62]

Mauss' observation is crucial since it allows us, through the myths and taboos surrounding the potlatch and through this "exchange of spiritual matter," to understand how a virtual *writing* of cyberspace has been able to engender, in the space of a few years, an almost full-fledged world bustling with incredible activity.

Bataille's *The Accursed Share* takes up Mauss' potlatch and excess and clothes it in even more sumptuous attire. In his first part entitled "Consumption," Bataille studies various societies and the way their consumption methods betrayed exuberance. Continuing from where Mauss had left, Bataille sees the value of the potlatch in terms of loss:

> But the wealth that is actualized in the potlatch, *in consumption for others*, has no real existence except insofar as the other is changed by the consumption. In a sense, authentic consumption ought to be solitary, but then it would not have the completion that the action it has on the other confers on it. And this action that is brought to bear on others is precisely what constitutes the gift's power, which one acquires from the fact of *losing*.[63]

What immediately strikes is the Bakhtinian importance of the other, and the potlatch becomes with Bataille a dialogic exchange where gifts replace words and are as easily disposed of as in a narrative that is only measured by its surpassing itself. This surpassing, this going *beyond* oneself to reach the other, is also reminiscent of the way myth functions to give humanity, through a simple narrative, a glimpse of what cannot be understood otherwise. Bataille writes that the "exemplary virtue of the potlatch is given in this possibility for man to grasp what eludes him, to combine the limitless movements of the universe with the limit that belongs to him."[64] The Aztecs and human sacrifices, the North American Indians and potlatch, Islam and conquest, Lamaism and the absence of militarism, the Soviets and industrialization are all drawn by Bataille on his map of the excesses of civilizations, and one can only wonder how, had he still been alive, he would have added the virtual society of cyberspace which, in one move, captures the essences of potlatch, conquest, and hyper-advanced technologies.

At this stage one is reminded of the important role played by fiction both in the representation of reality and in the creation of cyberspace. Hence the subversive aspect of virtuality: it is not only that virtuality threatens to diminish our hold on everyday reality or that the new technologies are alienating humanity from itself and giving up control to supposedly autonomous AIs; the problem is also one of language and power. What cyberspace has created is a new language, a new discourse which has probably forever altered our view of reality. Barthes, talking about the subversiveness of the Sadean language, writes these words equally applicable to our context:

> The deepest subversion (counter-censure) does not necessarily consist in saying what shocks public opinion, morality, the law, or the police, but to invent a paradoxical discourse (free from all *doxa*): *invention* (and not provocation) is a revolutionary act: the latter can only be accomplished in the foundation of a new language.[65]

The perversion of cyberspace doubles as the perversion of a discourse which runs counter to the established *doxa*, the revered doctrines presiding over what we have, for millennia, thought language to be. For there is a myth of language which is dissipated with difficulty, even after thirty years of postmodernism, a myth which has survived until now and about which Barthes says: "We find here the old modern myth according to which language is only the docile and *insignificant* instrument of the serious things taking place in the spirit, the heart, or the soul."[66] With the advent of cyberspace, the glossolalia of writing has decentered language once and for all from its age-old pedestal of representation-only. Cyberspace, from its programming to its dissemination to its use clearly evinces a language which can completely, from the bottom up, *create* worlds and realities.

The power of software programming as fiat combines with the myth of a speech which creates realities seemingly coming out of nowhere to deliver the most striking mixture of writing, magic, and creation known to humanity so far. A shamanistic incantation, cyberspace as *écriture* is plainly recognized by Stephenson in *Snow Crash* and given the Mesopotamian name of "nam-shub," "incantation":

> A *speech with magical force*. Nowadays, people don't believe in these kinds of things. Except in the Metaverse, that is, where magic is possible. The Metaverse is a fictional structure made out of code. And code is just a form of speech—the form that computers understand. The Metaverse in its entirety could be considered a single vast nam-shub.[67]

What is worthy of notice is that the Metaverse is a "fictional" structure, i.e., a structure using fiction as a model, and if we recall the basic definition presented earlier of fiction as "literature created from the imagination, not presented as fact, though it may be based on a true story or situation," then the notion of cyberspace/Metaverse acquires new dimensions. Not only is cyberspace a fictional construct, a matrix consisting of a "consensual hallucination experienced daily by billions of legitimate operators" devoid of tangible physical reality, but it is also a *narrative* construct, a work of fiction, a vast world of signifiers constantly pointing, hypertextually, to each other without ever reaching a primary point of reference, without reaching the forever-slipping ultimate signified. Indeed, cyberspace can be seen as a Metaverse and considered a single vast signifying incantation. Gibson's equation between the matrix and "the sum total of the works, the whole show," is not surprising anymore, neither is the closing scene where Case, jacked in, sees himself and Linda alive in cyberspace. Narrative as writing assumes full power in cyberspace and also problematizes the reality of our own existences, rejoining, with full blast, the postmodern assumptions making of all human experience a fictional construct.

Cyberspace elucidates, in true tangible form, ideas like those expressed by Terry Eagleton on the nature of a language which "now begins to look much more like a sprawling limitless web" in which "there is a constant interchange and circulation of elements, where none of the elements is absolutely definable and where everything is caught up and traced through by everything else." [68] Explaining one of the main tenets of Derridean deconstruction, Eagleton writes:

> Just as Western philosophy has been 'phonocentric', centred on the 'living voice' and deeply suspicious of script, so also it has been in a broader sense 'logocentric', committed to a belief in some ultimate 'word', presence, essence, truth or reality which will act as the foundation of all our thought, language and experience.[69]

Obviously, the above words can be applied to the binary reality/virtuality, making of reality the ultimate yardstick by which we measure the "appropriateness" of virtuality and by which we cast judgment upon cyberspace's truth value. Virtuality thus takes on a secondary role, an abnormal excrescence which can—and, to many, *should*—be safely excised in order to return to a "normal," "real," and "natural" world. Virtuality is portrayed as a *supplement* only. But supplements are always a dangerous proposition to say the least, especially since Derrida's *Of Grammatology* shook the precarious base over which Western philosophy had built, for centuries, a whole system of thought the results of which can be seen even now in the opposition between "good" reality and "bad" virtuality. Derrida warns that the notion of the supplement arises out of an essential lack:

> But the supplement supplements. It adds only to replace. It intervenes or insinuates itself *in-the-place-of*, if it fills, it is as if one fills a void. If it represents and makes an image, it is by the anterior default of a presence…As substitute, it is not simply added to the positivity of a presence, it produces no relief, its place is assigned in the structure by the mark of an emptiness.[70]

Cyberspace as supplement adds only to *replace*, and this is what Neo-Luddites and what Western culture fear most, the replacement of a cherished reality with what is thought to be unreal and intangible, a mere software gimmick. Yet what is happening is that virtuality is slowly invading reality, attempting to replace it in many fields, not only adding but filling an absence which was not recognized as such. And if reality proves to be, in the final analysis, the locus of an absence, then the whole conception of this reality is challenged.

But if reality is the locus of an absence and can be replaced by virtuality, it is only logical to assume that virtuality can also be, at some point in the future, the locus of some absence in its turn, and will be again replaced by another concept. Derrida is aware of the conundrum and subsumes any binary pair to his concept of "archi-écriture," an arche-writing essentially present in both. Writing about the nature/culture binary, he says:

> I would wish…to suggest that the alleged derivativeness of writing, however real and massive, was possible only on one condition: that the "original," "natural," etc. language had never existed, never been intact and untouched by writing, that it had itself always been a writing. An arche-writing whose necessity and new concept I wish to indicate and outline here; and which I continue to call writing only because it essentially communicates with the vulgar concept of writing.[71]

This passage is extremely important in the context of the reality/virtuality binary: if we transpose Derrida's pair with ours, we see that the alleged derivativeness of cyberspace is only made possible because the "real" nature of the world we live in has never been untouched by virtuality, i.e., that our reality is always, in some form or another, "contaminated" by virtuality. We have seen how language has always been metaphorical, and can never be perfectly equivalent to what it purports to name and describe. We have also seen how the ultimate signified can never be caught: signifiers lead, in an uninterrupted and infinite chain, to one another. Reality has always been virtual. What stands above this pair is what can probably be called *arche-virtuality*, the representative of which, what we now see as virtuality, is only a mundane yet necessary concept to pit against reality. Can we thus say, echoing Derrida's famous "There is nothing outside of the text,"[72] that *there is nothing outside of virtuality*?

But cyberspace writing, whether it has to assume an arche-writing or not, definitely posits a writer, or what is here better called a cyber-writer. Gibson's AI, Neuromancer, explains his/its name: "Neuro from the nerves, the silver paths. Romancer. Necromancer. I call up the dead."[73] An interesting passage as it not only positions cyber-writing but also conjures up meditations on the act of writing and the cyber-writer. Case is caught, in this final passage, in cyberspace with Linda and Neuromancer, the main AI, is the writer of this matrix where life and death are mixed or, as it appears later on, where the difference between the two states becomes irrelevant. Cyber-writers are in a very privileged position not experienced before: their writing assumes, because of the power of software, a quality hitherto only dreamed of, that of actually giving life to their creation. "Neuro," the presence in life, is also "necro," the absence in death, and both unite in the romance of the narrative, in the *fiction* created. We are no longer content to say with post-structuralist thinkers, that the author is dead, we can also add that cyber-writers *are* dead, a dead-alive entity present in the cyberspace they have themselves created. The triangle writer-text-reader is caught in a matrix where death is undifferentiated from life and reality from virtuality. Once again, what were mere intellectual exercises at the close of the twentieth century have become palpable reality…or virtuality?

But what Gibson does not—at least explicitly—elaborate upon is that Neuromancer is also a "new" romancer, a new writer of fiction, a new kind of creator whose narrative not only instantaneously problematizes, *in-situ*, the writer, the writing, and the reader, but also for the first time allows almost anybody to partake in an activity hitherto reserved to the "intellectual" elite. This is what Dibbell describes when he writes:

> It took Samuel Pepys, 17th-century Englishman of affairs, about 150 years to get his diary published. It takes "Soul Reaver," 21st-century American teenager of Gothick tendencies, about 14 kilobits per second, tops…History will yet judge whether Soul Reaver's diary has the staying power of Pepys's, but keep in mind his doesn't exactly start out with a bang either.[74]

Dibbell acutely realizes that cyberspace and writing are one and the same. We have always been writing a text anyway, an arche-writing barely visible in the bewildering array of signification continuously inventing itself everyday. But it is the merit of cyberspace to have made this theoretical truth a tangible fact. The author, decentered by Derrida and erased by Barthes, passes from the status of privileged being to that of everyday user, from a professional craftsperson to an amateur who learns to *re-use* the powers of narrative. Barthes, in an interview given in 1975, prophetically wrote:

> I can imagine a future society, totally unalienated which, on the level of writing, would only know amateurish activities. Especially on the level of the text. People would write, would make texts, for the pleasure of it, would profit from the jouissance of writing without preoccupying themselves with the image they may conjure up in others.[75]

Has the Barthean vision been fulfilled? When we sit in front of our screens, we all become *amateur* writers again, partaking in the mythical re-creation of words and commands which *do* something, whether we use a word processor, play a game, buy and sell stocks, transfer money, or just send an e-mail. Not only has the age-old idea of the original been superseded by that of the *legitimate* copy, thus doing away with the idea of a single author, but cyber-writers have also all become *de facto* hackers, cyber-bricoleurs tinkering with the world around them with the help of words. We have, as cyber-writers, acted the ultimate sleight-of-hand and thus precipitated, beyond all predictions, the demise of a writing which has always tried to produce and then to control, through its narrative and through the voice of its author, a logocentric order of things. If the language of pre-cyberspace was Bakhtinian monologism, a discourse pointing back at itself, the language of cyberspace is pure dialogism where all participants, in the web of the text, weave a giant and constantly changing tapestry of signifiers.

Talking about the Sadean discourse and the loss or inter-changeability and decentering of authorial voice, Barthes says:

> [W]ith Sade, it is some libertine who, without any other preeminence except that of an ephemeral and practical responsibility, arranges the postures and directs the general movement of the erotic operation; there is always somebody to regulate (but not: to legify) the exercise, the séance, the orgy, but this somebody is not a subject; director of the episode, he is only a moment of it, nothing more than…a sentence operator.[76]

Calvino has Marco Polo describe the city of Marozia which can be taken to represent the way cybernauts construct the fiat of narrative space(s) as cyber-writers:

> It also happens that, if you move along Marozia's compact walls, when you least expect it, you see a crack open and a different city appear. Then, an instant later, it has already vanished. Perhaps everything lies in knowing what words to speak, what actions to perform, and in what order and rhythm; or else someone's gaze, answer, gesture is enough; it is enough for someone to do something for the sheer pleasure of doing it, and for his pleasure to become the pleasure of others: at that moment, all spaces change, all heights, distances; the city is transfigured, becomes crystalline, transparent as a dragonfly.[77]

Are the kaleidoscopic nature of cyberspace and the uncertainty of its narrative forms some of the reasons why it has attracted so much criticism and antagonism from a culture which puts so much effort into *centering* itself and is so anxious at *mapping* its bearings? Cyber-writing, on the contrary, opens up the map(s) of cyberspace and refuses to be held and pinned down on a flat *mappa mundi.* Absence and presence form the two unshakeable pillars upon which cybermapping is to be envisioned.

Neuromancer's injunction to Case, "If your woman is a ghost, she doesn't know it. Neither will you" acquires, in the context of cyberspace and the new writing, an undreamt opportunity for cyber-writers, that of being part of a collaborative *orgy of writing* where all, whether existing or not, willingly join in the game of production of narrative. Gaggi says in this context:

> The subject of the author, most significantly, is challenged by hypertext... notions of intellectual property and authorship, which are very much tied to the fixity and permanence of the book as an object for which an individual can take responsibility and credit, are challenged. The speed and ease of comment and response in hypertext makes it difficult to keep track of the specific contributions of various writer/readers.[78]

Gaggi is here echoing Landow's observation that, following along the lines of contemporary critical theory, hypertext "reconfigures—rewrites—the author in several obvious ways...the figure of the hypertext author approaches, even if it does not entirely merge with, that of the reader."[79] Both Gaggi and Landow are in fact restating what Gibson had fictionally predicted in *Neuromancer* in the passage cited above.

If all cybernauts have become, with varying degrees, cyber-writers, it is legitimate to ask, in a study which attempts to map cyberspace, where the hugely voluminous mass of writing goes or where it is stored. The role of the librarian, or cyber-librarian, is in the age of cyberspace of critical importance since everything is, in one way or another, a writing or a variation thereof. Stephenson envisions, quite humorously, the cyber-librarian of the future, a software program capable of seamlessly and almost instantaneously finding information in cyberspace:

> "Your information, sir," the Librarian says.
>
> Hiro startles and glances up. Earth swings down and out of his field of view and there is the Librarian, standing in front of the desk, holding out a hypercard. Like any librarian in Reality, this daemon can move around without audible footfalls.
>
> "Can you make a little more noise when you walk? I'm easily startled," Hiro says.
>
> "It is done, sir. My apologies."[80]

On a more serious note, Michael W. Giles, in his presidential address to the

Southern Political Science Convention, in Tampa, Florida, in November 1995, said:

> The virtual library places greater emphasis on information management, accessing, and retrieval skills. It, thus, emphasizes the unique skills of the library professional. Indeed, given the high rate of technological change, library staff will come to play an extraordinarily important instructional role in maintaining consumer access. Moreover, the Cyberspace Model of scholarly communication places a heavy emphasis on information management from the earliest stages of research process.[81]

Notwithstanding the appropriateness and accuracy of Giles' observations, our concern here is not specifically with "consumer access," nor with "research." The cyber-librarian and the cyber-library he/she runs are mythical figures engaged in acts of writing and in the management of cyber-discourse. John Thiem, in his "Myths of the Universal Library: From Alexandria to the Postmodern Age," likes to imagine the creation of a hypothetical "Universal Electronic Library," itself a "subdiscipline of comparative mythology known as bibliomythography," and links it to the ancient Library of Alexandria in Egypt as a symbol or mythological object. Thiem heavily uses Borges' "The Aleph" and "The Library of Babel" to make clear the relationship between the vastness and complexity of the world and the "modern megalibrary."[82] As a monstrous object, the "Universal Library" in cyberspace has become a mythical symbol: "Like its precursor in Alexandria, the UL is not only an enormous repository of information about every known mythology, it too has become the impossible object of mythological devotion and execration."[83] In this context, Allen writes that the present computer systems "seem to take us back to the medieval idea of the total library."[84]

The connection with Borges' "The Book of Sand" is clear, but it is to the Argentinean author's "The Library of Babel" that one must turn in order to fully understand the connection between myth (Babel), writing (Library) and mapping. What we notice from the beginning is, first, Borges' identification of the library with the universe and, second, his apparent attempts at giving a *very physical* identity to an otherwise indescribable building:

> The universe (which others call the Library) is composed of an indefinite and perhaps infinite number of hexagonal galleries, with vast air shafts between, surrounded by very low railings...The distribution of the galleries is invariable. Twenty shelves, five long shelves per side, cover all the sides except two; their height, which is the distance from floor to ceiling, scarcely exceeds that of a normal bookcase...There are five shelves for each of the hexagon's walls; each shelf contains thirty-five books of uniform format; each book is of four hundred and ten pages; each page, of forty lines, each line, of some eighty letters which are black in colour.[85]

Borges is faced with the seemingly impossible task of *mapping* a space which he knows is unmappable with the usual means of measurement available in the physical world. As I have been showing throughout, it is to myth and to writing that he resorts. First, the library has existed from all times, and mankind has been the imperfect librarian entrusted with its care. Here we see that the myth is serving its primary purpose, that of explaining, in short-hand fashion, the vast and mysterious ways of the universe by means of analogy. As the universe is infinite yet manifested in its details, so is a library which, through the infinite combination of the letters of the alphabet, is yet found in some physical location. Second, and this is logically deducted from the first point, the library's mythical infinity is constructed by the mere combination of a very limited number of letters. Indeed, Borges wastes no time in linking myth and writing, making of them the two axioms that govern any understanding of the library. The first axiom is that "[t]he Library exists *ab aeterno*," and the second is that "*[t]he orthographical symbols are twenty-five in number.*"[86] In order to reconcile the two facts, Borges reaches an elegant solution which denies both the infinity and the limitedness of the library:

> Those who judge it [the world] to be limited postulate that in remote places the corridors and stairways and hexagons can conceivably come to an end—which is absurd. Those who imagine it to be without limit forget that the possible number of books does have such a limit. I venture to suggest this solution to the ancient problem: *The Library is unlimited and cyclical.*[87]

Obviously, the analogy rests on the way our planet, as a sphere, is built. A traveler would cross earth and, moving in a straight line, would eventually reach the point of departure, yet no two voyages would be similar. Cyberspace takes this analogy to new heights as it provides a sphere which, unlike physical earth, constantly changes in volume, expanding and retracting according to what is at the time the movement of networks on the Internet. Cyberspace is both a myth in the problematization of its origin(s) and end(s), a genesis and an eschatology in the problematization of its boundaries; and a writing which, unlike Borges' twenty-five "orthographical symbols" uses only two, the 1 and the 0.

Yet another theme can be fruitfully used in our search for ways to map cyberspace. Unsurprisingly, it will contain within itself the two seeds of myth and writing, a myth because it will try to explain the universe (both in its physical and non-physical natures) and allow us to see it as it may really is, and a writing because reality and virtuality can only be apprehended and represented through a system of signs. Such theme is the city, and it is appropriate to end this chapter with a marvelously prophetic passage from Calvino's *Invisible Cities*:

> Relegated for long eras to remote hiding places, ever since it had been deposed by the system of nonextinct species, the other fauna was coming back to the light from the library's basements where the incunabula were kept; it was leaping from the capitals and drainpipes, perching at the sleepers' bedside. Sphinxes, griffons, chimeras, dragons, hircocervi, harpies, hydras, unicorns, basilisks were resuming possession of their city.[88]

Has our age unleashed the immemorial myths which it had jealously kept in the prison-house of language? Is Eliade finally right in saying that the modern world is devoid of myth and that the latter has sought refuge in writing? Yet, like in Calvino's delightful account of the city of Theodora in the above passage, myth has, through cyberspace, taken a sizeable leap and is already walking the streets of Cyberia.

NOTES

1 Maurice Leenhardt, *Do Kamo: La Personne et le mythe dans le monde mélanésien* (Paris: Gallimard, 1976), 247.

2 Roland Barthes, *Mythologies* (Paris: Seuil, 1970), 181.

3 Claude Lévi-Strauss, *Anthropologie structurale* (Paris: Plon, 1998), 239.

4 Jorge Luis Borges, *Atlas* (Harmondsworth: Viking, 1986), 60.

5 Lévy, *Intelligence*, 240.

6 Lévy, *Virtuel*, 34.

7 Ibid., 86.

8 Leenhardt, *Do Kamo*, 232–33.

9 Caillois, *Mythe*, 151.

10 *Webster's*, 400, and Auzanneau and Avril, *Dictionnaire latin*, 180.

11 Deleuze and Guattari, *Mille Plateaux*, 33. The narrative is strikingly similar to that of André Breton recounting his first attempts at automatic writing with his friend Philippe Soupault as told in the first Surrealist Manifesto of 1924.

12 *Webster's*, 1555.

13 Auzanneau and Avril, *Dictionnaire latin*, 642, 643, 657, 658.

14 The question whether all language is metaphorical or not, especially since Nietzsche's famous "What then is truth? A mobile army of metaphors, metonyms, and anthropomorphisms," in his "On Truth and Lies in the Extra-Moral Sense," in *The Viking Portable Nietzsche* (NY: Viking Press, 1954), 46–47, continued a long war between the literalists (beginning with Aristotle) and the figuralists, and acquired giant dimensions with Derrida and most post-structuralist critics. Michael Arbib and Mary Hesse's *The Construction of Reality* (Cambridge: Cambridge UP, 1986), Northrop Frye's *Words with Power: Being a Second Study of the Bible and Literature* (NY:

Harcourt Brace Jovanovich, 1990) and *Myth and Metaphor: Selected Essays, 1974–1988* (Charlottesville: Virginia UP, 1990), and George Lakoff's "The Contemporary Theory of Metaphor" in *Metaphor and Thought*, 2nd edition, Andrew Ortony, ed. (Cambridge: Cambridge UP, 1993), are also of interest as far as the relationship between metaphor and reality is concerned.

15 Stephenson, *Snow Crash*, 95. My italics.

16 Michael Riffaterre, "Intertextuality vs. Hypertextuality," *New Literary History* 25.4 (Autumn 1994), 779–88, 779. My italics.

17 Gibson, *Count Zero*, 40.

18 Miller, *On Literature*, 21.

19 Worthington, "Bodies," 195.

20 George P. Landow, *Hypertext 2.0: The Convergence of Contemporary Critical Theory and Technology* (Baltimore: The Johns Hopkins University Press, 1997), 2.

21 Ibid., 38–39.

22 Jean-François Lyotard, *La Condition postmoderne* (Tunis: Cérès Editions, 1994), 64.

23 See Sokal (cited above).

24 Miller, "Moving Critical Inquiry On," 416.

25 Ryan, "Cyberspace," 96.

26 Lévy, *Virtuel*, 36.

27 Ibid., 42.

28 Ibid., 46.

29 Ibid., 48.

30 Landow, *Hypertext 2.0*, 3.

31 Barthes, *S/Z*, 6.

32 Lévy, *Technologies*, 29.

33 Ibid., 31.

34 Barthes, *S/Z*, 14.

35 Ibid., 13.

36 Silvio Gaggi, *From Text to Hypertext: Decentering the Subject in Fiction, Film, the Visual Arts, and Electronic Media* (Philadelphia: University of Pennsylvania Press, 1998), 103.

37 Sven Birkerts, "The Fate of the Book," *The Antioch Review* 54.3 (Summer 1996), 259–70, 261.

38 Jacques Derrida, *Of Grammatology* (Baltimore: The Johns Hopkins UP, 1976), 86–87.

39 J. Hillis Miller, "The Ethics of Hypertext," *Diacritics* 25.3 (Autumn 1995), 26–39, 31.

40 Lévy, *Intelligence*, 204.

41 Shawn P. Wilbur, "An Archeology of Cyberspaces: Virtuality, Community, Identity," in Bell and Kennedy, *Cybercultures*, 45–55, 46.

42 Heim, *Metaphysics*, 3.

43 Kittler, "There is no Software."

44 Stephenson, *Snow Crash*, 69.

45 Herodotus, *Histories* (Ware: Wordsworth Editions, 1996), 117–18.

46 Auster, *New York Trilogy*, 20–22.

47 Lévy, *Virtuel*, 45.

48 Stephenson, *Snow Crash*, 239.

49 Ibid., 64, 101.

50 Ibid., 260.

51 Add to the above C++, Python, Perl, Java, Lisp, and a multitude of other, more-or-less obscure, low and high-level languages.

52 *Webster's*, 602, 1365, and 802.

53 *The Bible*, King James' Version, Acts 2:2–2:4.

54 Ibid., 2:6–2:8.

55 Lévy, *Technologies*, 29.

56 Stephenson, *Snow Crash*, 193.

57 Barthes, *Sade, Fourier, Loyola*, 168–69.

58 Mikhaïl Bakhtine, *Esthétique et théorie du roman* (Paris: Gallimard, 1991), 109.

59 Ibid., 119. My italics.

60 Ibid., 144–45.

61 Marcel Mauss, "Essai sur le don: Forme et raison de l'échange dans les sociétés archaïques," in his *Sociologie et anthropologie* (Paris: Quadrige, 2001), 153, 152.

62 Ibid., 163–64.

63 Georges Bataille, *The Accursed Share* (New York: Zone Books, 1998), 69–70.

64 Ibid., 70.

65 Barthes, *Sade, Fourier, Loyola*, 130.

66 Ibid., 45.

67 Stephenson, *Snow Crash*, 197.

68 Terry Eagleton, *Literary Theory: An Introduction*, 2nd edition (Oxford: Blackwell Publishers, 2001), 112.

69 Ibid, 113.

70 Derrida, *Of Grammatology*, 145.

71 Ibid., 56.

72 Ibid., 158.

73 Gibson, *Neuromancer*, 289.

74 Julian Dibbell, "My Modem, Myself: Online Diaries," *The Village Voice* 45.43 (Oct. 31, 2000), 151.

75 Roland Barthes, *Le Grain de la voix: Entretiens 1962–1980* (Paris: Seuil, 1981), 233.

76 Barthes, *Sade, Fourier, Loyola*, 9.

77 Calvino, *Invisible*, 155.

78 Gaggi, *From Text to Hypertext*, 106.

79 Landow, *Hypertext 2.0*, 90.

80 Stephenson, *Snow Crash*, 102.

81 Micheal W. Giles, "From Gutenberg to Gigabytes: Scholarly Communication in the Age of Cyberspace," *The Journal of Politics* 58.3 (Aug. 1996), 613–26, 619.

82 John Thiem, "Myths of the Universal Library: From Alexandria to the Postmodern Age," in Ryan, *Cyberspace Textuality*, 256–66.

83 Ibid., 260. For a unique–and quite hyper-textual–account of the stories surrounding the Library of Alexandria, see Luciano Canfora's *The Vanished Library: A Wonder of the Ancient World* (Berkeley: University of California Press, 1990).

84 Allen, *Intertextuality*, 200.

85 Borges, *Labyrinths*, 78–79.

86 Ibid., 79, 80.

87 Ibid., 85.

88 Calvino, *Invisible*, 160.

CHAPTER SIX

Cyberspace as City

The imminent awakening is poised, like the wooden horse of the Greeks, in the Troy of dreams.

Walter Benjamin, *The Arcades Project*[1]

The Metropolis strives to reach a mythical point where the world is completely fabricated by man, so that it absolutely coincides with his desires.

Rem Koolhaas, *Delirious New York*[2]

As builders of cities for millennia and dwellers of megalopolises for more than a hundred years, twenty-first-century humans have naturally envisioned the new digital realm as a full urban space where the storing, exchange, and travel of information mirror the life and movement of dwellers of real-world cities. Not only does computer memory reside in "addresses," but we also speak of the "architecture" of processors, of "buses" linking, like street and avenues, different processes, of "ports" giving access not to tankers, ships, or liners, but to external or peripheral hardware or software, and of "drivers" allowing hardware to be recognized by the operating system. In addition, even casual cybernauts have heard—or are the owners—of email "addresses," Internet "sites,"—which are usually, at the beginning, "under construction,"—and "domain names." Beyond these rather mundane appropriations of the city metaphor, however, lies a more fundamental need to map out cyberspace on the urban grid, translating, as it were, the desire to order experiential phenomena onto the realm of the intangible, the ethereal, and the magical.

The implications of seeing cyber-cities as models of new ways of dealing with reality have not escaped the attention of architecture theoreticians who have, sadly, remained silent about the problem of cybermapping. Bermudez and Gondeck-Becker, building on the theories of Ledoux, Piranese, Woods and others, have come to the conclusion that since cyberspace offers a totally new environment where real-world limitations are lessened, digital space does not have to follow the rules of reality, and it becomes thus acceptable to try and reflect on the potentials of cyber-architecture by investigating the rules that are definitely alien to those governing the physical world in which architecture has developed for centuries. But the most important point, to Bermudez and Gondeck-Becker, is that if architecture can loosen up its grip on hard physical reality, then any other discipline can follow suit.[3] Amy Bruckman, founder of two virtual communities on the Internet, MediaMOO and MOOSE Crossing, was writing, in 1996, that the new dimensions offered by cyberspace present architects with a hitherto unheard-of medium wherein to explore the limitless possibilities of the virtual. Citing Marcos Novak's notion of "liquid architecture," Bruckman envisions a cyber-city where citizens become creators of their own environment(s).[4]

Yet Bermudez, Gondeck-Becker, and Bruckman are repeating, in their own words, what Jameson was writing years before about the way architectural problems lead to theoretical issues in the other disciplines:

> It is in the realm of architecture, however, that modifications in aesthetic production are most dramatically visible, and that their theoretical problems have been most centrally raised and articulated; it was indeed from architectural debates that my own conception of postmodernism…initially began to emerge.[5]

We can say with Jameson that it is in the realm of cyber-cities that modifications, such as Novak's "liquid architecture," are most remarkable, and that it is the way we define our cyber environment—and we have indeed begun to do so, witness the growing number of virtual communities—that has, as I have shown earlier, forced us to raise questions in other fields. Even though we might find ourselves, at first, uncomfortable with the dramatic changes living in cyberspace entail, the cyber-city is the first step toward the building of new theories of reality. Jameson, talking about postmodern architecture, and calling it the "new hyperspace," echoes the initial fear experienced by cyber-dwellers:

> I am proposing the notion that we are here in the presence of something like a mutation in built space itself. My implication is that we ourselves, the human subjects who happen into this new space, have not kept pace with that evolution; there has been a mutation in the object unaccompanied as yet by any equivalent mutation in the subject. We do not yet possess the perceptual equipment to match this new hyperspace, as I will call it.[6]

The leap from mutated space and hyperspace to the fantasy of myth and magic is understandable. Cyberspace as a writing of myth and as a mythical writing is a discursive space constructed in the image of the city. Numerous cyberspace writers have pointed at the connection. Benedikt writes:

> In fact, all images of the Heavenly City—East and West—have common features: weightlessness, radiance, numerological complexity, palaces upon palaces, peace and harmony through rule by the good and wise, utter cleanliness, transcendence of nature and of crude beginnings, the availability of all things pleasurable and cultured.[7]

He adds that the need for a Heavenly City is still as pressing as ever and that if this need is to be fulfilled, it can only be actualized in cyberspace.[8] Lévy says in this respect:

> Cyberspace: nomadic urbanity, software civil engineering, liquid *ponts et chaussées* of the Space of knowledge…It is an architecture of the interior, an unfinished system of the collective equipment of intelligence, a whirling city with roofs of signs. The construction of *cyberspace*, the converging center of communication and thought of human groups, is one of the principal esthetic and political stakes of the coming century.[9]

Lévy's challenge has been echoed by Heim's concept of the relationship between virtual and physical architecture, or "avatecture."[10]

Indeed, cyberspace can be seen as Benjamin's ideal labyrinthine city, as the quasi-mythical qualities of a maze-like discourse in cyberspace are also served by a model based on the city. Featherstone and Burrows, writing about cyberpunk fiction, say:

> The world of cyberspace is itself an urban environment…a digitized parallel world which from 'above' might appear as a rationally planned city…but from 'below' reveals itself a Benjaminesque labyrinthine city, in which no one can get the bird's eye view of the plan, but everyone effectively has to operate at street level.[11]

Benjamin's labyrinthine city is best demonstrated in this passage from Gibson's *Virtual Light* where the precise intersection of "information and geography," or of cyberspace and the real world, is seen as necessary for the sanity of travelers in both realms, but more so for that of dwellers of cyberspace. In a reversal of situations, physical movement in a physical city is seen as a return to an already archaic sense of stability:

> Was it significant that Skinner shared his dwelling with one who earned her living at the archaic intersection of information and geography? The offices the girl rode between were electronically conterminous—in effect, a single desktop, the map of distances obliterated by the seamless and instantaneous nature of communication. Yet this very seamlessness, which had rendered physical mail an expensive novelty, might as easily be viewed as porosity, and as such created the need for the service the girl provided. Physically transporting bits of information about a grid that consisted of little else, she provided a degree of absolute security in the fluid universe of data.[12]

Conversely, some see cyberspace intimately connected to the dismaying conditions existing in real-life cities. Röetzer writes: "The entry into cyberspace is interconnected, above all, with the urban reality of cities: the decay of public areas, increasing suburbanization, and the setting up of the dual city."[13] In a process not unlike that imagined by Calvino in his city of Eusapia, this real postmodern city is also becoming more and more similar to the virtual landscape as far as technological modes of communication are concerned. Ostwald, in "Virtual Urban Futures," says that the postmodern city is "gradually becoming more and more reliant on systems which are both simulated and transient. The idea that technology is erasing the perceived distance between points and the relationship between time and space is not unfamiliar."[14]

The recurring—and pressing—juxtaposition between the two cities has made some theorists of urban spaces—both physical and virtual—ponder the issue more seriously. Rem Koolhaas, in his monumental *Delirious New York*, ends his book with the following words:

> The City of the Captive Globe is devoted to the artificial conception and accelerated birth of theories, interpretations, mental constructions, proposals and their infliction on the World. It is the capital of Ego, where science, art, poetry and forms of madness compete under ideal conditions to invent, destroy and restore the world of phenomenal Reality.[15]

The cyber-city is indeed a hothouse where experiments, theories, interpretations and proposals are conducted in the world of simulation and where madness and sanity live side by side in order to invent a new reality, question the old one, and refresh our conception of what both mean. What Koolhaas is doing in *Delirious New York* is to provide a "blueprint," a "theoretical" Manhattan of which the real city is but a "compromised and imperfect realization,"[16] making thus of "Manhattanism" a virtual-city concept.

Similarly, I want to present a "theoretical" cyberspace of which the representatives in reality can be the Internet, simulated worlds, chat rooms, RPG worlds of fantasy, simulators, VR goggles, and others. All these are by no means the perfect realizations of the blueprint, but they all *tend*, each in its own way, toward achieving what I believe is a mode of reality which combines myth and writing to problematize our existing theories of physical reality. Koolhaas' Manhattan analogy is appropriate, for he attempts to extract, from the real Manhattan, a rarefied concept, an "interpretation that intends to establish Manhattan as the product of an unformulated theory, *Manhattanism*, whose program—to exist in a world totally fabricated by man, i.e., to live *inside* fantasy—was so ambitious that to be realized, it could never be openly stated."[17] Koolhaas' point is that Manhattan's driving force was the construction of a world poised at the antipodes of reality, where steel would mix with sheer fantasy to create another reality altogether, beginning with the magic of Coney Island and ending with the dream of world peace as embodied in the United Nations building. Writing in 1978, could Koolhaas have imagined that before the end of the century the Manhattan dream, to exist in a totally constructed world of fantasy, would be realized? In a world as ambitious as cyberspace where steel is replaced by writing, where virtuality is doubled by the element of language and augmented by myth, can we now "openly" state the program which will invent, question, and refresh our concepts of reality?

A starting point is how both worlds-as-cities can be represented as forming two mutually including realms. Ernest J. Yanarella, taking Calvino's *Invisible Cities* as model, asks in 1998: "How can these inchoate 'soft cities' unfolding before and around us and the 'hard cities' of our past be integrated and democratically controlled?"[18] If it is doubtful that the new technological revolution has passed, as Yanarella says, "largely unacknowledged," his comment is interesting in that it explicitly assumes that the cities we live in now are constructions of the past and that virtual communities, or "soft cities," will become the norm. Yanarella's answer to his own question is that cyberspace is *not* meant to be an alternative to human habitation but "merely another form of habitation within a more encompassing built environment enclosed within an even more encompassing set of relations in nature."[19]

Yet the connection with Calvino's *Invisible Cities* is too tempting to be ignored. Linking writing and the city, Calvino says about the city of Tamara:

> Your gaze scans the streets as if they were written pages: the city says everything you must think, makes you repeat her discourse, and while you believe you are visiting Tamara you are only recording the names with which she defines herself and all her parts. However the city may really be, beneath this thick coating of signs, whatever it may contain or conceal, you leave Tamara without having discovered it.[20]

The city-as-book is open to different readings and misreadings and is constructed gradually by its different readers, hence compounding the initial problem of mapping cyberspace as city. If the cyber-city is constructed as reading a text, it is then open to the same aleatory processes of intertextual readings. Indeed, city streets, to Benjamin, are the locus of writing: "This revolution in language was carried out by what is most general: the street.—Through its street names, the city is a linguistic cosmos."[21]

As mentioned above, the attempt to present a blueprint of cyberspace will not offer a tour of the premises—it has already been attempted by others—for they are, because of the nature of virtuality, as shape-shifting as can be; what can be achieved is pointing to the *discourse* of cyberspace without ever being able to arrest the cybernaut/cyber-writer's gaze on one possible landscape feature for too long. As such, "hard cities" have become so bloated with meaning that the more subtle signification opportunities provided by cyberspace are slowly prevailing. As Kublai Khan, we are overwhelmed with imperial cities too heavy to offer new avenues of discourse and we surprise ourselves enjoying the more boundless cities of virtual discourse:

> "The empire is being crushed by its own weight," Kublai thinks, and in his dreams now cities light as kites appear, pierced cities like laces, cities transparent as mosquito netting, cities like leaves' veins, cities lined like a hand's palm, filigree cities to be seen through their opaque and fictitious thickness.[22]

It is interesting to note that Calvino's invisible cities are not only "fictitious," i.e., pertaining to fiction and to writing, but also, more admirably, that they are represented as lace, netting, veins, filigree, all features equally applicable to the "Net" of our Internet and to the "tissue" of the text. This relationship between the cyber-city and writing is nowhere made more explicit than in *Snow Crash*. The "Street," mentioned previously, is an urban-like virtuality constructed from scratch with computer programming language, a fact which does not make it, to its cyber-denizens, less liveable:

> Hiro is approaching the Street. It is the Broadway, the Champs Élysées of the Metaverse...It does not really exist. But right now, millions of people are walking up and down it...The Street seems to be a grand boulevard going all the way around the equator of a black sphere with a radius of a bit more than ten thousand kilometers. That makes it 65,536 kilometers around, which is considerably bigger than Earth...The only difference is that since the Street does not really exist—it's just a computer-graphics protocol written down on a piece of paper somewhere—none of these things is being physically built.[23]

It is this feature of cyberspace, this propensity on the part of human beings to map out liveable space similarly wherever they migrate, that makes virtual space so akin to a city. What better way to anchor one's bearings in an otherwise totally new and totally alien environment as cyberspace than to duplicate the existing urban plans and transpose them, almost *word for word*, into the realm of virtuality? Writing unveils its total creative power as never before as it becomes clear that what we have taken for granted in the "real world" can simply—and dramatically—be explained by the putting into play of discursive strategies. A city, read as text and, what is more revolutionary today, *written* as software, is found to be no less liveable than a "real" city.

And it is here that writing and myth combine in the construction of the virtual polis, for there can hardly be anything more myth-like than an *écriture* which actually *builds*, through the sheer volition of the cybernaut, spaces which are immediately liveable and hence potentially mappable. The old dream of giving language magical qualities is fulfilled.

It is indeed as an urban space that cyberspace harbors mythical images and constructions. Graeme Gilloch, in his *Myth and Metropolis*, writes: "While the phantasmagoria of modernity finds its most palpable expression in the architecture of the city, the individual and collective experiences of the metropolis are also imbued with mythic forms."[24] The city is not just an urban construction, but encompasses utopias of ordered and structured existence. It acquires ontological status and comes to represent humanity's deepest aspirations, expectations, and fears. Greg Bear, in *Queen of Angels*, describes the "Country of the Mind" virtually accessed by mid-twenty-first-century scientists in similar urban myth terms:

> "It is a region, an unceasing and coherent dreamstate, built up from genetic engrams, preverbal impressions and all the contents of our lives. It is the alphabet and foundation on which we base all of our thinking and language, all our symbologies. Every thought, every personal action, is reflected in this region. All of our myths and religious symbols are based upon its common contents…"Is it truly a countryside?" "Something like a countryside or city or some other environment." "With buildings and trees, and people, and animals?" "Of sorts. Yes."[25]

And Cadigan's *Mindplayers* depicts the entry to the mind in architectural terms:

> All I had to do was move around a little. But in the beginning, I was moving around a lot, just to watch the way things changed…The cathedral—now, *there* was a surprise. I'd never imagined that *I* would have a church in *my* head, but there it was, taking up a healthy portion of space in whatever area of my mind I was in.[26]

Gilloch, by equating the city to a monad which contains, in its essence, the totality of human experience, is exactly re-phrasing one of the definitions of myth cited previously. The relationship between myth and the city is a reciprocal one: not only is myth constructing itself through the city, the city is also feeding and keeping intact the myths it creates itself. Here again the ambiguity presented by the problem of which comes first is one of the fundamental lessons taught by cyberspace.

One of the most durable equivalents to the urban myth of cyberspace in the real world is Paris, a city which has tormented the imagination of thinkers, writers, and artists throughout the centuries. Indeed, Benjamin writes: "Few things in the history of humanity are as well known to us as the history of Paris. Tens of thousands of volumes are dedicated solely to the investigation of this tiny spot on the earth's surface."[27] One of the reasons why Paris has often been seen as the city *par excellence* is the amount of myth it contains. In fact, a lot of mapping of Paris has been done with myth as the yardstick, sometimes actually providing travelers with maps better than those obtained by pure cartographic means.[28] Here again, the *writing* of myth, in a De Certeau manner, is better apt to render a space than a place. Benjamin, who devoted his major work, *The Arcades Project*, to Paris, says:

> Balzac has secured the mythic constitution of his world through precise topographic contours. Paris is the breeding ground of his mythology…it is from the same streets and corners, the same little rooms and recesses, that the figures of this world step into the light. What else can this mean but that topography is the ground plan of this mythic space of tradition…as it is of every such space, and that it can become indeed its key.[29]

The places of Paris become, through Balzac's writing, alive with innumerable characters marking their own paths in the city, transforming Paris into a space where myth springs out of the actions and reactions of its denizens. The city is constructed by the stories attached to its landmarks, and the more myth-like, the more secret, the better the topographical mapping. Benjamin again:

> To construct the city topographically—tenfold and a hundredfold—from out of its arcades and its gateways, its cemeteries and bordellos, its railroad stations…just as formerly it was defined by its churches and its markets. And the more secret, more deeply embedded figures of the city: murders and rebellions, the bloody knots in the network of the streets, lairs of love, and conflagrations.[30]

The city's convolutes twist and form, like cyberspace, passages and labyrinths where the unknown becomes secret and the secret becomes myth, the latter finally resurfacing as a written hieroglyph waiting to be deciphered. The underworld of real cities is a mirror image of another underworld, or *supraworld*, that of cyberspace. Both antipodal realms are built *with* and *on* myth and are peopled by mythological creatures thriving on legendary feats and prowess. Both worlds—the underworld of the dead and the supraworld of cyberspace—spill over onto the physical world and taint it, as it were, unalterably. Benjamin writes:

> Our waking existence…is a land which, at certain hidden points, leads down into the underworld—a land full of inconspicuous places from which dreams arise…By day, the labyrinth of urban dwellings resembles consciousness; the arcades (which are galleries leading into the city's past) issue unremarked onto the streets. At night, however, under the tenebrous mass of the houses, their denser darkness protrudes like a threat, and the nocturnal pedestrian hurries past—unless, that is, we have emboldened him to turn into the narrow lane.[31]

If the existence of the underworld is now, in our scientific age, seriously doubted, the supraworld of cyberspace is being constructed as a replacement.

Our waking existence, our real life, is a realm which hints at virtualities but we do not have to sleep—or die—in order to access the hidden points of the labyrinths, entrances to dreams or to the afterworld.

Cyberspace is a dream being realized before our very conscious eyes, a *third* mode of existence added to consciousness and unconsciousness. It is not even the surrealists' "inner man" mode which was to be accessed through automatic writing; it is actually dreaming awake. The monstrosity of this possibility transforms cyberspace into a dream-city the secrets of which await to be discovered, a dream-city the boundaries of which are never traced for good but the gates of which are guarded by mythical creatures:

> At the entrance to the arcade, to the skating rink, to the pub, to the tennis court: *penates*. The hen that lays the golden praline-eggs, the machine that stamps our names on nameplates and the other machine that weighs us (the modern *gnōthi seauton*)...the mechanical fortuneteller—these guard the threshold...They protect and mark the transitions.[32]

The myth city remains, however, untouchable and, as cyberspace, unreachable through the physics of real life. Calvino writes, talking about the effect Marco Polo's description had on the Great Khan:

> But what enhanced for Kublai every event or piece of news reported by his inarticulate informer was the space that remained around it, a void not filled with words. The descriptions of cities Marco Polo visited had this virtue: you could wander through them in thought, become lost, stop and enjoy the cool air, or run off.[33]

Caillois thought that when myth loses its moral coercive power, it becomes an object of aesthetic pleasure which finds its best representation in the city, and what he wrote about this phenomenon taking place in Paris can be easily transposed to cyberspace:

> [It is acceptable to affirm] that there exists...a representation of the big city, *powerful enough on the imaginations that its exactitude can never be practically questioned,* created bit by bit by the book, yet widespread enough to be now part of the collective mental atmosphere and possessing thus a certain coercive power. We can already recognize there the characters of mythical representation.[34]

Paris is a world dislocated, through the power of writing, into a myth powerful enough to create a representation that is collectively accepted and feared as the harbinger of truths too primordial to be uttered in the light of day. Readers of Paris know that the city

> is not the only one, not even the real one, and that it is only a make-believe stage brilliantly lit, yet too *normal*, one that the machinists will never unveil, and which dissimulates another Paris, the real Paris, the ghostly Paris, nocturnal, ungraspable,

> ever more strong because it is secret, and which comes in any place and at any time dangerously meddling with the other one.[35]

In other words, the writing of myth constructs a double-jointed reality hiding behind the appearances of order and structure. Here again, the pair Apollo/Dionysus resurfaces and helps us explain, both for the city and for cyberspace, how myth, by grafting itself on a seemingly simple entity, in fact deconstructs it and rebuilds it again, though differently, and ultimately helps us realize the fundamental uncertainty of what we had hitherto taken for granted. Cyberspace *is* the mythical writing of our real life and is instrumental in making us see, face to face, the quintessential nature of our representational practices, even at the cost of losing our bearings in real life and allowing the myth of cyberspace to *spill over*, as it is already doing, onto the domain of real life. Along these lines, Caillois wrote:

> The two Paris which, at the beginning, lived side by side without mixing, are now reduced to a unity. Myth was at first content to use the facilities of the night and of the peripheral suburbs, of the little unknown streets and the unexplored catacombs. But it has quickly reached the full light in the heart of the city. It *occupies* the most frequented edifices, the most official, the most reassuring…Nothing has escaped the plague, the mythical has everywhere contaminated the real.[36]

The above reads like a contemporary description of how cyberspace has encroached on the *places* allotted to reality, and how it is *writing* these places into a virtual *space* equipped with old myths clothed in new garbs. We are *writing over* reality with the myths of cyberspace, and our writing is itself a mythical practice, a magical writing which uses itself to build its own spaces in the virtual realm, to devour its old self like the *ouroboros* snake swallowing its own tail in a circle which knows no beginning nor end.

Furthermore, the physical city, to the cybernaut, can also be seen as only a pale shadow, almost a replica, of the *real* cyber-city, a Eusapia, the model after which we have unconsciously built our earthly polis. As such, cities can be *read* by those who have access to the master plan, the blueprint of cyberspace. Talking about Benjamin's notion of the city as readable space, Gilloch writes:

> The metropolis is a multi-faceted entity, a picture puzzle that eludes any unequivocal decipherment. There is no single picture, no overarching perspective, that can capture the fluidity and diversity of this environment. Insights into the character and experience of the city are to be gleaned, therefore, only from fleeting images and sudden moments of illumination, from the fragments stumbled upon in this complex and ever shifting social *matrix*.[37]

Gilloch's use of the term "matrix" brings to mind Gibson's AI, Neuromancer, as he explains to Case how, despite the bewildering array of diversity present in the city, cyberspace is the model against which the physical can be read. Neuromancer as cyberspace's ultimate AI is as complex as the "ever shifting" matrix he lives in and has become part of. As such, he foresees all possible events and specifically Linda's death: "I saw her death coming. In the patterns you sometimes imagined you could detect in the dance of the street. Those patterns are real. I am complex enough, in my narrow ways, to read those dances."[38] Short of transforming themselves into AIs, cybernauts can become Poesque "physiognomists" and, through their cyber-gaze, untangle the knots which are incessantly constructed in their cyber-cities. Gilloch explains that since the city, as a mythic construction, is never what it seems to be, "it is the gaze of the physiognomist which brings to light the true character of the city. Physiognomic reading is no superficial activity, no cursory glance. It must go beneath the surface of things, penetrate their core."[39] Cybernauts become, in the cyber-city—an invisible city *par excellence*,—cyber-flâneurs trying, like their real-life counterparts, to decipher the city-as-text they have themselves helped shape.

Benjamin's flâneurs can serve as the starting point for the construction of their cyber counterparts. To him, the flâneur is an individual who feels a deep alienation and who projects onto the city a tragic vision:

> The gaze which the allegorical genius plunges in the city rather betrays the feeling of profound alienation. It is the gaze of a flâneur whose way of life hides behind a mirage of goodness the anguish of the future inhabitants of our metropolises. The flâneur seeks a refuge in the crowd. The crowd is the veil through which the familiar city, to the flâneur, morphs into a phantasmagoria.[40]

Derrida's sailing metaphor mentioned previously is striking here as well. The flâneur is a ship sailing in a sea of people, anonymously drifting in the crowd, *surfing* among the faces, the gestures, and the gaits of the passers-by, driven from one place to another by the sheer forces of chance. The cybernaut as cyber-flâneur can easily be seen in the following passage from Benjamin:

> The crowd gives birth, to the man who abandons himself to it, to a kind of drunkenness accompanied by very particular illusions, in a way that he flatters himself, upon seeing the passer-by swept by the crowd, in having classified him, from his external appearance and recognized him in all the recesses of his soul.[41]

The cyber-flâneur, however, in one important point works in a way crucially different from Benjamin's late-romantic figure: in cyberspace the world is not alien; real life might be so, but not virtuality. The cyber-flâneur may be hiding in front of a monitor or behind VR goggles, but the cyber-city offers itself in all its intricacies to his/her wildest fantasies. The anguish created by modern and postmodern cities disappears as the virtual polis, a digital construct, is invisibly yet forcefully expanding in fascinating and unimaginable ways. True, the cyber-flâneur is still seeking refuge in the crowd, but it is not the physical, fleshy crowd of the real streets which hypnotizes the virtual surfer: it is the encounter with disembodied identities, with countless personas, each hiding behind an avatar, masquerading (from *mask*) in an endless pageant where truth and illusion double the existing simulation. Each cybernaut, in cyberspace, becomes a cyber-flâneur, trying to hide in order to better appreciate the intricacies of a world entirely made up of programming language, where only the voice/writing of the other carries through. How different yet how strangely familiar the cyber-flâneur's experience in cyber-cities is to that of the physical flâneur can best be measured in the following from Benjamin's *Arcades Project*:

> An intoxication comes over the man who walks long and aimlessly through the streets. With each step, the walk takes on greater momentum; ever weaker grow the temptations of shops, of bistros, of smiling women, ever more irresistible the magnetism of the next streetcorner, of a distant mass of foliage, of a street name...Like an ascetic animal, he flits through unknown districts—until, utterly exhausted, he stumbles into his room, which receives him coldly and wears a strange air.[42]

The similarity of this experience with "jacking out," to use Gibson's term, is striking, as both real-world flâneurs and their cyber counterparts acutely sense the relative harshness or uncouthness and inane materiality of the physical world. It is only in the crowd that the flâneur can regain what is lost; it is only in cyberspace that the cyber-flâneur surfs the crowded digital expanses like an invisible spirit in a magical world. Indeed, both types of flâneurs share the attraction for myth:

> The street conducts the flâneur into a vanished time. For him, every street is precipitous. It leads downward—if not to the mythical Mothers, then into a past that can be all the more spellbinding because it is not his own, not private...In the asphalt over which he passes, his steps awaken a surprising resonance.[43]

The double ground nature of cyberspace alluded to by Benjamin is acutely felt by every cyber-flâneur: what the digital world is offering is, among other things, an illumination into the nature of reality itself: short of leading to the "mythical Mothers," the source of creation, the cyber-city invites cybernauts to re-assess their existing concepts of what is and what is not; cyberspace has fulfilled, through writing, the role of myth in providing an encapsulated version of reality. The only difference is that, in the cyber-city, cybernauts are *actually inside* the myth itself.

Being *inside* the city-as-myth is best exemplified in Auster's story of Peter Stillman the father mentioned above in the context of the Tower of Babel myth. Walking on the streets of New York, Stillman is also writing his own illusions, his own search for an unattainable pre-Edenic language, and Quinn, the detective, is learning, in the process, how to do the same:

> For walking and writing were not easily compatible activities. If for the past five years Quinn had spent his days doing the one and the other, now he was trying to do them both at the same time. In the beginning he made many mistakes. It was especially difficult to write without looking at the page, and he often discovered that he had written two or even three lines on top of each other, producing a jumbled, illegible palimpsest.[44]

Interestingly, walking *and* writing are seamlessly done in cyberspace, especially in the early days of IF and RPGs mentioned earlier. In fact, walking could then *only* be done by typing out the commands or by voicing them out to the Dungeon Master before the era of computers. The sensation of discomfort experienced by cyberspace "newbies" can be attributed, among other things, to this very palpable, very physical relationship between moving and writing: the keyboard or the mouse becomes the site of repeated physical touching. Like disabled persons, cybernauts re-learn the art of moving in the cyber-city through the use, not of their physical body, but of language. And this cyber-city, these cyber-pavements they walk on with their cyber-bodies, are truly a *palimpsest*, temporarily "jumbled" and "illegible" for the likes of Quinn who have not become adept at *walking and writing at the same time*. The palimpsest, "a parchment or the like from which writing has been partially or completely erased to make room for another text,"[45] can be seen as the different writings on top of one another, vying, on the texture of the page, for survival. In *Neuromancer*, Gibson shows this palimpsest-like nature of cyberspace as it vies with reality when the physical realm—in this case music—tears Case from the language-as-code grips of the matrix:

> The music woke him, and at first it might have been the beat of his own heart...His vision crawled with ghost hieroglyphs, translucent lines of symbols arranging themselves against the neutral backdrop of the bunker wall. He looked at the backs of his hands, saw faint neon molecules crawling beneath the skin, ordered by the unknowable code.[46]

Case is able to live, even for a brief moment, in the twilight zone between the physical and the virtual worlds, and it is this glimpse which allows him, at the end, to understand that the latter is also the palimpsest of its physical counterpart.

The question I have raised throughout remains the same: is the mythical cyber-city we have created and in which we are beginning to live hiding the real physical polis in which we leave our body or is it the opposite? Is this why Quinn, in Auster's trilogy, disappears from the city—and from the physical world altogether—the moment he learns to walk and write at the same time, exactly at the moment when he can read the palimpsest he has himself constructed; exactly at the moment when, in a terrible flash, he and Case and all cyber-flâneurs discover that *all writings make up the text and none is more or less real than the other*?

The palimpsestic inter-connection between human beings, the city, and cyberspace is clear when Case looks up at Linda and describes her as having her hair "drawn back, held by a band of printed silk. The pattern might have represented microcircuits, or a city map."[47] Gibson was, as early as in 1984, able to voice the beginning of a theory of cybermapping where cyberspace—as a pattern, as a veil, as a text-tissue, and as a band of printed silk—and the city join in a microcircuit-like dimension. Yet he was also aware that the city model was to be used not only as a *place* where people live but also, in a way reminiscent of de Certeau's theory, as a *space* where new discourses are constructed: "But he [Case] also saw a certain sense in the notion that burgeoning technologies require outlaw zones, that Night City wasn't there for its inhabitants, but as a deliberately unsupervised playground for technology itself."[48] The new technologies have, as we have seen, used cyberspace as a "playground" on which to test new theories, and it is the city which serves as the model for these new experimental grounds. Adding to Koolhaas' "Manhattanism" project, Gibson goes a step further and sees the physical city itself as a digital representation:

> Program a map to display frequency of data exchange, every thousand megabytes a single pixel on a very large screen. Manhattan and Atlanta burn solid white. Then they start to pulse, the rate of traffic threatening to overload your simulation. Your map is about to go nova. Cool it down. Up your scale. Each pixel a million megabytes. At a hundred million megabytes per second, you begin to make out certain blocks in midtown Manhattan, outlines of hundred-year-old industrial parks ringing the old core of Atlanta.[49]

The city, seen from a distance, is a microcircuit and the microcircuit, examined the way a close reading examines a text, is built after the image of a metropolis. The physical world *is* the mirror image of cyberspace, and vice-versa; this is probably, for the purpose of the present study, the single most important message of Gibson's *Neuromancer*.

Are we ready, at the beginning of the twenty-first century, not only to inhabit cyberspace, but also to consciously spell out the new modes—among them Roy Ascott's vision of "moistmedia" mentioned earlier—such move has effected? What is striking is that cyberspace dwellers, like Ng in *Snow Crash*, simultaneously live, for the first time in history, in two—or more—different places. While cybernauts are quietly sitting behind a screen, their minds and their cyber-bodies are engaging in not less gratifying activities at the far reaches of the planet. A curse or a blessing? Paradise lost anew or, on the contrary, regained? But perhaps the question is, like many important questions, simply misleading. Maybe the answer lies somewhere beyond the mere duality of right or wrong, of true or false, of, again, reality or virtuality. If we insist on trying to understand the cyber-city in terms of opposition we will miss the point that, above anything else, the cyber-city is a city of *microcircuits*, and as such is the exemplary model for a theory based on relationship, not of intrinsic, isolated identity. Deleuze and Guattari's rhizomatic model:

> A book...does not have an object. As an assemblage, it is itself only in connection with other assemblages, in relation to other bodies without organs. We will never ask what a book means, signified or signifying, we will look for nothing to understand in it; we will ask what it functions with, in connection with what it transmits intensities or not, in which multiplicities it introduces and metamorphoses its own multiplicity, with what bodies without organs it makes its own body converge.[50]

If the objects in the physical world have no meaning and can only be defined in context, in their relationship with one another, cyberspace and the cyber-city, similarly, do not have objects to be defined per se. If we take this further, physical reality as a total concept has no object and has to be defined only in context, this time in its relationship with virtuality. The cyber-city provides the ultimate missing link without which the rhizomatic model is unable to go beyond the apparently totalizing nature of the physical world. With cyberspace, the balance is regained and the virtual is defined *and* defines the actual; with cyberspace as the ultimate body without organs, reality is suddenly stripped from self-reflecting meaning and acquires in the process full rhizomatic status. Marco Polo, in Calvino's fictional account, is aware of the inter-relationship between the cities of the real and those, "invisible," of his story-telling narrative. He tells Kublai:

> In vain, great-hearted Kublai, shall I attempt to describe Zaira, city of high bastions. I could tell you how many steps make up the streets rising like stairways, and the degree of the arcades' curves, and what kind of zinc scales cover the roofs; but I already know this would be the same as telling you nothing. The city does not consist of this, but of relationships between the measurements of its space and the events of its past.[51]

The cyber-flâneur is re-constructing a relationship and a rhizomatic assemblage through the measurements of cyberspace and the events of the real world's past, which have become, like Lévy's collective intelligence, a shared memory. As we surf what is now the Internet or as we "jack" into simulations, we recognize the familiar and build on it as studiously as Benjamin's nineteenth-century Paris flâneur:

> At the approach of his footsteps, the place has roused; speechlessly, mindlessly, its mere intimate nearness gives him hints and instructions...Often, he would have given all he knows about...the site of a surprise attack or even of a barricade, to be able to catch the scent of a threshold or to recognize a paving stone by touch, like any watchdog.[52]

Benjamin's "imminent awakening" is indeed poised now not in the Troy of dreams, hidden in the recesses of humanity's desires, but in the cyber-city. But the cyber-city and all of cyberspace mean nothing when not inhabited and furiously crossed day and night by cyber-citizens, cyber-flâneurs, and cybernauts of all kinds. If we remember de Certeau's distinction between place and space, we realize once again that our mapping of cyberspace is built not on fixed ephemeral maps but on a model of relationships, and that these relationships rotate around the "everyday" practices of cybernauts re-writing, in their cyber-cities, their pasts and their myths. It is these activities which transform mere cyber-places—lifeless series of digital 1s and 0s—into the cyberspaces we are still colonizing and expanding. To these cyber-citizens we now turn in our exploration of cybermapping.

NOTES

1 Benjamin, *Arcades*, 392.

2 Rem Koolhaas, *Delirious New York: A Retroactive Manifesto for Manhattan* (London: Thames and Hudson, 1978), 242.

3 Bermudez and Gondeck-Becker, "Emerging Architectures."

4 Amy Bruckman, "Finding One's Own Space in Cyberspace," *Technology Review* (Jan. 1996), 48–54. See also Ollivier Dyens, "The Emotion of Cyberspace: Art and Cyber-Ecology," *Leonardo* 27.4 (1994), 327–33, for a discussion of the ecology of liquid architectures.

5 Jameson, *Postmodernism*, 2.

6 Ibid., 38.

7 Benedikt, "Cyberspace: First Steps," 38.

8 Ibid., 40.

9 Lévy, *Intelligence*, 120.

10 Michael Heim, "The Feng Shui of Virtual Worlds," *Computer Graphics World* (Jan. 2001), 19–21, 19.

11 Featherstone and Burrows, *Cyberspace*, 10–11.

12 Gibson, *Virtual Light*, 85.

13 Röetzer, "Outer Space or Virtual Space?" 128.

14 Ostwald, "Virtual Urban Futures," 662.

15 Koolhaas, *Delirious New York*, 243.

16 Ibid., 7.

17 Ibid., 6.

18 Ernest J. Yanarella, "Plato Meets Lawnmower Man in the Virtual Polis: The Case of PS 776," *PS: Political Science and Politics* 31.4 (Dec. 1998), 792–96, 795.

19 Ibid., 796.

20 Calvino, *Invisible*, 14.

21 Benjamin, *Arcades*, 522.

22 Calvino, *Invisible*, 73.

23 Stephenson, *Snow Crash*, 23–24.

24 Graeme Gilloch, *Myth and Metropolis: Walter Benjamin and the City* (Cambridge: Polity Press, 1996), 171.

25 Bear, *Queen of Angels*, 109–10.

26 Cadigan, *Mindplayers*, 25.

27 Benjamin, *Arcades*, 82–83.

28 The French surrealists have abundantly supplied the literature on "secret" and/or "magical" Paris with wonderful texts. Aragon's *Le Paysan de Paris* and Breton's various works are just a few examples.

29 Benjamin, *Arcades*, 83.

30 Ibid., 83.

31 Ibid., 84.

32 Ibid., 88. The "penates" are the Roman gods of the household, and "gnōthi seauton" is Greek for "Know Thyself" (in the *Notes* section, 961).

33 Calvino, *Invisible*, 38.

34 Caillois, *Mythe*, 153.

35 Ibid., 157.

36 Ibid., 158–59.

37 Gilloch, *Myth and Metropolis*, 169–70. My italics.

38 Gibson, *Neuromancer*, 305.

39 Gilloch, *Myth and Metropolis*, 170.

40 Benjamin, *Écrits français*, 389.

41 Ibid., 390.

42 Benjamin, *Arcades*, 417.

43 Ibid., 416.

44 Auster, *New York Trilogy*, 76.

45 *Webster's*, 1039. Gerard Genette's fascinating *Palimpsestes* (Paris: Seuil, 1982) relentlessly pursues the palimpsestic nature of the text as hypertext, architext, hypotext, and others.

46 Gibson, *Neuromancer*, 286.

47 Ibid., 17.

48 Ibid., 19.

49 Ibid., 57.

50 Deleuze and Guattari, *Mille Plateaux*, 10.

51 Calvino, *Invisible*, 10.

52 Benjamin, *Arcades*, 416.

CHAPTER SEVEN

Mapping Socio-Cultural Cyberspace

Space is fundamental in any form of communal life; space is fundamental in any exercise of power.

Michel Foucault, *Power*[1]

I presented in the previous chapters some of the most important features that allow us to construct a model for mapping the new virtual space(s). From the humble beginnings when gamers were imagining dungeons and battling invisible gnomes and wizards, to hi-tech simulations, myth and writing have joined to enable human beings to come to terms with a cogent interpretation of their place and function within the new technologies. Cyber-citizens have arranged their space(s) according to the tested model of real-life cities and tried to anchor their bearings as best as they could. They have hacked their way in, surfed the increasingly high and increasingly exciting waves of the Internet, spent a sizeable portion of their time communicating with others across the globe, and engaged in the most fantastic simulations ever, whether in the name of science, warfare, or simply for the sake of entertainment. The inescapable fact is that cyberspace does not exist without these hardy pioneers and their descendants. If the real world has existed for billions of years without the species *homo*, not so with cyberspace which is the first full world created by mankind from scratch, continuously expanding, universe-like, solely through human agency. It is in cyberspace that issues which have tormented critical minds over the centuries, issues such as gender, race, class, power and the revolt against the tyrannical forms thereof, are divested of all external features and put to the test in the form of disembodied ideas and voices no less potent, no less human, than in real life.

That cyberspace is not only a testing ground for existing theories but is also way *ahead* of them is what worries, as mentioned before, Bailey when she accused thinkers of merely basking in the "delirious prospect" of leaving their bodies behind and of trying to apply old theories to completely new situations. To Bailey, questions of race and sexuality are kept in the margins of discussion. In fact, the genderless heaven envisioned in a disembodied world like cyberspace is, to her, an illusion, and the apparent virtuality provided to the cybersubject is, notwithstanding utopian claims, heavily gendered. Bailey says: "Freeing up movement, communication and sensation from the limitations of the flesh might be the promise of digital experience, but the body will not be abandoned so easily."[2] At the same conference, Nancy Paterson spoke another discourse, that of cyberspace as providing an opportunity for women to free their voice from patriarchal oppression: she saw the new technologies as having stretched existing notions of time and space so much that the physical body has been re-inscribed and re-written to fit the new environment. The body in cyberspace can be remodeled, left behind, and twisted as much as allowed by the current technology; women are faced with opportunities to break out of roles prescribed by patriarchal societies. Mostly because cyberspace is *not* modeled after a linear organization of information, i.e., because of its hypertextual quality, it has allowed women to transgress an order imposed by a male view of the universe.[3] In fact, changes are bound to happen just because the new configuration demands new appraisals. Doris A. Graber says in this context: "The needs and interests of specific audiences, such as groups differing in ethnicity, religious beliefs, or sexual orientation, or groups with special concerns related to their vocations and avocations are more likely to be addressed."[4] The new technologies are seen as having empowered users, and especially women, to transmit to the world a voice hitherto suppressed. Says Graber: "In cyberspace, a single private citizen can address hundreds of thousands of people via computer from the privacy of his or her home."[5] Yet is this as simple as Graber wants to picture it? Is the release of woman's voice a mere question of coverage? Mary Flanagan, in 2000, was raising the question of geography and the use of mapping terms that have been traditionally male dominated:

> [W]e ask in the Basic language for the computer to "run" (not process); other commands include "goto" and "get" or, in Lingo, "put" or "place" (rather than compute, display, or calculate input). Such descriptions using the language of geography must be carefully considered given linguistic ties to a historic use of geography as a site of male power.[6]

Flanagan accurately traces metaphors and myths related to cyberspace such as the frontier myth and colonization as typically male-constructed. Virtual spaces have to be conquered, tamed, and subjugated; Gibson's hero "jacks in" to the feminized "matrix" in order to experience orgasm-like situations. To

Flanagan, cyberspace has been visualized in terms of performance and control through the sheer force of mainly male will, although the nature of virtuality is contrary to this vision: networks and the multiplicity and open-endedness of hypertextual spaces favor models based not on ideologies of control, power, and competition, but ultimately on the uncontrolled and the fleeting. Here Flanagan is perfectly in tune with the basic tenets of postmodernism and post-structuralism. Seen from a Derridean and Barthean angle, cyberspace problematizes the hitherto sacrosanct differences between the sexes: the disembodiment and relative anonymity inherent in cyberspace restrict gender differences to matters of voice and/or writing. Gender in cyberspace can be switched at will, either through avatars or through impersonation, in a way not possible before, probably due to the visible and, at the same time, invisible nature of virtuality for, unlike in real life, encounters can be tailored to suit individual desires as far as what is to be revealed and what is to be hidden are concerned.

Donna Haraway's celebrated "Cyborg Manifesto" first lent weight, in 1991, to the inherent liberatory possibilities of cyberspace for women:

> By the late twentieth century, our time, a mythic time, we are all chimeras, theorized and fabricated hybrids of machine and organism. In short, we are cyborgs. The cyborg is our ontology; it gives us our politics. The cyborg is a condensed image of both imagination and material reality, the two joined centres structuring any possibility of historical transformation.[7]

Cyberspace, to Haraway, is an artificial space which can defeat the limitations of biological sexes and elevate humans, for the first time in history, to an asexual dimension. Such a world "without gender" can also be "a world without genesis, but maybe also a world without end," and can eventually offer a leap outside of "salvation history" altogether.[8] Of course, it is clear to Haraway that such a disappearance can only be accomplished through writing:

> Writing is pre-eminently the technology of cyborgs, etched surfaces of the late twentieth century. Cyborg politics is the struggle for language and the struggle against perfect communication, against the one code that translates all meaning perfectly, the central dogma of phallogocentrism. That is why cyborg politics insist on noise and advocate pollution, rejoicing in the illegitimate fusions of animal and machine.[9]

Haraway's enthusiasm for a mythical cyborg-hero able to transcend differences through a new discourse is echoed by Sadie Plant: "The Internet promises women a network of lines on which to chatter, natter, work and play; virtuality brings a fluidity to identities which once had to be fixed; and multimedia provides a new tactile environment in which women artists can find their space."[10] Expectedly, the promises offered by the new spaces have generated extreme pronouncements such as the following by "Legba," a participant of LambdaMOO: "We exist in a world of pure communication, where looks don't matter and only the best writers get laid."[11] Interestingly, both myth—in the form of the dream of pure communication fully disengaged from the flesh—and writing—in the form of the ultimate weapon of seduction and control—figure prominently in such visions.

Yet, one can argue that cyberspace, as a new geography, has allowed the same old actors with the same old clichés and stereotypes to come and inhabit its digital realms. Although *Snow Crash*'s male standard avatar, the Clint, is briefly described as "just the male counterpart of Brandy," and has "an extremely limited range of facial expressions," the female avatar, the Brandy, is given a generous paragraph fully showing that cyberspace is not very different from gender discrimination as it exists in the real world:

> When white-trash high school girls are going on a date in the Metaverse, they invariably run down to the computer-games section of the local Wal-Mart and buy a copy of Brandy. The user can select three breast sizes: improbable, impossible, and ludicrous. Brandy has a limited repertoire of facial expressions: cute and pouty; cute and sultry; perky and interested; smiling and receptive; cute and spacy. Her eyelashes are half an inch long, and the software is so cheap that they are rendered as solid ebony chips. When a Brandy flutters her eyelashes, you can almost feel the breeze.[12]

Indeed, Judith Squires, while recognizing the possibilities for women in cyberspace, is aware of the dangers of gratuitous and facile generalizations which whole-heartedly embrace new technologies mainly put in place by patriarchal societies:

> [W]hilst there *may* be potential for an alliance between cyborg imagery and a materialist feminism, this potential has been largely submerged beneath a sea of technophoric cyberdrool. If we are to salvage the image of the cyborg we would do well to insist that cyberfeminism be seen as a metaphor for addressing the inter-relation between technology and the body, not as a means of using the former to transcend the latter.[13]

She adds: "Far from exploring an ungendered ideal, cyborg imagery has created exaggeratedly masculine and feminine bodies."[14]

If the discursive construction of cyberspace, through its insistence on mythifying "pure" types, is finding itself proposing more masculine males and more feminine females, it is also doing the same for most binary oppositions. As a mythical writing and as a writing of myth, cyberspace quite effortlessly divests itself from the "dross" of "irregularities" or "bugs" in its system and can encourage simplistic black-or-white representations. When voice only is heard, it is all too easy to disembody it and mythify it. Indeed, the construction of gender in cyberspace is intimately connected to that of class, and the assumptions of the former are carried to the latter. Elmer-DeWitt enthusiastically describes how cyberspace helps transcend class barriers: "The usenet newsgroups are, in their way, the perfect antidote to modern mass media...the newsgroups allow news, commentary and humor to bubble up from the grass roots."[15]

Such a paean of joyful liberatory self-expression can be very attractive and Lévy, for example, tries to incorporate this social dimension of cyberspace into his grand project of collective intelligence. To him, cyberspace is the dream of democracy come true: the site of a "virtual agora," true democracy is a "direct democracy assisted by computer," which is better suited than present political systems to "help us cross the tumultuous waters of anthropological mutation."[16] Far from being a technology reserved to the elite, cyber-politics is now available for all: "As to the barriers facing use, contemporary digital instruments are less and less difficult to use. An increasing part of the population is now using computers at work and knows how to handle one or two software programs."[17]

Lévy's obviously simplistic generalizations are too good to be true—and his dismissive "one or two software programs" rather slighting. It seems that once the machines are in place, all is well in the best of worlds. Yet over-simplification is not lacking. How true is the famous 1993 *New Yorker* cartoon which proclaimed that on the Internet "nobody knows you're a dog?"[18] How true are such assertions that "[s]tripped of the external trappings of wealth, power, beauty and social status, people tend to be judged in the cyberspace of the Internet only by their ideas and their ability to get them across in terse, vigorous prose"[19]? How true is it that the cybernaut, freed "from the baggage of a biasing body; elevated into the connective flow of the digital stream" becomes "a kind of technological angel"[20]? As Kandi Tayebi and Judy A. Johnson warn, "it is important to recognize that cyberspace exists within a social framework, which is deeply sexist and racist. Computers do not automatically obliterate hierarchies, blur gender, and produce class free communities."[21] More bluntly, Lisa Nakamura said in a recent interview: "Certainly the Net is as racist as the societies that it stems from. How could this not be true? Is it not true of all other media forms, including literature, film, and television?"[22]

Allen, in the context of intertextuality and the new technologies, believes that "it remains difficult to imagine that technological changes by themselves will produce more active and productive 'author-readers' and an increased 'democratization' of language, reading and the communication and possession of information."[23] Dery, like Squires above, cautions that "cyber-Rapture" is blinding us to the realities of the “devastation of nature, the unraveling of the social fabric, and the widening chasm between the technocratic elite and the minimum-wage masses.”[24] Despite the many utopian dreams—some would say nightmares—of leaving the body behind and becoming pure disembodied beings, the fact that we are still creatures of flesh and blood should act as a safety valve reminder. Dery warns:

> As we hurtle toward the millennium, poised between technological Rapture and social rupture, between Tomorrowland the *Blade Runner*, we would do well to remember that—for the foreseeable future, at least—we are here to stay, in these bodies, on this planet. The misguided hope that we will be born again as “bionic angels,”…is a deadly misreading of the myth of Icarus. It pins our future to wings of wax and feathers.[25]

The myth of Icarus, Daedalus’ son, serves here as a warning: imprisoned by Minos with his father, Icarus makes himself wings of feather held by wax and, as he flies too near the sun, the wax melts and he falls to his death. Pieter Brueghel the Elder’s famous painting *Landscape with the Fall of Icarus* (circa 1554–1555) portrays this event in a setting of prosperous and bustling countryside life: Icarus’ fall only occupies a tiny space in the landscape. To the unaware, the splash in the right-hand corner of the painting, the tiny feet still visible as Icarus plunges headlong, are almost invisible. But as the lure of cyberspace intensifies, isn’t the situation reversed and the greatest threat becomes that the unheard splash is that of the minority who have refused—or who are unable—to enter “live into simulation”? Indeed, *Snow Crash*’s Brandys and Clints make up the vast majority of the virtual population because real life users cannot afford more expensive models. Far from being a free-for-all new world, cyberspace replicates real-life social differences. Graber, in 1996, was saying:

> In practice, cyberspace riches are available only to individuals with superior education and financial resources. These are the publics who already participate far more in politics than their less privileged fellow citizens. As technology continues to evolve, the knowledge gap between the information privileged and the information underclass is likely to grow. Since knowledge means power, an information-deprived class is likely to suffer other power deprivations.[26]

Even such a practical attempt like Dodge and Kitchin’s *Atlas of Cyberspace* begins with the following warning:

> The…way that maps can create false impressions is through omission. For example, many maps of infrastructure and cyberspace focus their attention—either deliberately or unconsciously—on the developed world in the West, especially the United States…Pushing countries to the periphery reinforces, visually at least, the existing

> world hegemony in relation to the Internet.[27]

Kevin Robins plays on Gibson's famous "consensual hallucination" to show that our attitude to cyberspace is also a hallucination which refuses to see the grim facts of reality: to Robins, this vision is "a tunnel vision" which "has turned a blind eye on the world we live in."[28] The possibility of taking up different personalities or inventing new ones in cyberspace has been one of the much-vaunted achievements of virtual online communities, yet Robins also sees in this apparent richness and diversity only "banal identities," adding:

> Only the technology is new: in the games and encounters in cyberspace, it seems, there is little that is new or surprising...All this rhetoric of 'age-old' dreams and desire—which is quite common among the cyber-visionaries—is unspeakably vacuous and devoid of inspiration...It is the aesthetic of fantasy-gaming; the fag-end of a Romantic sensibility.[29]

Another attack, in the context of this study, is also launched by Robins who says that the "mythology of cyberspace is preferred over its sociology."[30] A utopian vision, cyberspace is alluring because of the rich world it so easily presents. This is a realm where people don't die, where most actions are "undoable," where even eternity can be envisioned. Obviously, virtuality, especially when it is only accessible to a well-to-do minority, is bound to make its users ignore that a real world exists where *real* humans feel hunger, pain, and death. Dodge and Kitchin write: "The reality is that cyberspace is dominated by white, middle-class males from Western nations who can converse in English, are computer literate, and are generally in their late teens or early twenties."[31] Dery uses the word "insulated" to describe such a phenomenon: "[M]any of *Mondo*'s readers are sufficiently insulated from the grimmer social realities inside their high-tech comfort zones to contemplate the power of positive hedonism without irony."[32] Theoreticians of the virtual have received their share of attacks when they were perceived as insulating themselves and their enthusiastic readers from everyday reality. Vivian Sobchack delivered such an attack on Baudrillard:

> I wish Baudrillard a little pain—maybe a lot—to bring him to his senses. Pain would remind him that he doesn't just *have* a body, but that he *is* his body, and that it is in this material fact that 'affect' and anything we might call a 'moral stance' is grounded...If we don't keep this subjective kind of bodily sense in mind as we negotiate our techno-culture, we may very well objectify ourselves to death.[33]

If the above turns out to be true, then the prospects are far from reassuring. If language forms, as I have shown, the basic structure of cyberspace, educated users will have an edge over their less fortunate fellow-citizens and will yield more power as their knowledge increases. In a virtual world where physical advantage is not a concern anymore, the battle for survival is fought with digital wit, software know-how, and informational power. Since everything in cyberspace is, in some way or another, information, it is the possession of information that will decide who holds power. It follows quite naturally that those who control information are in the position to give it and withhold it at will.

This new social configuration, the first *fully* informational in the history of humanity, is not only threatening to consecrate, and probably to seal for good, the social gap between privileged and unprivileged, but it has also created, and this in an unprecedented manner, a new class, almost invisible, operating solely on the acquisition, use, and dissemination of digital information. This new class, for some, can be defined as the virtual class. Kroker and Weinstein have defined it at length in "The Political Economy of Virtual Reality: Pan-Capitalism," equating it with the appearance of the new technologies as it "fuses with the high-speed backbone of the Net," and "[i]ts expression as the emergent class of post-history is coterminous with the sovereignty of the re-combinant commodity."[34] The virtual class is the first class to appear outside of geographical boundaries, thus fully mirroring the cyberspatial characteristic of non-physicality. Unlocatable yet human, this paradox makes Kroker and Weinstein ascribe amphibious qualities to the new class:

> A mutant class born at that instant when technology acquired organicity and became a living species, the technological class is itself a product of combinatorial logic. It stands as the first, self-conscious class expression of the universal net of post-human bodies.[35]

Postmodernism heralds the end of history and the end of the human body as flesh only or, as Case would put it, as "meat" and, in a Kurzweilian-like scenario, human and machine—or analog and digital—would merge to the extent of indifferentiation. The end of flesh and the full entry into the pure realm of the mind is portrayed as a victory over the death instinct.

Are new technologies, such as ultra-sophisticated media and the Internet, instead of keeping us in touch with world events and allowing us to actively participate in shaping our future and fighting injustice, acting instead as a mere screen behind which we have left our impotent bodies for a simulacrum of decision-making capability? Will the end of the "meat" and the emergence of the virtual class signal a full de-localization, as we have seen before, leading to the incapacitation of will and the hijacking of the users' digital power? Virilio writes, in the context of televised media at the end of the twentieth century: "We are in the grips of a videoscopic technology that has nothing to do with film analysis or the critique of domestic television, a logistics of perception necessary for the progressive acquisition of the neural targets that we have become."[36] In a scenario reminiscent of the movie *The Matrix*, humanity is hooked on and unknowingly pooling its neural power for the service of the virtual class. Time and its immediate, *live*, use, are becoming more important than space itself. If classes in the physical world are predominantly built on a carefully regulated space, the virtual class, by the attempted diminishing of the "flesh," relies in contrast on a controlled use of time: uptime, time online, time-out and other network terms betray the sliding from a body in space to a mind—or an attention—in time. Experience, which is partly experience through the body is, to Kroker and Weinstein, the target set to be destroyed by the virtual class; our twenty-first-century culture, falsely hailed as "wired," is the sad result of a plot to achieve full digitality:

> Not a wired culture, but a virtual culture that is wired shut: compulsively fixated on digital technology as a source of salvation from the reality of a lonely culture and radical social disconnection from everyday life...for virtualizers, the good is ultimately that which disappears human subjectivity, substituting the war-machine of cyberspace for the data trash of experience.[37]

Ironically, Kroker and Weinstein's pronouncements are only accessible through the same cyberspace they are attacking. Ctheory's main repository of articles is accessible online at www.ctheory.net and even the books they offer are digital scans—as pdf files—of actual hardware copies meant to be easily read on a computer screen. But what is of note in our context is that even Kroker and Weinstein find difficulty in locating and positioning this virtual class and the locus of its operational base mainly because of the merger between analog and digital, between the "meat" and the digital, between the real and the virtual. The problem is solved by a highly technical—or "wired"—but metaphorical language which still uses physical models to describe a-physicality. The virtual class achieves dominance "because its reduced vision of human experience consists of a digital superhighway, a fatal scene of circulation and gridlock, which corresponds to how the late twentieth-century mind likes to see itself."[38]

Another question is raised: will we lose, as Kroker and Weinstein say, along with our humanity and our history, our space as well? Don Mitchell's 1995 essay in the *Annals of the Association of American Geographers*, "The End of Public Space?" illustrates the shift in perspective. Mitchell argues that public space is disappearing not only because of privatization but also, and more insidiously, because of the changes in communications technology. If these new technologies empower users because "citizenship no longer requires the dichotomy between public and private *geographies*; access to a television set, radio, or computer with a modem is sufficient," yet at the same time political debate can only be possible through the media and their digital spaces and therefore a "fully electronic public space renders marginalized groups such as the homeless even more invisible to the working of politics" and, as such, "their needs, desires, and political representations [can never] be *seen* in the manner that they can be seen in the spaces of the city."[39]

McKenzie Wark believes that instead of empowering users, virtuality and, more specifically, multimedia, are in fact fully putting the user at the mercy of the creator or programmer. Unlike books where we can skip to the end and browse at our leisure, multimedia forces us along a specific path and ending(s) can be hidden for as long as the programmer wants.[40] What Wark is hinting at is that the virtual class can, under the guise of "interactivity," domesticate common users into either choosing the "correct" answer or having to repeat the whole procedure in a Pavlovian-like scenario. Users become helpless in front of a technology which will only deliver upon full compliance with a carefully designed path; physical rebellion, for the first time in history, is ruled out by the mere nature of the medium involved, and cybernauts, instead of freely navigating the reaches of cyberspace, are in fact forced to turn in circles and re-map atrophied and artificial spaces.

Elaborating on Foucault's disciplinary societies which, through the prison, the hospital, the factory, the school, and the family, enclose the individual, Deleuze, in his "Postscript on the Societies of Control," applies the distinction between the two modes onto the current real-virtual problem. If disciplinary societies, through enclosure, detain the individual, it is essentially in a physical world, visibly and solidly mapped out; the problem quite simply is, as Deleuze says, analogical. But the present societies of control operate through what he calls a numerical model, through modulation, like a flexible cast which continuously takes on the shape of the person wearing it; in a virtual world, the apparent elasticity of the boundaries of control give the illusion of freedom. Individuals have become "dividuals," and human beings have become "samples," "data," "markets," and, most importantly, "banks" of information. The user in pre-virtual disciplinary societies was, despite physical enclosure, producing physical energy in a physical world; the user in societies of control is "in orbit," in a "continuous network." Deleuze sarcastically adds: "Everywhere *surfing* has already replaced the older *sports*."[41]

Kroker and Weinstein do not mince their words and call this society of control, along with pan-capitalism, a "virtual fascism" quite different from its historical real-life precedents, a "reinvention" consisting of "a set of political symptoms of the hatred of existence, the will to will, the will to virtuality, the (death) wish to be replaced,"[42] and in another—online—article written by Arthur and Marilouise Kroker reviewing Bill Gates'—hardcopy—book *Business @ The Speed of Thought*, the digital nervous system of the future is envisioned:

> An analytically abstract, fast circulating, highly coded, feedback loop of "good digital information flows" and "good analytical tools," Gates' model of post-human business is the key interface by which human flesh will migrate to the machine in the digital future. Once fully operational, the digital nervous system can be quickly installed in every form of organization.[43]

To Kroker and Weinstein, Microsoft is not about products but about a certain model which heralds the coming of a new technological age where human memory, instead of being contained in physical bodies, will be virtual and downloadable—and by the same token fully mapped and thus potentially erasable—enabling the new virtual class, in a cyber-panopticon-like scenario, full access—past, present, and future—to the totality of that memory.

In that context, Armitage, in a work cited earlier, describes the current technologies as "Neoliberal," that is, as a species of liberal fascism characterized by free enterprise, globalization on the economic level, and the rise of national corporatism. Human beings will be gradually transformed into cybernetic machinery docilely executing the orders of their Neoliberal masters who will have themselves lost their humanity in a cyborgian mixture of flesh and machine. To Armitage, all technology is the carrier of totalitarianism and the new technologies, by allowing humans to adopt a virtual model, looms high at the pinnacle of control.

The implications to mapping cyberspace as the meeting *place* for the digitalized twenty-first-century human are clear: control exists in the virtual mode as it has existed in the physical one; the will to surveillance has not abated but, on the contrary, it has adopted the characteristics of the new technologies such as networking and sharing and has attempted, with varying success, to infiltrate and occupy these new channels. In a fast-moving and fast-expanding world such as cyberspace, control has to keep shifting shapes in order to keep up with the changes in the technology. David Lyon, in his "Surveillance in Cyberspace," writes: "Unlike the panopticon, where the body is subject to surveillance, it is now information flows that are under scrutiny. Personal data is abstracted from bodies to be re-constituted as data images, about which automated decisions are routinely made."[44] The physical, as Lyon says, is translated into the digital, and what were hitherto human experience, feelings, and emotions suddenly become strings of 1s and 0s neatly archived in the data banks of control centers. Routes and paths, whether as traces in the physical world or as traces in organic parts like the brain and the body, are becoming obsolete because they are deemed transitory and thus unaccountable for, largely unmeasurable, and mostly non-repeatable. If we remember de Certeau's practices of everyday life, it becomes clear that non-repeatability is both a threat to the establishment and the warrant of the users' freedom. Attempting to freeze these practices and transpose them into binary data tips the balance in favor of the emerging virtual class and threatens to transform experience into information.

In 1979, Lyotard was already warning against the shift in emphasis heralded by the new technologies and the loss of experience as it is transformed into binary language:

> In this general transformation, the nature of knowledge does not stay intact. It cannot pass through the new channels and become operational unless it is translated into quantities of information. We can therefore predict that everything in our constituted knowledge which is not thus translated will be forsaken, and that the orientation of new research will limit itself to the translatability condition of the eventual results into machine language.[45]

The end of traditional ways of power and the emergence of new means of surveillance generated by new designs and concepts of space and the ways to map them are heralded by Baudrillard. Mapping itself is a means of power for the new technologies:

> *End of the panoptic system.* The eye of TV is no longer the source of an absolute gaze, and the ideal of control is no longer that of transparency. This still presupposes an objective space (that of the Renaissance) and the omnipotence of the despotic gaze. It is still, if not a system of confinement, at least a system of mapping.[46]

The panoptic system of surveillance, built on physical space, is replaced by a strategy of deterrence centered around virtual spaces occupied not by people but by information:

> No more subject, no more focal point, no more center or periphery: pure flexion or circular inflexion. No more violence or surveillance: only "information," secret virulence, chain reaction, slow implosion, and simulacra of spaces in which the effect of the real again comes into play. We are witnessing the end of perspectival and panoptic space...and thus to the *very abolition of the spectacular*.[47]

Classical notions of space no longer apply to a sociology of cyberspace where objectivity, or the positing of an individual gaze focusing, as subject, on an object in a perspectival mode, is made obsolete by the new technology; old notions of surveillance are replaced by the race for informational supremacy. Classical space is replaced by hypertextual or hyperspatial vortices criss-crossed by the almost instantaneous exchange of information in various forms. A map of cyberspace would have to take into account the principle of chaos inherent in any information exchange. Baudrillard says:

> Such a blending, such a viral, endemic, chronic, alarming presence of the medium,

without the possibility of isolating the effects—spectralized, like these advertising laser sculptures in the empty space of the event filtered by the medium—dissolution of TV in life, dissolution of life in TV—indiscernible chemical solution.[48]

What is apparent is that once mapping concerns are translated onto a space where humans interact, the problems are bound to increase in complexity. This, in itself, is not new and has been, as shown before, the object of heated debate. What is interesting is that if this space is *inherently unstable* as with cyberspace, the human element exponentially aggravates the situation: the hypertextuality of human discursive interaction seamlessly blends with the hypertextuality and cybertextuality of the new space; fluidity, uncertainty, and undecidability meet virtuality, open-endedness, and expansibility on a dynamic map. Bey, echoing Baudrillard's viral model, writes in this context:

If we were to imagine an *information map*—a cartographic projection of the Net in its entirety—we would have to include in it the features of chaos, which have already begun to appear, for example, in the operations of complex parallel processing, telecommunications, transfers of electronic "money," viruses, guerilla hacking and so on.[49]

In this dangerous and highly unstable world, information becomes the only commodity; surveillance subtly shifts to deterrence; and cyber-control is met by cyber-anarchy in a virtual battle for survival. To Bey, the new anarchy, "Post-Anarchism Anarchy," combines myth, language as "poetic terrorism," and mapping the "despatialized" emerging cyberspace(s):

How can we separate the concept of *space* from the mechanisms of *control*? The territorial gangsters, the Nation/States, have hogged the entire map. Who can invent for us a cartography of autonomy, who can draw a map that includes our desires? AnarchISM ultimately implies anarchy—& anarchy is chaos. Chaos is the principle of continual creation . . . & *Chaos never died.*[50]

The empty and unlocalized spaces of Virilio can, to Bey, be turned into a haven: the physical landscape has been hijacked by sites of power and control and the only refuge left is cyberspace. True, the virtual is also the locus of a loss, a loss of nature and a loss of identity, but the risk is worth taking and the "territorial gangsters" are met in cyberspace by the cyber-anarchists who have honed the skills of moving in an a-physical landscape the map of which is drawn by desire and chaos. As Bey very well says, the question of land refuses to disappear, that is, the problematization of a space which is not prone to mechanisms of control is paramount. Sterling, in "A Brief History of the Internet," shares this view: "Why do people want to be 'on the Internet?' One of the main reasons is simple freedom. The Internet is a rare example of a true, modern, functional anarchy. There is no "Internet Inc." There are no official censors, no bosses, no board of directors, no stockholders."[51] The land of opportunities *par excellence*, cyberspace holds, deeply buried within itself, the two extremes of total surveillance and total anarchy.

In this context, Bey is keen on differentiating between the "Net," and the "Web," also known as the "Counter-Net": the first, as the name implies, is a construct which is used to trap, as a fishing net, the unwary cybernauts into a system of control and dependance; the second is the natural outgrowth of and reaction to oppression and, as "web," weaves, spider-like, its own paths through the "interstices" and "broken sections" of the net.[52] The relationship between Bey's web and the text as *tissue* is obvious. These tendencies, then, remind us of de Certeau's practices of everyday life: places as net and spaces as webs of narrative(s). Interestingly, "interstice" comes from the Latin "intersistere" which means "to stay between, to insert oneself in; to stop in the middle (of discourse)."[53] Not only are interstices *places* to be filled by an entity which will transform it by the mere fact of its presence, but they are also intimately related to speech, discourse, and language. Bey and Sterling may have come close to essential element in the cyberspace equation: when we actively seek refuge within the interstices of the virtual landscape, when we scour the *text* of the matrix for "broken sections," we are also stopping or in fact deviating discourse from its path, misreading *ortho-doxy*, applying violence to the weakest points of the fabric, re-creating our own discourse in the place where the language of power is stopped.

By occupying the haven of interstices, cyber-rebels have become viruses, from the Latin "virus," meaning "sap, juice, humor; drool, venom, poison; bad breath, infection, bitterness,"[54] threatening and challenging what is taken to be good, "virtus." The virus functions as malevolent juice, as a viscous liquid which spills, unstoppably, through the interstices of the Net, viscous as the secretions of a spider weaving its web. Of course, the imagery is taken from the physical world, as myth does, and history has witnessed proto-cyber-states spilling, virus-like, onto the accepted norms of society. Bey uses the model of the medieval Assassins as one of these networked entities, as they "founded a 'State' which consisted of a network of remote mountain valleys and castles, separated by thousands of miles, strategically invulnerable to invasion, connected by the information flow of secret agents, at war with all governments, and devoted only to knowledge."[55] The network nodes scatter an otherwise centralized control and, in a post-structuralist vein, *disseminate* the text which can henceforth never be read by authoritative voices. As the reader is freed from the tyranny of both the author and the critic, the cyber-anarchist is freed, through the same networked hypertext, from the tyranny of the programmer as well as that of governments. Our mapping of cyberspace, then, has also to take into account precisely that which cannot be accounted for, the text which lies *outside* of the accepted discourse, the marginalized and supplementalized interstices into which we become viruses, virulent stoppers of a speech which always poses itself as authoritative and final.

As virus, cyber-anarchy is just re-presenting and re-enacting the lessons learned—and taught—since the break, the post-1960 *brisure*, and the almost magical efflorescence of post-structuralism. As early as 1971, Barthes was writing the following telltale words:

> The only possible counter-attack is achieved neither by facing nor by destroying, but only by stealing: to fragment the old text of culture, of science, of literature, and to disseminate its traits according to unrecognizable formulas, the same way one masks stolen merchandise. Faced with the old text, I thus try to erase the false sociological, historical, or subjective blooming of determinations, visions, and projections; I listen to the excited movement of the message, not to the message itself, I see...the victorious deployment of the signifying text, of the terrorist text.[56]

The post-*brisure* text as terrorist text, as text of excess, as guerilla text; not destroying, but subtly and elegantly deconstructing and destabilizing the old nefarious concepts; appropriating the otherness of the margin by tactically displacing, transforming, playing with, and disseminating meanings; masking and masquerading; appearing and suddenly vanishing in an ever-moving and ever-expanding sphere. Bey writes: "Beyond the temporary autonomous zone, beyond the insurrection, there is the necessary revolution."[57]

It should be clear by now how naturally and how effortlessly was cyberspace able to acquire, from its inception, the fundamental qualities and capabilities of contemporary textual theories. The effort at upsetting the established interpretive maps found fertile ground in virtuality, and the sometimes insurmountable difficulties faced by underground movements of protest against oppressive control are, in cyberspace, addressed from a different perspective. George Woodcock, in his seminal book on anarchism, both deplored the end of anarchism as a movement and gave hope to it as an individual endeavor. In the prologue he prophetically wrote that, although the historical anarchist movement is dead, "it is possible that the theoretical core of anarchism may still have the power to give life *to a new form under changed historical circumstances*."[58]

I maintain that cyberspace may be this new major historical circumstance that could allow the idea of anarchism to take on, with the help of post-structuralist theories, a new shape and renewed vigor. How else can we interpret the numerous and daily calls, on the Internet, for the freeing of virtual territory before it is too late? The "mirroring" of threatened and subsequently banned protest sites is now an established practice: when authoritarian control threatens to shut down a web page, individuals, maybe located thousands of physical miles apart, volunteer to "mirror" the entire contents of the site in an attempt to thwart the silencing of voices. Without a centralized body, with minimal financial costs, with only a wild thirst for truth and freedom, anarchists are born again in cyberspace.

Indeed, De Certeau describes the practice of everyday life as the "delinquent narrativity in a society" when and where pedestrians create their own mapping paths, criss-crossing the city with memories and stories, imposing and inscribing their own bodies in movements on the city grid: "The opacity of the body in movement, gesticulating, walking, taking its pleasure, is what indefinitely organizes a *here* in relation to an *abroad*, a 'familiarity' in relation to a 'foreignness'."[59] Similarly, cyber-users inscribe, through their hypertextual jumps, links, and mirrors, a virtual map where the obvious foreignness of the new medium is tamed, appropriated, and familiarized. It is a "delinquency" which at the same time firmly anchors the cyber-users in unfamiliar territory and allows them to paradoxically extend and reduplicate their presence and make themselves invisible to centers of control.

These invisible spaces, these islands in the Net, Bey calls the "TAZ," or "Temporary Autonomous Zones," the title of his most famous book. He writes:

> The TAZ is like an uprising which does not engage directly with the State, a guerilla operation which liberates an area (of land, of time, of imagination) and then dissolves itself to re-form elsewhere/elsewhen, *before* the State can crush it…The TAZ is an encampment of guerilla ontologists: strike and run away. Keep moving the entire tribe, even if it's only data in the Web.[60]

The TAZ is temporary because its nature is that of simulation itself: a collection of binary data exposed to hardware loss anytime, threatened by network failures and memory leaks. Yet it is this very uncertainty—which, in a way, mirrors the uncertainty of physical reality—which gives the TAZ its chances of survival: similar to Baudrillard's nihilism, the Temporary Autonomous Zone uses the enemy's own weapons to carve out a niche for itself. The cyber-rebel acquires a strange double nature, living in both worlds, moving virtual encampment like American Indians escaping the onslaught of the white colonizer. Here we come to a reversal of the myth of the frontier presented above: the Net is not only a frontier to be expanded "westward," a happy-go-lucky adventure of exploration and discovery; the terrible truth of the colonization is that it must erase or deface the image of the colonized in the process. As Edward Said said about the United States' expansion westward, "[t]he broad tendency was to expand and extend control farther, and not to spend much time reflecting on the integrity and independence of Others, for whom the American presence was at very best a mixed blessing."[61] The Temporary Autonomous Zone is a forced and at the same time willed migration to the margins, to the places of real but invisible power, in order to masquerade as a supplement yet in reality to exist as a necessary presence, ambulant and ambivalent, that is, disseminated and uncertain, autonomous and temporary. De Certeau says:

> Every culture proliferates in its own margins. Irruptions happen, described as "creations" relative to stagnations. Bubbles emerging from swamps, a thousand suns go on and off on the surface of society. In the official imaginary, they appear as exceptions or as marginalisms...In reality creation is a disseminated proliferation. It pullulates. A multiform feast infiltrates everywhere.[62]

Bey similarly writes in *Hieroglyphica*: "In the Dark Ages the monasteries made points of light on a map of spilled and featureless ink. In these Lite Ages we need monasteries of darkness, holes of black light from which nothing emerges but a thin blue radiance of esotericism and some woodfire smoke."[63] Bey's points of lights and later, free enclaves on the Net carrying on their "festal purposes," echo de Certeau's "multiform feast," and both rejoin the essential Barthean and Derridean principles of game and playfulness.

Mapping this new social—or even anarchic—cyberspace is also one of Bey's main concerns:

> The TAZ has a temporary but actual location in time and a temporary but actual location in space. But clearly it must also have "location" *in the Web*, and this location is of a different sort, not actual but virtual, not immediate but instantaneous. The Web not only provides logistical support for the TAZ, it also helps to bring it into being; crudely speaking one might say that the TAZ "exists" in information-space as well as in the "real world."[64]

The double nature of cyberspace is what allows virtuality to provide cyber-anarchists with an alternative to real-world societies of control. Occupying virtual locations on what is now the Internet, cybernauts instantaneously lay claim to a new dimension of information space which can be switched at will, replicated almost to infinity, and disposed of at any moment. Barlow, in the "Declaration of the Independence of Cyberspace" cited previously, declares that the new space is "naturally independent of the tyrannies" governments try to impose on citizens; that the "legal concepts of property, expression, identity, movement, and context do not apply" and that citizens "must declare [their] virtual selves immune" to the supposed sovereignty of tyrannical powers.[65] If bodies are at the mercy of totalitarian regimes and oppressive government, not so with the mind that has taken cyberspace as its ultimate haven. Bey likes to compare the nature of the relation between cyber-anarchists and virtuality to that of 18th-century sea-rovers and corsairs and the oceans around them: both can only function, in an otherwise unmappable medium—the digital matrix and watery expanses—through information networks linking the outlaws' hideouts—islands both physical and virtual—with each others.[66]

However, it is the notion of nomadism that can best put the mapping of socio-cyberspace in a fresh perspective. In Deleuze and Guattari's famous twelfth chapter in *Mille Plateaux* entitled "1227–Traité de nomadologie: la machine de guerre," they posit their first axiom which possesses all the features I have been leading to: the concern for mapping, myth, writing, and ludicity:

> Axiom I: The war machine is external to the state apparatus.
>
> Proposition I: This exteriority is first attested by mythology, epic writing, drama, and games.[67]

Deleuze and Guattari write that, seen from the point of view of the State, "the originality of the man of war, his eccentricity, necessarily appear under a negative form: stupidity, deformity, madness, illegitimacy, usurpation, sin."[68] Expectedly, cyberspace will be painted as a waste of time, as mass hysteria, as an illegitimate mode of existence, as a usurpation of reality, and, most importantly, as *the* cardinal sin against Creation: the arrogant appropriation of the Creator's prerogative in creating the world.

The main threat to centers of control and to novice users is that cyberspace functions on a fundamentally different concept of territory and movement. To Deleuze and Guattari, nomads situate themselves according to points of reference, but these points are used or subordinated to wider trajectories; these points, which to migrants would be points of arrival, are to nomads there only to be left behind. In cyberspace, hypertexts are never final resting places for cybernauts: the very essence of hypertextuality resides in the un-stoppable and ultimately unpredictable movement from one information node to the other. Another important difference Deleuze and Guattari make between nomadic space and sedentary space—our cyberspace-physical space pair—is that the state apparatus, primarily sedentary, distributes closed spaces to individuals by allotting parts and opening communication channels between them, thus enabling full surveillance and control; nomadic space, on the contrary, takes individuals and distributes them in open spaces; communication, if it does take place, remains within individual free will.[69]

Paradoxically, nomads in their smooth space *do not move*. Keeping to a forever changing trajectory, they ride, as it were, the crest of a wave which, while immobile, allows them to cross huge distances; the analogy is perfect:

disembodied Internet "surfers" intersect and interweave the vast tissue of cyberspace without actually moving; leaving what they see as the gross body in physical space, they are free to roam at will in playful response to the prison of reality created by the state apparatus. Deleuze and Guattari explain:

> [I]t is wrong to define the nomad by movement...the nomad is on the contrary *the one who does not move*. Whereas the migrant leaves a place which has become amorphous or ungrateful, the nomad is the one who does not leave, does not want to leave, sticks to this smooth space where the forest recedes, where the steppe and the desert increase, and invents nomadism as a response to this challenge.[70]

Indeed, cybernauts, far from being the embittered and a-social creatures cynically portrayed by Neo-Luddites, are the last of the nomads and, as such, present us with alternative ways to stake our individuality and free choice amidst mounting informational oppression.

The "war machine" can be translated as Bey's TAZ, cyber-anarchism, the smooth space of cyberspace as opposed to the striated space of physical reality. Indeed, Bey makes use of Deleuze and Guattari's notion of the war machine in order to bring his TAZ theory forward and come up with what he calls "psychic nomadism" tactics:

> These nomads practice the *razzia*, they are corsairs, they are viruses; they have both need and desire for TAZs, camps of black tents under the desert stars, interzones, hidden fortified oases along secret caravan routes, "liberated" bits of jungle and bad-land, no-go areas, black markets, and underground bazaars.[71]

In a surprisingly familiar description of the Internet underworld, Bey is able to put together Barthes' notion of the readerly and the writerly, de Certeau's practice of everyday life, and the hacker's mode of existence. More, Bey is also aligning himself with a long tradition which makes of the writing of myth an essential feature of defense against oppression: "If the TAZ is a nomad camp, then the Web helps provide the epics, songs, genealogies and legends of the tribe; it provides the secret caravan routes and raiding trails which make up the flowlines of tribal economy."[72] In Lévi-Straussian terms, Bey writes:

> Whether through simple data-piracy, or else by a more complex development of actual rapport with chaos, the Web-hacker, the cybernetician of the TAZ, will find ways to take advantage of perturbations, crashes, and breakdowns in the Net...As a bricoleur, a scavenger of information shards, smuggler, blackmailer, perhaps even cyberterrorist, the TAZ-hacker will work for the evolution of clandestine fractal connections.[73]

Lévy, likewise, is very interested in this kind of new-technology nomadism: "we have become nomads again...To move is not to travel from one place to another on the terrestrial surface, but to cross universes of problems, lived worlds, and landscapes of meaning."[74]

Whether as islands or as Mandelbrot-like fractals, the TAZ's areas of "chaos" are embedded—as cyberspace—in the very fabric of physical reality, disappearing at will but always present in a map made up of the light-speed control, appropriation, hijacking, and camouflaging of information. Kroker and Weinstein also picture the new "wired body" as "perfect," since it is now able to travel "like an electronic nomad through the circulatory flows of the mediascape," having become, after its many metamorphoses, not much more than the "virtual biological form of a multi-layered scanner image." Relieved from the fetters of a heavy and awkward body, the wired body has finally "crack[ed] its way out of the dead shell of human culture,"[75] and the zones crossed by wired bodies are, because of their specific nature, invisible to normal mapping processes and have to remain so. The classical mapping spree which ended with the twentieth century is indeed powerless when it comes to the new landscapes of virtual space, and has allowed private space to acquire renewed meaning. Bey says:

> The "map" is a political abstract grid, a gigantic *con* enforced by the carrot/stick conditioning of the "Expert" State, until for most of us the map *becomes* the territory...Hidden enfolded immensities escape the measuring rod. The map is not accurate; the map *cannot* be accurate...Revolution is closed, but insurgency is open...the map is closed, but the autonomous zone is open.[76]

What Bey proposes is the coining of a new term to replace the defunct "cartography of Control," what he calls "psychotopography" which, for the first time, will be able to draw 1:1 maps of reality based on the individual human mind, and not on state concerns. At a genuine 1:1 projection scale, the new map will have no room for control because it will be virtually identical to itself. What can be obtained from these psychotopographic maps will be approximations and hints, for they can "only be used to *suggest*, in a sense *gesture towards*, certain features." Bey is "looking for 'spaces' (geographic, social, cultural, imaginal) with potential to flower as autonomous zones...Psychotopology is the art of *dowsing* for potential TAZs."[77]

Dowsing is the search for underground currents—water, minerals, metals—by the use of divining tools, usually a rod, a bricoleur's creation *par excellence*. An uncertain and thus marginalized attempt at mapping what cannot be seen; a myth, the utopian dream that we can, through magic, escape the two forces that have oppressed us as humans from the beginning of time: first, a government where injustice, inequality, and tyranny are the rule and, second, a nature which, though it bestows the gift of life, is perpetually reminding us that it can take it back anytime.

NOTES

1 *Essential Works of Foucault: 1954–1984*, vol. 3, James D. Faubion, ed. (London: Penguin Books, 2000), 361.

2 Bailey, "Virtual Skin."

3 Nancy Paterson, "Cyberfeminism," *Sixth International Symposium on Electronic Art (ISEA)*, Montreal, Canada (Sep. 18–22, 1995).

4 Doris A. Graber, "The 'New' Media and Politics: What Does the Future Hold?" *PS: Political Science and Politics* 29.1 (Mar. 1996), 33–36, 33.

5 Ibid., 34.

6 Mary Flanagan, "Navigating the Narrative in Space: Gender and Spatiality in Virtual Worlds," *Art Journal* 59.3 (Fall 2000), 75–85, 76.

7 Donna Haraway, "A Cyborg Manifesto: Science, Technology and Socialist-Feminism in the Late Twentieth Century," in Bell and Kennedy, *Cybercultures*, 291–324, 292.

8 Ibid., 292.

9 Ibid., 312.

10 Sadie Plant, "On the Matrix: Cyberfeminist Simulations," in Bell and Kennedy, *Cybercultures*, 325–36, 325.

11 Qtd in Randal Woodland, "Queer Spaces, Modem Boys and Pagan Statues: Gay/Lesbian Identity and the Construction of Cyberspace," in Bell and Kennedy, *Cybercultures*, 416–31, 416 (note the Voodoo allusion in the user's avatar). See also Graham Brown, Bruce Maycock, and Sharyn Burns, "Your Picture is your Bait: Use and Meaning of Cyberspace among Gay Men," *The Journal of Sex Research* 42.1 (Feb. 2005), 63–73, on Internet usage by gay men in Perth, Western Australia.

12 Stephenson, *Snow Crash*, 35.

13 Judith Squires, "Fabulous Feminist Futures and the Lure of Cyberculture," in Bell and Kennedy, *Cybercultures*, 360–73, 360.

14 Ibid., 364.

15 Elmer-DeWitt, "Welcome," 10.

16 Lévy, *Intelligence*, 65.

17 Ibid., 70.

18 *The New Yorker* 69.20 (Jul. 5, 1993), 61.

19 Elmer-DeWitt, "Welcome," 9.

20 Wertheim, "The Medieval Return of Cyberspace," 56.

21 Kandi Tayebi and Judy A. Johnson, "Feminism's Final Frontier: Cyberspace," *Academic Exchange* (Winter 2004), 190–95, 191. See also Michelle M. Wright, "Finding a Place in Cyberspace: Black Women, Technology, and Identity," *Frontiers* 26.1 (2005), 48–59, for a discussion of African American users of the Internet.

22 Geert Lovink, "Talking Race and Cyberspace: An Interview with Lisa Nakamura," *Frontiers* 26.1 (2005), 60–65.

23 Allen, *Intertextuality*, 206.

24 Dery, *Escape*, 17.

25 Ibid., 17.

26 Graber, 34.

27 Dodge and Kitchin, *Atlas*, 5.

28 Kevin Robins, "Cyberspace and the World we Live in," in Bell and Kennedy, *Cybercultures*, 77–95, 77.

29 Ibid., 80.

30 Ibid., 92.

31 Dodge and Kitchin, *Mapping*, 42.

32 Dery, *Escape*, 39.

33 Vivian Sobchack, "Beating the Meat/Surviving the Text, or How to Get out of this Century Alive," in Featherstone and Burrows, *Cyberspace*, 205–14, 213.

34 Kroker and Weinstein, *Data Trash*, 78.

35 Ibid., 78. It is interesting to note that the language used below to describe such a class is highly technical and, ironically, geared to quite a sophisticated, elite readership. Kroker and Weinstein's readers are definitely not hungry, illiterate, citizens of third-world countries.

36 Virilio, *Desert Screen*, 22.

37 Kroker and Weinstein, *Data Trash*, 4, 6.

38 Ibid., 6. An interesting parallel can be found in Marshall Berman's classic *All that is Solid Melts into Air: The Experience of Modernity* (London: Verso, 1999), where Robert Moses' "expressway world" is pitted against Jane Jacobs' "shout in the street" in the struggle for New York; the current struggle for the control or the liberation of cyberspace is also opposing the information highway to the nomadic spaces.

39 Don Mitchell, "The End of Public Space? People's Park, Definitions of the Public, and Democracy," *Annals of the Association of American Geographers* 85.1 (Mar. 1995), 108–33, 122–23.

40 McKenzie Wark, "The Virtual Sensoria: Notes on New Media Art," *Sixth International Symposium on Electronic Art (ISEA)*, Montreal, Canada (Sep. 18–22, 1995).

41 Gilles Deleuze, "Postscript on the Societies of Control", *October* 59 (Winter 1992), 3–7.

42 Kroker and Weinstein, *Data Trash*, 63–64.

43 Arthur and Marilouise Kroker, "Digital Ideology: E-Theory (1)," *Ctheory* (Sep. 15, 1999), online at http://www.ctheory.net/articles.aspx?id=116, as article a073 [Last accessed Oct. 12, 2006].

44 David Lyon, "Surveillance in Cyberspace: The Internet, Personal Data, and Social Control," *Queen's Quarterly* 109.3 (Fall 2002) 345–56, 349. John Perry Barlow's article "Decrypting the Puzzle Palace," *Communications of the ACM* 35.7 (Jul. 1992), 25–31, describes the NSA's role in using cyberspace for surveillance and intelligence.

45 Lyotard, *La Condition postmoderne*, 14.

46 Baudrillard, *Simulacra*, 29.

47 Ibid., 29–30.

48 Ibid., 30.

49 Hakim Bey, *T.A.Z.*, 110.

50 Ibid., 63.

51 Bruce Sterling, "A Short History of the Internet," originally published as "Internet," in *The Magazine of Fantasy and Science Fiction* (Feb. 1993), later available online at http://w3.aces.uiuc.edu/AIM/scale/nethistory.html [Last accessed Oct. 12, 2006].

52 Bey, *T.A.Z.*, 106–14.

53 Auzanneau and Avril, *Dictionnaire latin*, 334.

54 Ibid., 666.

55 Bey, *T.A.Z.*, 96.

56 Barthes, *Sade, Fourier, Loyola*, 15–16.

57 Hakim Bey, *Millennium* (New York and Dublin: Autonomedia and Garden of Delight, 1996), 30.

58 George Woodcock, *Anarchism: A History of Libertarian Ideas and Movements* (Harmondsworth: Penguin Books, 1963), 443. My italics.

59 De Certeau, *Practice*, 130.

60 Bey, *T.A.Z.*, 99–100. It is interesting to note how Bey rejects his previous enthusiastic espousal of the Internet in his preface to the second edition of *T.A.Z.* in 2003: "I think perhaps the least useful part of the book [*T.A.Z.*] is its section on the Internet. I envisioned the Net as an adjunct to the TAZ, a technology in service to the TAZ, a means of potentiating its emergence. I proposed the term 'Web' for this function of the Net. What a joke. *Time* magazine identified me as a cyber-guru and 'explained' that the TAZ exists in cyberspace. 'Web' became the official term for the commercial/surveilliance [sic] function of the Net, and by 1995 it had succeeded in burying the anarchic potential of the Net (if any really existed) under a mass of advertizing and dot-com scams. What's left of the Left now seems to inhabit a ghost-world where a few thousand 'hits' pass for political action and 'virtual community' takes the place of human presence. The Web has become a perfect mirror of Global Capital: borderless, triumphalist, evanescent, aesthetically bankrupt, monocultural, violent—a force for atomization and isolation, for the disappearance of knowledge, of sexuality, and of all the subtle senses," xi. Previously, in Arthur and Marilouise Kroker's *Digital Delirium*, Bey was already beginning to have doubts as to the future of cyberspace. Venting his frustration in a piece called "Notes for CTHEORY" (152–55) he wrote: "No matter how much more exploitation of conceptual space occurs, the structure of the space is now *defined* for all practical purposes. Hasn't something similar happened with the Internet?" (152).

61 Edward Said, *Culture and Imperialism* (New York: Vintage Books, 1993), 289.

62 Michel de Certeau, *La Culture au pluriel* (Paris: Seuil, 1993), 213–14.

63 Anonymous, *Hieroglyphica* (New York: Autonomedia, 2002). Although "anonymous," the booklet is believed to be the work of Hakim Bey.

64 Bey, *T.A.Z.*, 107.

65 Barlow, "Declaration," 18–19.

66 Bey, *T.A.Z.*, 95–96. See also Zhou Yongming, "Living on the Cyber Border: *Minjian* Political Writers in Chinese Cyberspace," *Current Anthropology* 46.5 (Dec. 2005), 779–803, on the political activities of *minjian* online writers, and Birgit Bräuchler, "Islamic Radicalism Online: The Moluccan Mission of the Laskar Jihad in Cyberspace,"

The Australian Journal of Anthropology 15.3 (2004), 267–85, which explores the ways in which radical Muslim Indonesian groups acquire and develop an extended visibility and reach through cyberspace.

67 Deleuze and Guattari, *Mille Plateaux*, 434.

68 Ibid., 437.

69 Ibid., 471–72.

70 Ibid., 472.

71 Bey, *T.A.Z.*, 105.

72 Bey, *T.A.Z.*, 107–8.

73 Bey, *T.A.Z.*, 111.

74 Lévy, *Intelligence*, 10.

75 Kroker and Weinstein, *Data Trash*, 1.

76 Bey, *T.A.Z.*, 101.

77 Bey, *T.A.Z.*, 101.

CONCLUSION

What Lies Ahead

> Once upon a time, I, Chuang Tzu, dreamt that I was a butterfly, flitting around and enjoying myself. I had no idea I was Chuang Tzu. Then suddenly I woke up and was Chuang Tzu again. But I could not tell, had I been Chuang Tzu dreaming I was a butterfly, or a butterfly dreaming I was now Chuang Tzu? However, there must be some sort of difference between Chuang Tzu and a butterfly!
>
> *The Book of Chuang Tzu*[1]

> It was the Cat who persuaded me to write down these memories. I don't know what to call it yet…I might just call it after my name, or after what I am. What I have become. Maybe you're reading it now. Or maybe you're playing the feather. Or maybe you're in the feather, thinking that you're reading the novel, with no way of knowing . . . No matter. The game is over soon. Just one more moment . . . And then it's gone.
>
> Jeff Noon, *Vurt*[2]

We have entered into a new age where, like in the story by Zhuang Zi, reality and virtuality are so similar, and so overwhelmingly *real* to our senses, that we hesitate to decide which is anterior, i.e., more *genuine* than the other; Zhuang Zi's impatience, more than two thousand years ago, is not only understandable but is also a pressing problem today: there *must* be some way to differentiate between the two worlds. Yet what has survived from this wonderful story is not the tomes of Daoist wisdom produced as much as the *seduction* created by the tantalizing hint that we already are on the side of the simulation. Too long have we been occupied by our own reflection to realize that the mirror's function is not only to present another image of ourselves but also to problematize the very existential nature of this image. We have become, in Derrida's words, so "attentive, fascinated, glued to *what it is* that presents itself," that "we are not able to see its real *presence* which itself is not present [does not introduce itself, 'ne se présente pas']."[3]

Our tentative journey in cybermapping, from myth to *écriture* to the virtual city and its denizens, has allowed us to realize, first, that *not all spaces are similarly or equally mappable*. The lesson is a humbling one, and rejoins, again through the different paths of contemporary critical theory, the great mystical traditions of unnameability and silence. What this mapping demands is a sideways glance, one that does not look directly but, paradoxically, sees more things which are invisible to a frontal gaze, and sees them more clearly as well.

Second, our journey has led us to a tragic—in the Greek sense of the word—realization of our own physical and social limitations. The nature of a new space where the old myths of humanity can be experienced and enacted again and where the fiat of an instantaneously performative writing act can be practiced anytime has made our situation all the more tragic because it has allowed us to glimpse a dimension where the equivalent limitations in everyday life can be, for the first time, surpassed.

But *should* they be surpassed?

Homo Sapiens Cyberneticus, for all the hype surrounding the new challenges facing us today, may just be a gimmick born out of technological advances so fast that they bring with them an illusion of power we are loathe to forsake. Although the real world can be a daunting place to live in, yet it is the only one we human beings were created for, and we cannot remain for long glued to a cyberspace which denies us a panoramic view of the sometimes dire social realities surrounding us. Are world conflict, world hunger, the atrocities of war, only simulations, or are there indeed *real* people with *real* pain suffering out there?

But then, are we to dismiss the whole of cyberspace and relegate it to a by-product of the new technologies as a toy which served its mechanical purpose and nothing more? Or should we rather give it its due as a necessary step in our on-going evolutionary history, a window into another cognitive and interpretational dimension from which, as if from a vantage point, we are able to see what we call the "real world" with different eyes? Is the distancing thus offered a terribly catastrophic event which threatens the whole species, or is it a salutary jump out of the bound, saturated, overworked, and overserious self?

If writing, that best means of expressing oneself, is given for all to use without the traditional constraints, if the ability to voice one's emotions and ideas is given free rein, and if this language proves to be, by the same token, the key that will open the rich mythical stores buried in humanity, shouldn't we at least acknowledge these obvious benefits and wisely weigh them against the equally obvious shortcomings which have accompanied—and always will—hand-in-hand, all technological advances?

Cyberspace is, beyond doubt, calling us, *en masse*, and offering its forever-changing vistas for us to explore, to collectively write, and to enact our fantasies and myths. If our mapping of cyberspace is in fact our creation of new realms which we may one day inhabit, then what beckons to us from behind the mirror, what begs to introduce itself, may not be, after all, just our reflection, but that of a new species of humanity feverishly asking to be born.

NOTES

1 *The Book of Chuang Tzu* (London: Penguin Arkana, 1996), 20.
2 Noon, *Vurt*, 341–42.
3 Jacques Derrida, *La Dissémination* (Paris: Seuil, 1993), 381.